A CLASH
OF DESTINIES

The Arab-Jewish War and the Founding of the
State of Israel

by

JON AND DAVID KIMCHE

FREDERICK A. PRAEGER, *Publishers*

New York

BOOKS THAT MATTER

Published in the United States of America in 1960
by Frederick A. Praeger, Inc., Publishers
64 University Place, New York 3, N. Y.

Copyright © Jon and David Kimche 1960

Library of Congress catalog card number 60-6996

Printed in the United States of America

Jon and David Kimche

CONTENTS

PREFACE

INTRODUCTION
On Writing Contemporary History

PART ONE
Imperial Disengagement

PART TWO
The Unofficial War

PART THREE
The Official War

EPILOGUE
Israel and the Arab Revolution

APPENDIX

INDEX

MAPS

In memoriam
MONES KIMCHE
May 20th, 1958

PREFACE

$\mathbf{W}$ E have been writing this book for something like five years and we had to overcome many initial difficulties before we managed to get down to the real story. One of these difficulties has stayed with us to the end. For we were confronted with the one problem which faces every attempt to write about contemporary affairs. Many of our essential sources were serving generals, ministers in office, civil servants and diplomats—Arab, British, Israeli and others—and some of them are still in office or in command. But fortunately most of those whom we approached—well over a hundred—were fully prepared to help with information and, in important cases, also with documents—provided we did not quote them. We were thus faced with the dilemma of either getting the information without the name-tags attached or going without it.

We had no doubt about the course we should take, but we were also conscious of the resulting responsibility to the reader. We have therefore been almost pedantically careful not to make any statement or quote any opinion without having the necessary supporting evidence in our possession.

We would now like to thank all those who have helped us and we prefer, in justice to all of them, to name none of them. We feel, however, that we must make two exceptions: David Ben-Gurion, whose help and encouragement provided us with the necessary access to the Israeli documentation, and to Gabriel Cohen, whose unique detailed knowledge of the course of the war saved us from many an error of fact or of opinion. But the responsibility for both fact and opinion is ours alone. We would have liked to thank our Arab friends for their help, but under existing conditions discretion is the highest form of gratitude. And the same goes for the British who have helped us unstintingly. And once again Barbara Bundock, now Brosselin, has given us her efficient help with the manuscript.

J.K.

April 1960.   D.K.

ix

We have used five passages from the *Seven Fallen Pillars*. These were either eye-witness accounts or documents. They will be found on pages 154/6, 196/8, 229/30, 233/4 and 251.

INTRODUCTION

On Writing Contemporary History

In the fateful spring of 1938 one of us began to keep a scrapbook of significant items in the Press which expressed the attitudes of different people and parties to the prospect of another war. The scraps soon became too complicated. As we came nearer to war the effort was abandoned. But the first, now faded, entry, dated March 4th, 1938, is a cutting from the *Manchester Guardian*. It reported an address given the previous day to the Manchester Luncheon Club "by Mr. B. H. Liddell Hart." In his talk Liddell Hart had drawn some conclusions from his twenty years' study of the documents of the First World War. Governments had opened their archives and generals their hearts in time for their records to be checked by personal examination of other witnesses.

After twenty years' experience of such work Liddell Hart concluded that nothing could deceive like a document. Pure documentary history was akin to mythology. Many were the gaps found in official archives—tokens of documents destroyed so as to conceal what might impair a commander's reputation. The French were rather more subtle; a general would safeguard the lives of his men as well as his own reputation by writing orders based on a situation that did not exist, for an attack that nobody carried out, while everybody shared in the credit, since the record went into the file. "I have often wondered how the war went on at all," he said, "when I have found how much of their time the commanders spent on preparing its history."

Long before Liddell Hart, Thucydides came across the same problem when recording the history of the Peloponnesian War. He also found that the first accounts of commanders did not always tally with the facts, that general impressions were apt to be misleading, and that even eye-witnesses had to be

11

checked, for many of them suffered either from "partiality for one side or the other or else from imperfect memories." Now, when we began this book four years ago, we thought that we had the advantage over both Liddell Hart and Thucydides. One of us had participated in the war as an Israeli soldier; the other had been a newspaper correspondent with exceptional facilities which had enabled him to observe virtually every battle from the commander's or commander-in chief's perspective. We thought we knew it all.

Our subsequent experience in reconstructing the Palestine War from the available documentation in the official archives, from an endless chain of interviews which we conducted, and from the published memoirs, made nonsense of many of the accepted assumptions about the nature and course of the war. We discovered that it was not even enough to be an eye-witness in order to establish an event clearly; appearances were sometimes as deceptive as documents. We found it necessary to distrust the testimony of many witnesses. It was as if some camouflaged curtain had intervened between the appearances and the realities of the war. We found that the official Israeli archives—even those still on the secret list—suffered from gaps and from much impressionist documentation. Some minor encounters appear as major battles, and some decisive battles are totally unrecorded or appear as trivial engagements. The formal Arab archives on the actual war are very much like Liddell Hart's French examples: any relation to real events is purely coincidental.

This is not accidental. For in many ways, the actual fighting in the Palestine War played a secondary role in the conflict. What really mattered was the clash of wills, the battle of commands, and this is almost wholly unrecorded in the archives—except in the personal notebooks of David Ben-Gurion, the Israeli Prime Minister and Commander-in-Chief[1] at the time. In fact, the actual fighting of the war (certainly until October 1948) played a much smaller part in the wider aspect of the conflict than one would conclude from the some-what stylized accounts of the military side of the war which

[1] Until May 15th, 1948, Ben-Gurion was Chairman of the Jewish Agency and in charge of its Security Department. After May 15th, he became Prime Minister and Minister of Defence with the authority of Commander-in-Chief.

have become familiar by repetition, each according to his needs: the Israeli, the Arab and the British. We have, therefore, devoted rather more attention to the "wills" on both sides that set the troops in motion and respectively succeeded and failed in the end. If ever there was a war of commanders, this was it: supreme commanders, field commanders and local commanders. They were decisive; and without knowing the conflicts and purposes within their ranks, it is impossible to appreciate what really happened in Palestine in 1948.

Because of its failure to understand their conflicts and purposes, most of the new generation of Israelis is already becoming somewhat ashamed of its "war of liberation"; only about half a million of Israel's two million population actually experienced and can remember the war. The others (over a million) either arrived later or grew up only after the war had been won. Thus, when Israel celebrated her first decade as a state in 1958, the great majority of the population had no personal link with the war of 1948 and did not identify itself with it as it did with the Sinai war of 1956. As fact was catching up with legend, and with the "How-I-won-the-war" memoirs, the David and Goliath theme became somewhat tarnished in the eyes of the new generation of Israelis. The triumph over the divided, incompetent and hapless Arab armies appeared less a cause for pride and jubiliation than as a dangerous source of over-confidence. The Israel of 1958 was therefore much more inclined to look back only two years to the campaign of the Israel Defence Forces in the Sinai Peninsula for a more valid measure of its strength than to the seemingly puny engagements of the 1948 war.

The new generation of Israelis thus made the mistake which so many others have made before them: it measured the significance of the battle of 1948 by the size of the armies who engaged in them or by the nature of the equipment which they used. Both were, of course, of importance, but only of secondary significance in the international political setting in which the war was fought. Much more to the point, given these circumstances, was the will to survive on the part of the Palestinian Jews, and perhaps even more, the political and military expression of this will in the person of Israel's first Prime Minister, David Ben-Gurion, and in the military instruments of Palestinian Jewry: the Haganah, its clandestine national defence organisation, and the Palmach, the hand-picked striking force which together provided the foundation and framework of the future Israel Defence Forces.

Nevertheless, the conflict in Palestine in 1948 appeared to the Palestinian Jews as their triumphant war of independence. In Arab eyes it was an unmitigated catastrophe brought about by the perfidy of the Great Powers, especially of Great Britain and the United States, and as a great betrayal by the selfish and incompetent leadership of the Arab ruling classes. No credit is given or allowed to the Palestinian Jews for their will and their capacity to fight it out. Only a few isolated and largely ignored Arab voices[1] tried vainly to advance the more fundamental assertion that the true cause of the Arab defeat lay more deeply embedded within the Arab world itself.

Their analysis was ruthless. The conflict with Zionism was going to be long and arduous. "Palestine and the self-respect of the Arabs must be recovered," wrote Musa Alami in 1949. "Without Palestine there is no life for them. This our ancestors understood truly as of old. Their understanding was better than ours, when Europe attacked and took Palestine from them. They were willing to die for it and continued to struggle until they recovered it. Thus it is today. This is the first phase of a long war."[2]

Zurayk, who was later to become the acting head of the American University in Beirut, argued likewise. In 1948 he wrote:[3]

> If we have lost this battle that does not mean that we have lost the whole war or that we have been finally routed with no possibility of a later revival. This battle is decisive from numerous points of view, for on it depends the establishment or the extinction of the Zionist state. If we lose the battle completely, and the Zionist state is established, the Jews of the whole world will no doubt muster their strength to preserve, reinforce and expand it, as they mustered their strength to found it.

[1] Principally, Constantine R. Zurayk in *The Meaning of the Disaster* (Arabic in 1948, English translation in 1956) and Musa Alami's *The Lesson of Palestine (Ibrat Falastin)*, published in Arabic in March 1949. An English summary, still well worth reading, appeared in October 1949 in the *Middle East Journal*, Washington, D.C.

[2] *The Lesson of Palestine*, p. 386.

[3] *The Meaning of the Disaster*, p. 7.

To achieve this end, the ultimate defeat of the Jews in Palestine, both Musa Alami and Zurayk argued that a total internal revolution of Arab society was required. Arab society could be equipped for this combat only by a total political and social renaissance. The old regime must be ended; there must be genuine Arab unity, freedom of the masses, equality for the Arab woman, and education for all. Writing still in the immediate aftermath of battle and disaster, both Musa Alami and Professor Zurayk set a fashion which every other Arab writer on the Palestine War has followed, and which was given a new lease of life ten years later, when in 1958 Sir John Glubb published his version of the war. A dangerous legend was launched on the Arab world which credited the Jews with a unified and efficient command, "wide-scale military training, complete modern armament, heavy mechanical equipment, expert and strong defences" and so on.[1] Zurayk made much the same point,[2] and so did virtually every Arab writer and leader who followed these two.[3]

This was to become increasingly the accepted—and self-comforting—view of the Arab world. It was to become a firm belief that was to inflict incalculable damage on the course of Arab revolution and renaissance which followed in a kind of zig-zag course in the wake of the Palestine catastrophe. In Egypt, Syria, Iraq and Jordan, it forced the new movements into political blind alleys and made it impossible for them to achieve as much as they might have done. It forced the Arab revolutions to preoccupy themselves with false issues and to tilt against non-existing windmills.

In this book we have, therefore, attempted to go back to the starting-point and establish what really took place. Perhaps, in the light of this additional knowledge, the Arab world of the 1960s will be able to free itself from the legends of the 1950s and face the reality of the lesson of Palestine, instead of perpetuating a self-created myth which has prevented these revolutions from fulfilling the more pressing

[1] *The Lesson of Palestine*, pp. 374, 378.

[2] "It is, therefore, our duty to acknowledge the terrifying strength which the enemy possesses and to take it into account when we view our present problem and try to remedy it." (*The Meaning of the Disaster*, p. 5.)

[3] Especially President Nasser.

need of the Arab world: to bring about fundamental changes in traditional Arab society, a society which, in 1948, proved itself weak, incompetent, unrealistic and unable to adjust itself to the needs of the times or to the interests of the Arab peoples. And, by the standards of Musa Alami and Zurayk, these criticisms were still true of Arab society as we enter the 1960s.

The Israelis, as we shall show, were also far from united and in many ways quite unprepared for the ordeal which lay ahead. They had their adequate share of internal personal, political and military crises and we shall follow their course though this may appear to tarnish the popular contemporary image of the Israeli war effort during its formative period. But only the image will be tarnished, not the reality. For despite the differences and clashes even in the hours of crisis, emergent Israel had one instrument which the Arabs lacked— the spirit of the Haganah. It was this that made possible the improvisations, the adjustment and the sense of unity which gave the Israelis the advantage not only in battle but also in the spirit of their soldiers and their commanders. It is the imponderable element of this story for which there are no records, no proofs, no witnesses other than the actual account of the war. It was this spirit of the Haganah which Arab intelligence failed to take into account then, and one has the impression that today, they—and many Israelis—are still inclined to forget and overlook the part which it played in the Palestine war of 1948. It was possibly the most important single lesson of that war for Arab and Israeli alike, for both soldier and statesman. And it found its most emphatic military expression in the doctrine of independent action and flexibility which had been established by Itzhak Sadeh in May 1946. The Haganah—especially its commanders—had this doctrine in their bones. It was the military explanation for their night-fighting and their infiltration tactics, for their ability to seek out the weak points of their enemies, and for their ultimate victory in battle; but for the victory in the war that now loomed ahead something more was required.

PART ONE

Imperial Disengagement

1

THE CRISIS IN DOWNING STREET

MOST empires—the French, the Russian and the Chinese, for example—have reached the climax of disintegration as a consequence of tyranny, corruption and misgovernment; others—the Roman and especially the British—entered the period of their disintegration in the hour of their greatest enlightenment, progress and egalitarianism. Both the latter came into conflict with the Jews in Palestine at this turning-point in their history.

Palestine—the Roman Palestina—came into existence as a consequence of the defeat of the Jews in Judaea in their final rebellion against the Roman mandatory authority under Bar-Kochba in A.D. 135. Palestine, as a country, ceased to exist as a consequence of a successful rebellion of the Jews 1813 years later. Both rebellions were in the nature of national uprisings against ruling empires; both were brought about by conditions which were thought by the Jews to be intolerable; both broke out when the imperial overlords—Rome and Great Britain—were faced by an imperial crisis. They differed, however, in the strategy and tactics adopted by the revolutionaries, and in the fact that one rebellion failed and the other succeeded. Why was the Jewish War of 1948 successful, whereas the last three Jewish uprisings against the Romans had failed with catastrophic consequences?

Both Rome and the British Empire were at the commencement of a long period of disintegration when the Jewish wars broke out. But for the crisis of empire in ancient Rome and modern Britain, it is questionable whether the Jewish leaders, then or now, would have embarked on a military challenge to the imperial power, which in both cases had the same limited objective—to loosen the imperial grip on Palestine and so bring about the political independence of the Jewish nation. In

neither case did the Jewish leaders set out to encompass the
defeat and destruction of their imperial opponent; they
wanted, like the American colonists, no more than to achieve
a loosening (not necessarily even the complete abandonment)
of the imperial stranglehold on Jewish life in Palestine. They
failed against Rome because the success of the rebellion
threatened the very existence of the Empire; they succeeded
against the British because the British did not, in the end,
consider the successful Jewish rebellion as a serious threat to
their Empire—for, among other things, the whole concept of
Empire had undergone a revolutionary change in the three
fateful years between 1945 and 1948.

In this book we seek to establish an agreed diagnosis of what
happened—and why it happened. In doing this we must
avoid digging back into the all-too-familiar deeper roots of the
relationship of the Zionists, Arabs and British. For Zionism
underwent a catalytic transformation between 1939 and 1945;
the post-1945 Zionist had basically little relation to the pre-
1939 Zionist. From 1945 onwards the British and the Arabs
were therefore confronted by something that was quite different from the pre-war Zionism they had come to know during
the previous twenty years. The new Zionism was emotionally
super-charged by the catastrophe that had befallen the
European Jews and was politically conditioned by the urge to
do something for the survivors. It intended to provide a
physical existence for those who had been emotionally and
practically despoiled by the Germans and their allies, and to
secure a moral and political re-insurance for the millions of
Jews who remained outside the range of the German "final
solution," but who felt that, "but for the grace of God" and
the Allied victory, they would probably have suffered the
same fate.

It was these two factors that gave post-war Zionism its
essential character, not the "Jewish longing for the home-
land." It was the European catastrophe that turned this
passive, abstract, religious, emotional, but *politically* almost
ineffective longing of centuries into an irresistible political
urge. It also provided this urge with a supporting moral
argument for which the gentile world had no answer and could
have no answer.

But for the British Labour Government at the beginning of

1947 this was no abstract moral problem. 100,000 British troops in Palestine were concerned with it; so were another 200,000 stationed throughout the Middle East, and many more on duty in occupied Germany, Austria and Italy. These widely dispersed forces were all involved in the refugee movement to Palestine.

The Palestine dispute was thus, at the beginning of 1947, impinging on the duties of some half-million British troops in three continents. Yet, even so, the Labour Government in Whitehall could not isolate the Palestine problem from its other difficulties, which reached a climax during these winter weeks of 1947 such as no other British Government has had to face in peace-time.

In Egypt, Syria and Transjordan governmental crises raised new Governments into office. The new Egyptian Government led by Nokrashy Pasha denounced the draft treaty with Britain negotiated by his predecessor, Ismail Sidky Pasha. In Palestine, terrorists flogged a British major and five N.C.O.'s as a reprisal for the flogging of a Jewish youth. But these were Britain's lesser worries. More menacing than these man-made troubles was the imponderable aftermath of the Second World War, the shortage of manpower, the pressure on inadequate supplies of raw materials, especially coal and wheat. During January 1947, Britain received less than half of her wheat requirements. Coal supplies dwindled, factories began to close for lack of fuel. Then the elements struck their body blow at Britain's reeling economy.

On February 2nd, 1947, the sun was seen over the British Isles for the last time for four weeks. On the 3rd the Austin Motor Works, and many others, closed down; unemployment was increasing; potatoes disappeared from the shops. On the same day the United States Ambassador in Athens reported to the State Department that there were strong rumours that the British were about to withdraw their troops from Greece. On the next day the Cadbury Chocolate Works stopped work because of the lack of fuel, and on February 6th a snow blizzard isolated parts of northern England from the rest of the country. It was announced that food and milk supplies were in danger, and by the 7th coal stocks were declared to be "critically short." Severe cuts in the supply of electricity were imposed over the whole of southern England.

In this setting, in the midst of an electricity cut which plunged the entire Foreign Office into darkness, the Foreign Secretary communicated the last word of the British Government to the Jewish Agency delegation, and later also to that of the Arab States. There was to be a British Trusteeship for a period of four years, followed by independence if Arabs and Jews could agree on it. A hundred thousand Jewish immigrants would be admitted during the first two years. After that "economic absorptive capacity" would guide the High Commissioner in deciding on the number to be admitted. "Failing agreement," Ernest Bevin said, "His Majesty's Government will send the whole Palestine issue to the United Nations." As the lights went out at the meeting, Bevin joked with his brute trade unionist humour that there was no need for candles as they had the Israe*lites* present. It was symptomatic of the strained mood of the meeting that afterwards Ben-Gurion and Shertock expressed themselves strongly about Bevin's bad taste and lack of sensibility. The nerves of both British and Jewish leaders were by now on edge. Both had ample justification.

Three days later both Jews and Arabs informed the Foreign Secretary that his "final" proposals were unacceptable to them. It was the end of negotiations with the British. But against the background of the howling tempest that seemed to force the country almost to its knees, the implications of this rejection were not immediately apparent. There was no electricity in Britain that day, except for emergency use. Heat and light were cut to zero; electric trains were running skeleton services; unemployment rose into the millions; food supplies were jeopardised; industry was almost at a standstill. London worked by candle-light as the Cabinet met to face the imperial consequences of its domestic breakdown. Even without the immediate catastrophe of the weather, it was both vast and grave.

For, in the midst of elemental chaos, the Labour Cabinet was called upon to decide irrevocably and finally the future of Burma, Palestine, India and Greece in terms of British commitment and policy. The decision on Burma had been taken on January 28th, but now came the three days that were to change the course of British history.

The legal advisers to the Foreign Office had ruled that,

under the terms of the Palestine Mandate, the British Government had no authority to "award" the country either to the
Jews or the Arabs, or to partition it. Now Bevin, unlike the
Prime Minister, was convinced that the British could not and
should not withdraw from the Middle East; Britain's economic
interests (to use his own words, "the wage-packets of the
workers") were too deeply involved in the area to be lightly
abandoned. He therefore welcomed the latest Foreign Office
ruling; with its backing, he had no difficulty in persuading the
Cabinet to drop a tentative proposal to partition Palestine
which had been drawn up by Arthur Creech Jones, the
Colonial Secretary. The Cabinet—supporters and opponents of Zionism alike—were only too glad to clutch at these
legal straws and so escape the onus of a decision that could no
longer be postponed. Clearly, in the unanimous opinion of the
Cabinet, only the United Nations could now propose a
Palestine settlement. On Tuesday, February 18th, 1947,
Bevin accordingly told the House of Commons that it had been
decided to submit the Palestine question to the United
Nations.

Bevin's announcement of this in the Commons was one of
his more insensitive performances. He denounced President
Truman's interventions[1] as unhelpful meddling and argued
against excessive haste in reaching a decision. "After 2,000
years of conflict, another twelve months will not be considered a long delay," Bevin told Parliament. His speech was
badly received, even though the decision to surrender the
Mandate was widely welcomed. President Truman later
described it as noteworthy for "the callousness" of "its dis-
regard for human misery" and this was also the general
Jewish reaction.

Nevertheless, when Bevin spoke on that day he was an
angry and frustrated man. He felt that he alone in the Cabinet
understood what the decision to take the Palestine question to
the United Nations meant for the Commonwealth, especially
when taken in conjunction with the two other withdrawals
that were to be initiated later in the same week: those from

---

[1] The President had, in 1946, sent his own representative to the
Displaced Persons' camps in Germany and Austria, and subsequently
addressed a letter to the Prime Minister, Mr. Attlee, urging the entry of
100,000 Jewish immigrants into Palestine (see also below, p. 46).

India and from Greece. If faced by the choice, he would rather have abondoned the British position in Greece than in Palestine.

On this score Bevin was isolated, and his principal opponent was neither Bevan nor Morrison, as so often, but the Prime Minister himself. It was Attlee more than anyone in the Cabinet who refused to accept Bevin's arguments about the importance of the Middle East being so great that it called for the maintenance of British troops and of direct British influence; it was Attlee who pressed all along the line for the withdrawal of British troops and direct control. The Prime Minister had overruled the arguments of the Chiefs of Staff against rapid withdrawal; he also overruled Bevin's political and economic objections. Attlee wanted to get out of Palestine without any further involvement, and the Cabinet supported him.

It was not an isolated decision. Two days after Bevin had told Parliament that the responsibility for the future of Palestine would be handed over to the United Nations, Attlee himself appeared before the Commons—on Thursday, February 20th. He told Parliament that the Government intended to transfer the government of India "into responsible Indian hands" not later than June 1948. Once again the Service chiefs had been overruled in the time-table of withdrawal; speed seemed to be Attlee's overwhelming consideration.

Before this momentous step had been fully appreciated in the world at large, barely twenty-four hours later, in the late afternoon of Friday, February 21st, the British Ambassador in Washington called on the Secretary of State, General Marshall, with an urgent message from the Foreign Secretary in London. Marshall was away, but Dean Acheson was given a copy of the document that would be formally presented on the following Monday. The gist of it was simple and stark: the British Government would have to give up its military and financial committments in Greece by March 30th. Thus, within seventy-two hours during this cold February week the Labour Government had handed over its responsibility for Palestine to the United Nations, its control over India into "responsible Indian hands," and its commitments in Greece to the United States. At home that day coal stocks dwindled to fourteen days' supply and unemployment figures marched towards the two million mark.

It was in these circumstances that the British Government abandoned the Palestine Mandate; it was part of the greatest voluntary abdication in modern imperial history. But unlike the Indian or the Greek withdrawal, the transfer of the Palestine question to the United Nations was only the beginning, not the end of this chapter. For at the Foreign Office the idea was taking root that the withdrawal from Palestine need not be an unmitigated disaster; it was a view shared also by the Chief of the Imperial General Staff, Field-Marshal Montgomery.

As far back as October 1946, a conference had met at the War Office to consider the practicability of an alternative Mediterranean strategy and a War Office spokesman had subsequently described its conclusions in these words:

> The Imperial general staff has proposed tentatively to withdraw the British administrative and supply bases from the eastern Mediterranean—including Palestine—to the African colonies of Kenya and Tanganyika. The proposal envisages retention of Britain's forward operational bases as long as practicable in such countries as the Sudan, Palestine, Transjordan and Iraq.

Montgomery in his memoirs surprisingly ignores this whole strategic episode, though it is by no means his only omission, as we shall see later, in the record of his Palestine policy.

However, there was no echo from Washington of these rosy views of the implications of this British decision. At the Cabinet luncheon on February 24th, 1947, General Marshall reported that the British had informed him that they could no longer be the reservoir for the financial-military support of Turkey and Greece, and added his own opinion that this was tantamount to British abdication from the Middle East. But that was not the British Government's view—Ernest Bevin, alone perhaps, held it.

In the event the Labour Government proceeded, apparently unaware of the extent of the governmental crisis in which it was involved. It was possible to shrug off responsibility from now on for the future of India or Greece, but Palestine and the Middle East were more complicated, for there was no one as yet who would or could take over this responsibility. Furthermore, there were still 100,000 British troops and a complete

British administration in Palestine. It was these, and not the United Nations, who continued to govern, and the hand on the wheel that controlled the Palestine Government was still in Downing Street. But now the Labour Government made an unpleasant political discovery: the more they sought to disengage themselves from Palestine on the international scene, the more deeply they were becoming involved locally in Palestine. This contradiction was brought about by the inability or reluctance of the Government to formulate a decisive Palestine policy, and their consequent tendency to allow the soldiers in Palestine to shoulder the burden of responsibility, at a time when purely military problems were becoming increasingly serious. For the relations between the British and the Jews in Palestine had reached rock bottom. The Jews hated the British for their policy of deporting "illegal" immigrants to Cyprus; the British despised the Jews for the terrorist activities of the Irgun Zvai Leumi and the Stern Gang.[1]

How did the Government face up to this contradiction between its political and military intentions? To provide an accurate answer to this question has been one of the most difficult features of our investigation, and probably its most important. For the British Government's position at the centre of the emergent Middle Eastern crisis, as it was at the time and not as it became rationalised later by hindsight, had a

---

[1] As the toll of terrorist activities increased daily, the British authorities on the spot tended increasingly to exaggerate the importance and size of the two terrorist organisations. In fact, however, the Stern Gang had not more than 150 active fighting members, while the Irgun Zvai Leumi (National Military Organisation) had a nucleus of several hundred "fighters," with an additional two to three thousand active sympathisers, who would provide the necessary funds, allow their homes to be used as hiding-places etc. The I.Z.L. was an offshoot of the Revisionist Zionist Organisation, which did not recognise the authority of the Jewish Agency and the official Zionist leaders. It became particularly active during the 1936-39 Arab rebellion in Palestine and after the British Government White Paper of 1939. With the outbreak of war, however, it decided to suspend operations against the British, a decision which was repudiated by an extremist section of the I.Z.L., led by Avraham Stern. He left the organisation and founded his own group in 1941. Stern was subsequently caught by the British and shot while attempting to escape, but his group continued to operate until the establishment of Israel.

greater bearing on the future of Palestine, and also of British interests and influence in the Middle East, than any other single factor.

In reconstructing this situation we endeavoured to use contemporary and first-hand evidence as much as possible, and we were fortunate on both counts: we had almost constant contact with many of the principal members of the Labour Government during the period here described, and we have since interviewed almost all the leading personalities who were in any way connected with the formulation and execution of this policy. The picture which we obtained in this way is frequently contradictory and sometimes irreconcilable as between different interests, but that is natural and understandable. The memory of the Cabinet Minister for whom Palestine was one item on a long agenda to be dealt with every so often—but not too often—in ten minutes' discussion, and thus settled for the time being, may be rather different from that of the administrator or soldier on the spot who had to deal with it almost every hour of every day during many trying months.

In order to do justice to the difficulties which overwhelmed the men who were at the helm of affairs in Whitehall, it is necessary not to isolate the events concerning Palestine from the general circumstances in which the Government of the day had to operate. They found themselves called upon to govern a course of events which had been uncharted in the anticipatory programmes of the Labour Party, which were wholly unfamiliar to the civil servants who advised them, and for which there was no ready theory to guide their practice.

Thus, no sooner had the Government escaped from the incipient crisis produced by the weather at home than they found themselves facing the threatening collapse of Europe's economic framework on the one hand, and the political absorption of Eastern Europe into the Soviet orbit on the other. Furthermore, the carefully laid plans for the transfer of power in India had belied Labour's fond hopes. Instead of a phased shift from the British to the Indians and the Pakistanis which would be concluded by June 1948, the communal differences between Hindu and Muslim had exploded in a refugee migration accompanied by a mass slaughter on a scale rarely experienced even in the history of the Orient.

Accordingly, by the early summer of 1947 the Cabinet was forced to face situations in India and Europe for which it had been wholly unprepared. In India the act of partition had to be advanced by almost a whole year in order to limit the anarchy and the slaughter.

As happens so often in politics, the Labour Government proceeded to turn this inescapable necessity into a virtue. A theory of wise disengagement from imperial burdens was evolved as accompaniment to the act. India, Burma, Egypt, Greece and Palestine were to be "set free," so that they should shape their own future and so that the Labour Government would be able to face its responsibilities at home and in Europe. No real difficulties were experienced (by the British) in the abandonment of India and Burma, or in Greece, despite the shattering consequences and the great loss of life which followed in some of the countries from which the British were withdrawing.

But it was different with Palestine, where, on the face of things, it ought to have been much easier to carry through a transfer of power than in India. Yet British policy in Palestine was oddly schizophrenic: there was to be a deliberate British withdrawal of troops and authority, accompanied by an apparent determination not to relax the grip of authority until the last possible moment. There were also differences and doubts as to whether the withdrawal was seriously intended, and, above all, there was an angry, almost emotional, attitude in the Cabinet towards the Palestinian Jews and their Zionist supporters who had added so many additional difficulties to those which were already besetting the Cabinet.

There was also one other factor that set the Palestine difficulties apart from the others. The Labour Ministers were not directly, emotionally engaged in the formulation of policy for India or Burma or Greece. It was different with Palestine. Many of the members of the Cabinet had been, in the years before they had become Ministers, ardent supporters of the Zionist cause, others had been equally ardent opponents or ardent neutrals. But every one had been ardent on some side. Morrison, Greenwood, Dalton, Jowitt, Creech Jones, Bevan and Williams had supported Zionism; Bevin, Alexander and Cripps had opposed; and most of the neutrals, including Attlee, Addison and Shinwell, generally supported the opposition to the Zionists. But now that the climax in Palestine had come, there was no longer any real opposition in the Cabinet to the policy advocated by the Foreign Secretary.

Briefly, Bevin's policy was to leave the matter in the hands of the United Nations, in the confident belief that either the United Nations would be unable to come to any agreement on the subject, or, even if it did agree, that it would have to request Great Britain to remain in Palestine in order to enforce its proposals.

Without exception, Ministers had become convinced that this policy was the only possible way for the Government to disengage themselves;[1] they found the ruthlessness of terrorist attacks on British troops and the unbending attitude of the Jewish leaders to any proposed compromise as strong enough evidence to justify their new tough policy towards the aspirations of the Zionists. But in this context it would be wrong to state that the policy of the Cabinet was either pro-Arab or anti-Zionist, for the policy never reached out this far. It was rarely more than a purely hand-to-mouth improvisation.

The Palestine policy was decided by a variety of authorities, often completely opposed to each other. Thus at the time when the British Government had informed the United Nations Organisation that it proposed to hand over responsibility for the Palestine Mandate to the United Nations, the Chief of the Imperial General Staff, Field-Marshal Montgomery, was pressing the Government in London to impose strict martial law over all Palestine in an all-out effort to break the Jewish underground organisations—the terrorists and the Haganah.[2] The authorities in Palestine, military and civil, were, however, opposed to such a step, and in March 1947 the High Commissioner, Sir Alan Cunningham, and the G.O.C. Palestine, General Sir Gordon Macmillan, were ordered to come to London for further discussions. During their stay in London

[1] Field-Marshal Montgomery, in his *Memoirs* (Collins, 1958), p. 472, indicates that this switch in the Cabinet's mood took place in the course of the summer of 1947.

[2] Montgomery's own account of this period in his *Memoirs* (pp. 471-472) is singularly imprecise and conveys the impression that he shared the opposition to imposition of martial law, whereas the record shows him to have been the principal advocate of all-out military measures—including martial law.

the two generals were asked to attend a Cabinet meeting in Downing Street.

They turned up and were ushered into an ante-room, given an agenda, and requested to wait. To their horror they discovered that Palestine ranked fairly low in the order of priorities: it was item four on the Cabinet agenda, squeezed in between arrangements for the Olympic Games and amendments to the National Health Bill. They should not have been surprised. For the Foreign Secretary and his advisers were still unconvinced that the decision to withdraw was final. They remained convinced of their appraisal of events: that the United Nations would have to ask the British Government to continue to act as policeman in Palestine. They could not imagine any other possible agent to ensure law and order. At the Colonial Office, also, all the ingrained conscientiousness of the Colonial Service revolted at the prospect of abandoning the orderly government of the Mandate to the utter chaos which they were convinced would follow on the heels of the departing British. And at the War Office Field-Marshal Montgomery added his own scepticism about the intended withdrawal from Palestine.

This dichotomy of British policy was further illustrated both at the United Nations and at home. On April 2nd, 1947, the British Government had addressed a request to the Secretary-General to summon a special assembly for the purpose of considering the future of the Palestine Mandate, but in the mind of the Foreign Secretary, and in the opinion of his principal advisers, that was not the same thing as handing over actual responsibility to the United Nations. Even six weeks later, on May 29th, Bevin told the Labour Party annual conference that the reference to the United Nations was essentially conditional. He personally would not be bound by any United Nations decision about the future of Palestine unless it was unanimous, he assured the conference. But that this proviso would never be fulfilled was the only thing that seemed certain in the whole Palestine situation. Meanwhile, during April a Special Assembly of the United Nations, called at the request of the British Government, had appointed a Commission of Enquiry into the Palestine question.

But the events of the summer brought a reappraisal of the situation. The growing tension in Palestine, the increased pressure of the so-called illegal immigration and the resulting commotion in the United States,[1] the tenacious insistence of the Prime Minister on the withdrawal from Palestine, and, most of all, the rapid rush of events in India (which in June compelled the Government to advance the handing over of responsibility by almost a year), finally convinced the Foreign Secretary and the Foreign Office that there was no alternative to withdrawal. This conviction was translated into policy in August 1947, and from then onwards was maintained with a tenacity that surprised both the United States administration and the Jewish Agency representatives.

Yet there was a curious ambivalence in this British policy. The Foreign Office—especially Bevin and his adviser on Palestinian affairs, Harold Beeley—were pressing for withdrawal, but at the same time believed firmly that either the Jews or the Arabs, or both, would ask the British to stay on and save the country from chaos.

But it was one thing to decide on withdrawal and another to translate such a decision into a policy which would ensure the continuity of British interests in Palestine and the neighbouring countries. It was at this stage that the Cabinet again showed its limitations. Having decided as a body on the withdrawal from Palestine, and the handing over of responsibility to the United Nations, it now washed its hands, albeit somewhat righteously, of any further interest in the outcome. It accepted and based its policy on the unrealistic formula that it would take no initiative in the United Nations, nor would it support with British troops or authority in Palestine any United Nations decision which was not unanimous and accepted by both Jews and Arabs. Since this possibility did not arise at any time, and was never likely to arise, the

---

[1] The so-called illegal immigration had proved to be a great moral weapon in the hands of the Jews. The sight of displaced persons, remnants from Nazi concentration camps, being turned back from the shores of Palestine by Royal Navy warships was not kindly received by world public opinion, and nowhere less kindly than in the United States. This American resentment flared into open and widespread denunciation of British policy when, in July 1947, the British authorities decided to deport back to Europe the 4,500 Jews on the immigrant-runner *Exodus*. The three-hour battle on board the ship, followed by the long-drawn out drama of the actual deportation (which only ended when the immigrants were forcibly taken back to German soil), caused a wave of anti-British sentiment both in the United States and in France.

decision of the Cabinet was equivalent to complete dissociation from the course of coming events in Palestine.

So far as we have been able to establish there was not one discussion in the Cabinet on British policy during and following the withdrawal, or during the discussions at the United Nations, other than in these escapist terms. Throughout 1947 the Palestine issue was discussed only in the most cursory manner. The decision to withdraw had been agreed on by most of the Cabinet in the spring, it was accepted by the Foreign Secretary in the summer, and there was no longer any need for the Cabinet to bother. The rest was a purely administrative question which could be left to the Foreign Office, the War Office, the Mandatory administrations and the troops. That was the situation at the heart of the Government.

But now let us turn to the men in Palestine itself. As Palestine had increasingly become a military problem, the day-by-day administration was falling more and more on the shoulders of the soldiers in Palestine, in Egypt and in the Middle East generally. In many ways they were the decisive element in the story, and, fortunately, also the least inhibited. Let us, therefore, see how these men, who were charged with the execution of the Labour Government's Palestine policy, assessed the situation in the summer of 1947.

The situation had been altered very considerably during those summer months. The United Nations had set up a special committee, comprising the representatives of eleven countries, which was to study possible solutions of the Palestine problem. The committee's proposals were published on August 31st. They advocated the termination of the Mandate at the earliest possible date, and the partition of Palestine into an independent Jewish and an independent Arab State, with Jerusalem as an international enclave. The Jewish State would include the Negev, the coastal strip from Isdud to Acre,[1] the Plain of Esdraelon and the Eastern Galilee, while the Arabs would receive the Western and Central Galilee, Samaria and the Judaean Hills, and the coastal strip from Isdud down to the Egyptian frontier. The Jews welcomed the decision; the Arabs and the British did not. On September 23rd Mr. Creech Jones, the Colonial Secretary, declared that the British Government had decided

[1] But just leaving these two towns as Arab territory.

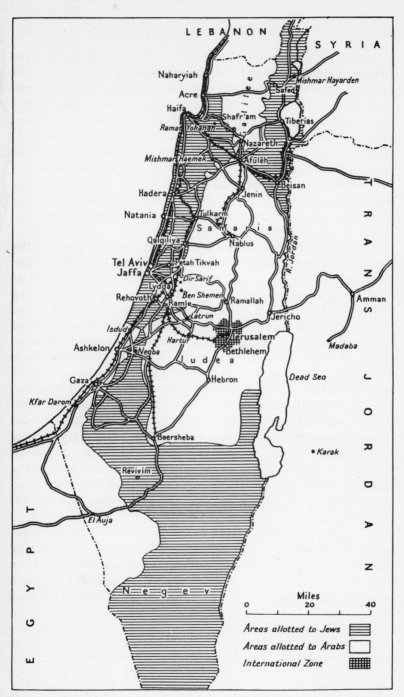

LEBANON

SYRIA

Naharyiah

Mishmar Hayarden

Acre

Safed

Haifa

Shafr'am

Tiberias

Ramat Yohanan

Nazareth

Mishmar Haemek

Afuleh

Beisan

Hadera

Jenin

Natania

Tulkarm

Qalqiliya

Samaria

Nablus

Tel Aviv

Petah Tikvah

Jaffa

Dir Sarif

Lydda

Ben Shemen

Ramallah

Rehovoth

Ramle

Latrun

Jericho

Isdud

Hartuf

Jerusalem

Ashkelon

Negba

Bethlehem

Madaba

Judea

Gaza

Hebron

Dead Sea

Kfar Darom

Beersheba

Karak

Revivim

El Auja

N e g e v

E G Y P T

T R A N S J O R D A N

Amman

R. Jordan

Miles

0   20   40

Areas allotted to Jews

Areas allotted to Arabs

International Zone

Map. 1. The plan for the partition of Palestine approved by the U.N. Assembly on November 29th, 1947.

to plan for the early withdrawal of the British forces and the British Administration from Palestine. At the same time he made it clear that unless the committee's decision was acceptable to both the Jews and the Arabs (and it was by then amply clear that it was not) the British Government would not feel able to implement the recommendations made by the committee. These proposed that the independent Jewish and Arab States should come into being after a transitional period of two years, during which Great Britain was to carry on the Administration under the auspices of the United Nations, and was to admit 150,000 Jewish immigrants into that part of Palestine allotted to the Jewish State.[1]

Mr. Creech Jones's statement, and British reaction to the partition proposal in general, made it clear that it was the announced British intention to pull out of Palestine as fast as possible, without at the same time doing anything to help put into effect the United Nations partition proposal. Thus, an entirely new situation emerged. But neither the Cabinet nor the Chiefs of Staff appeared to have an over-all appreciation of this changed position; neither provided their respective "men on the spot" with any indication of what were the political objectives of the Government other than the purely military and administrative measures connected with the security situation and the forthcoming withdrawal of troops from Palestine. Thus, the British G.O.C. Egypt was ordered to get the Egyptian authorities to agree to the greatly increased number of British troops in the Canal Zone as a consequence of the intended withdrawal from Palestine, but he was at no time acquainted with any wider objectives which the Government may have had in mind.

The great problem, therefore, which faced the British civilian and military authorities in the Middle East was that none knew what was the Government's ultimate intention, or what their own policy objectives should be. The contact between the Embassy in Cairo and the General Officer

---

[1] These proposals were made in a majority report supported by the representatives of Canada, Czechoslovakia, Guatemala, the Netherlands, Peru, Sweden and Uruguay. A minority report, advocating a form of cantonisation with a Federal Government, was submitted by the representatives of Iran, India and Yugoslavia. The eleventh member of the committee, Australia, abstained from supporting either of the two reports.

Commanding was purely social. Similarly, the army commanders in Egypt were not apprised of events or of special
information available to the adviser on Arab affairs at the
Embassy, General I. N. Clayton. One reason for this was that
the soldiers largely suspected this source, which was the main
provider of Arab information to the Foreign Office. Clayton,
the soldiers felt, had "gone native" and could not be trusted
as an objective provider of information. But these shortcomings were but the symptoms of a much graver fault. As
these men on the spot saw it, there was no central direction of
policy, and, what was worse, no central and responsible
authority. No one in the Middle East was in a position to take
a decision on policy, neither the High Commissioner in
Jerusalem, nor the officers commanding the troops in either
Palestine or Egypt. Every request for a decision was passed
from authority to authority until it found its way back to the
Chiefs of Staff in London: Montgomery, Tedder and Cunningham. But they also refused to take a firm line and left the
principal decisions to the Cabinet.

In the Cabinet the Prime Minister's main characteristic
would assert itself. Attlee would delay and put off making a
political decision until events had overtaken the need for
action. Instead he would be tough about secondary matters,
or about issues which served only to underline the failure to
take political decisions. Thus he would insist on cutting down
the time for the military withdrawal from Palestine and from
India far beyond the point demanded by the soldiers, or even
requested by Bevin. In the end Attlee carried the day but the
cost in actual loss of life and in political consequence of this
over-hasty withdrawal without an accompanying policy has
become evident only in later years. At the time, however, it
served to prop up the myth of the Labour Premier getting
tough with the soldiers and insisting on getting his own way.
The soldiers drew their own conclusions about the Government's ability or inclination to govern during this critical period.

This view was further reinforced by the realisation that
there was no one in the Cabinet who had any independent
or first-hand knowledge either of the Middle East or of military
affairs. The Cabinet, the soldiers soon understood, was as much
at the mercy of its expert advisers on these matters as it was
at that of the Chiefs of Staff. The soldiers on the whole

distrusted the Foreign and Colonial Office advisers, whether they were pro-Arab or pro-Zionist. As the year wore on the commanders in the Middle East began to understand that Attlee was concerned at all costs to avoid a conflict with the United States over Palestine,[1] and that to make sure of this he was inclined to delay his final decision and his policy directives as long as possible. Not so Bevin. He was known to be bellicosely inclined to support the Arab position. But that was not enough to lead to a decision.

Thus, responsibility which had been passed from hand to hand until it reached the Cabinet was now passed back again until it was returned into the hands of those who had first disclaimed it. The administrators and soldiers in Palestine, and elsewhere in the Middle East, were left with the authority and responsiblity to carry out the unstated and apparently non-existent policy. Not having any directive, clear or otherwise, they were left with considerable latitude in interpreting what was supposed to be the Government's policy. Many of them, especially in Palestine, already held strong feelings against the Jews because of their support or apparent condonation of terrorist activities against the British. They knew also that the Foreign Secretary largely shared their opinions and prejudices.

It was, therefore, not surprising that when they came to execute the only two aspects of policy which were explicit— to withdraw from Palestine with the least possible disruption. and to maintain law and order meanwhile as well as possible— they had their own views on how this was to be done without getting into trouble with the authorities at home, while at the same time satisfying their own inclinations. The prevailing "pro-Arab" bent among the soldiers and administrators was thus given its head. But the fault was not that of the men on the spot; it was the Cabinet which had the ultimate authority and did not exercise it. By irresponsibly refusing to take decisions, or to give orders, it demonstrated, in the eyes of the soldiers, its unwillingness to govern.

[1] United States policy, at that time, was still in avowed support of the recommendation of the Anglo-American Commission of Enquiry, contained in the Commission's report published in May 1946. The chief of these recommendations was that 100,000 Jewish refugees should be admitted into Palestine over a period of two years.

This is not an occasional or personal opinion; it appears to be the almost unanimous conclusion of the military men in the field who had the job of carrying out British policy in the Middle East. The army commanders were equally outspoken about the Foreign Office—which had, however, in theory, no direct standing in relation to the execution of policy in Palestine (for this was still within the province of the Colonial Office) but which made its impact felt most effectively through the strong personality of Ernest Bevin, the Foreign Secretary. But whatever was his policy in Washington and at the Embassy in Cairo, it was not conveyed to the soldiers in Palestine or Egypt. The Foreign Office may or may not have had its own objectives and manner of achieving them, but the diplomats on the spot did not confide in the soldiers on the spot. These were therefore inclined increasingly to withdraw from involvement in higher policy, especially as there was the additional conflict between Montgomery, the Foreign Office and the Colonial Office to contend with.

Field-Marshal Montgomery describes the course and nature of the differences in his *Memoirs* (Chapter 29), though the details which he gives and the emphasis which he places would probably not be accepted by either the Foreign Office or the Colonial Office. Creech Jones's authority was qualified by Bevin's overiding veto and initiative. The difference was essentially one between a tough policy proposed by Montgomery and vaguely and hesitatingly supported, with some uneasy second thoughts, by Attlee and Bevin, and a more concilatory policy proposed by Creech-Jones, with occasional support from Herbert Morrison and Arthur Greenwood.

The soldiers on the spot therefore became increasingly inclined to look after their own back garden: they were to get out without getting involved, without considering political or moral implications. So they stuck to the letter of their instructions, and left it to the civilians and politicians to cope with the political implications.

But it so happened that the graver and more far-reaching these became, the less was the attention being paid to the military on the spot. The commanders were not kept informed either of the British Government's intentions, or of what the British Government knew of Arab intentions. Thus the soldiers fumbled in the political dark and acted as they felt

inclined or considered best against a background provided by
the chain of indecision which in these decisive months operated
as follows: the local administration was responsible to the
Colonial Office, presided over by Arthur Creech Jones; but the
Colonial Office would not act without the approval of the
Foreign Office, presided over by Ernest Bevin; this, in turn,
would not act without the advice of the Service Chiefs—
Montgomery, Tedder and Cunningham; but these refused to
assume the responsibility, which they claimed was the
Cabinet's. The Cabinet, however, refused to take the decision
and left it to the Service Chiefs, the Foreign Office, the
Colonial Office and their local officials to interpret this general
state of indecision into a workable day-to-day policy. That,
in the words of one who had a key role in its application, was
the real explanation of the allegedly Machiavellian subtlety
of British policy in Palestine in the months before the
evacuation. It was a mixture of ignorance, blundering,
indecision and local bias against the Jews, encouraged by the
known bias of the Foreign Secretary.

If we now revert to the London scene it will be recalled that
by August 1947 Bevin and the rest of the Cabinet were
unanimous that the British must withdraw from Palestine.
But the accounts that we have had from Bevin's principal
advisers, and from their opposite numbers at the Colonial
Office, provide a disconcerting picture of the manner in which
the Government approached the surrender of authority in
Palestine. No one had prepared an appreciation of the likely
consequences of the British withdrawal or of the course which
events might take in Palestine. Bevin was apparently not
concerned with this aspect, nor was Attlee. The main pre-
occupation was to get out with the least possible trouble and
the greatest possible speed. There had been some cursory
speculation at a Cabinet discussion during which Creech Jones
had voiced his view that there would be no war. Bevin
thought otherwise. He believed that there would be some
fighting, but he thought the Arabs would not do too badly.

It was this belief of the Foreign Secretary, which was shared
also by his advisers and by the Prime Minister, which gradually began to colour the day-to-day practice of British policy
in Palestine and also in the United Nations. The assumption
from which both the United States and the Jewish Agency

appeared to shrink became increasingly the accepted basis of British policy: the British withdrawal would be followed by an outbreak of some fighting, and the future geography and politics of Palestine would then be decided on the battlefield and not in the Special Assembly in New York. As the Arab leaders also inclined to this trend of thought an almost natural British-Arab coalition emerged at the United Nations—and also in Palestine, where the administrators and soldiers had to keep their ears close to the ground to comprehend what the Home Government expected of them.

As they did not receive directives they began to interpret any and every possible sign of a policy or an inclination. As they saw British spokesmen at the United Nations discussions side ever more firmly with the Arab cause, they trimmed their sails accordingly, and, as their own inclinations often urged them in the same direction, they added their own embellishments to so imprecise a policy.

Thus, as the prospect of war became more real in the opinion of the Foreign Office experts and the soldiers, and also in the conviction of the Arab leaders, the informal discussions between them tended to turn into speculation on what would come after partition. So far as we could establish from extensive enquiries among all those most intimately concerned, there was at no stage a formal arrangement between the British and the Arab leaders about the precise details of what should happen on the morrow of the British withdrawal. The only agreed and officially admitted arrangement was that King Abdullah of Transjordan should occupy those parts of Palestine not allocated to Israel.

But actually the arrangement went further. It was understood by Bevin's advisers that an agreement had been reached with King Abdullah which provided that some areas allotted to the Jews would be occupied by the Arab Legion and that, as a result of any fighting, there would be a much smaller Jewish State than the United Nations had recommended. This rump of a state would then probably seek the protection of the British for an arrangement with its Arab neighbours. These plans for the morrow centred essentially on the future of Haifa, but they never achieved firm translation into either an agreement with Abdullah or an orderly, worked-out plan.

But enough had been said and done to cancel out to a large

extent the Cabinet's fond hope that the disengagement in
Palestine could be as complete as it had been in India. And so,
as the hour of decision approached, as the United Nations
voted for partition in November and the United States and the
Soviet Union (contrary to British prophecy) joined hands to
see it through the Special Assembly and thus end the British
connexion with Palestine, the Labour Government found itself
suddenly locked in a struggle with the Jews of Palestine, and
allied to the Palestinian Arabs and the countries of the Arab
League in the endeavour to frustrate the decision of the Special
Assembly and the establishmnet of an independent Jewish
State in Palestine. The Cabinet was thus to discover that in
the very hour of the ending of the Mandate on May 14th,
1948, it had become more deeply involved in the future fate
of Palestine, and in this other revolt of the Jews, than it had
ever been in all the twenty-five years of the Mandate. It found
itself tied and committed by actions and decisions taken far
from the Cabinet room, because the members of the Cabinet
had repeatedly contracted out, under Attlee's guidance, from
making decisions when it was their competence, and theirs
alone, to make them.

They had tried to pass on this responsibility to the United
Nations but at the same time used their remaining authority
in Palestine to frustrate the United Nations' decisions and
intentions—and they had also tried to involve the United
States in the future organisation of Palestine. But though
Britain had successfully forced President Truman's hand in
Greece and so produced the Truman Doctrine, and though the
United States had accepted a far-reaching involvement in
Europe during the summer of 1947, it turned down any direct
involvement in Palestine. Thus, as we close this picture of the
muddled governors in London and Washington approaching
the hour of decision in Palestine, we find that the British, who
had set out to withdraw, were now involved more deeply
than ever before, and that the Americans, who were becoming
deeply involved, withdrew completely from direct intervention
in Palestine. Thus the stage was set. Palestinian Jewry was
largely unaware of what lay ahead. It had prepared, but had
it prepared for the right kind of war? The British leaders had
some idea of what might happen. "You are going to have quite
a party," were Field-Marshal Montgomery's farewell words to

General Macmillan when the G.O.C. Palestine left him at the War Office after consultations in the summer of 1947.

But who was going to fight whom? The time has come to leave London and New York and to look in at the Arab conferences which had been proceeding in a leisurely manner, alternately in Egypt and in the hill resorts of the Lebanon. The third side of the triangle was taking shape: the Arab countries were being drawn into this conflict which had started as a Jewish revolt against a British administration which had refused entry into Palestine to the remnant of European Jewry after the Second World War. How then did this Jewish revolt against British rule turn into the Arab-Israeli war of 1948?

2

HOW THE ARAB COUNTRIES WERE DRAWN INTO THE PALESTINE WAR

THE real attitude of the Arab leaders, in Palestine and elsewhere in the Middle East, towards the project of a Jewish State in Palestine had for long been something of a mystery. For the same Arab statesman who would give contradictory opinions, depending on whether they were voiced in public or in private, would also follow his divergent opinions by equally contradictory deeds. Thus it was never easy for the outsider, and especially for the governments of Europe and the United States, to be sure which was the valid expression of the Arab mood: the publicly voiced determination to fight against the Jewish aspirations in Palestine, or the privately uttered assurances that some kind of amicable arrangement was quite possible. In the end, British and also United States officials, and public opinion generally, concluded that the endlessly reiterated public hosility of the Arabs to the notion of a Jewish State in Palestine was the genuine voice of the Arabs.

Now, largely as a result of the publication of the German Foreign Ministry archives captured by the Allies, and also by the publication of the State Department papers, especially those for 1938, new and rather more authentic light has been thrown on the real position taken by the Arab leaders, political and royal. Taken together, the confidential information which the Arab leaders conveyed at that time to their German and American friends must rank among the important contributions to the understanding of their actual position on this issue.

Before the Second World War, the British, and to some extent also the Americans, were too deeply involved in the politics of Palestine to be able to play the part of confidante for the Arab nationalists. These, as we can see from the captured German documents, were far more inclined to turn to the Germans for frank discussion of the Palestine problem. The results of a long series of such discussions were recorded by the able head of the Near and Middle East Division of the Political Department of the German Foreign Ministry, Otto von Hentig.[1]

Thus it came about that on July 29th, 1937, von Hentig circulated a significant memorandum for the guidance of Germany's policy makers. This dealt frankly with the proposal made by the Royal Commission presided over by Lord Peel (in July 1937) to partition Palestine into a Jewish and an Arab State, while maintaining British interests in Haifa and the Negev. It is most instructive in retrospect to place von Hentig's conclusions next to those presented by the Foreign Office in its reports on the anticipated Arab reactions to the Peel Report. For the Foreign Office conclusions emphasised the depth of Arab opposition to the proposal to partition Palestine and the serious consequences which would flow from its implementation. The German conclusion was very different, very much more thorough, and more understanding of the Arab mind. The man who wrote this important piece of evidence in 1937 was employed after the war in 1947 as one of King ibn Saud's political advisers. In 1937, he had concluded, on the strength of detailed reports from the German representatives in Jerusalem and in the Arab capitals, that there was a great gulf between what the Arab leaders were saying and what they were prepared to do. This is how he put it:

> There is, of course, in the whole Islamic world a widespread aversion to permitting the Jewish State to come into being, but on the other hand there is not the least inclination to quarrel with England over this question. The Arabs are well aware that England considers the question important enough to impose her point of view by force of arms, without restrictions.

Hentig then explains that the only strong protest against the partition proposal had come from Iraq and from the Mufti of Jerusalem, Haj Amin. King ibn Saud had refused to commit himself about the Palestine question, the Egyptians

[1] *Documents of German Foreign Policy*, Series D, Vol. v, June 1937–March 1939; Document 569, pp. 758–760.

had been lukewarm and did not seem greatly to care, and the Emir Abdullah of Transjordan had declared bluntly that he would do what the British wanted; only the Zionists were actively opposing the partition solution.

The Hentig Memorandum was followed two weeks later by an important policy statement which appeared to have the stamp of approval of the head of the German Foreign Ministry. This assumed that it was a British imperial interest to see a Jewish State established in Palestine, and concluded that since Germany did not want at that time to come into conflict with the British, it was "out of the question" to support the Arabs with either arms or money, or to oppose actively the establishment of a Jewish State in Palestine.[1] All this in 1937.

From the American State Department Documents for 1938, which have also been made public, we can see that even the two most active Arab opponents to partition noted in the Hentig memorandum—Iraq and the Mufti—were at the time engaged in secret negotiations with Palestinian Jewish representatives. Both General Nuri and the Mufti had meetings with Dr. Judah Magnes, the then head of the Hebrew University in Jerusalem, in the hope of negotiating a settlement which would make partition unnecessary.[2] In a long letter to the Chief of the Division of Near Eastern Affairs, the United States Minister in Baghdad tells the full story as told to him by Nuri. Once again, the contrast between the German and the British, or the American, appreciations of the situation stands out starkly. The Germans knew and understood that the Arabs were not prepared to fight against a determined British policy; the American Minister, Knabenshue, showed far less insight into the situation. He reported faithfully what Nuri had said to him, without attempting, as Hentig had done, to provide himself with an independent opinion.

But from the moment when the Germans and Arabs saw the British waver over partition (after the presentation of the Royal Commission report in July 1937) the whole situation changed. As the British weakened, Arab and German opposition gathered strength and courage. The Arab moderates, who

[1] *Ibid.*, p. 759.
[2] It is a pity that Professor Norman Bentwich does not deal more thoroughly with this illuminating episode in his biography of Magnes.

were generally also the pro-British elements, were silenced and discredited; the Arab extremists, who were generally the most anti-British elements, were encouraged. The Germans were at first incredulous, then amazed, and lastly encouraged by the display of British indecision in the Middle East which followed the presentation of the Royal Commission's report.

Without this background, the events ten years later, in 1947, cannot be fully appreciated. For once again the future of British rule in Palestine was at stake. Once more the Arab world watched and waited to see how the British would act. Until March 1947, the policies of the Arab states were largely orientated on those of the British. So long as the British remained the dominant factor in the shaping of the future of Palestine, none of the Arab states was prepared openly to challenge them. But in February 1947 there came the unmistakable decision of the British Government to ask the United Nations to decide on the future of Palestine. The Arabs, including the newly anointed King Abdullah, were frankly sceptical. They could not imagine that the British really meant to leave Palestine. But by mid-March they had been convinced of the genuineness of the British retreat.

The process of gradual Arab involvement in the conflict between British and Jews in Palestine had begun in the wake of the publication of the report of the Anglo-American Commission of Enquiry in May 1946. Its principal recommendations, that 100,000 Jewish refugees from Europe should be admitted into Palestine over a period of two years and that land sales to Jews should no longer be restricted as before, came as a great shock to the Arab leaders. This was not lessened by the denunciation of the report's "inadequacies" by the Zionist leaders, who had anticipated recommendations more favourable to their demands for national independence.

But in the view of the Arab leaders it presented an immediate challenge to which they had to respond. Arab public opinion was in an uproar. The British Government—and especially the Prime Minister, Mr. Attlee, and the Chiefs of Staff—considered the Commission's recommendations to be detrimental to British interests. There was thus from the outset a community of Anglo-Arab interest in their common opposition to the principal recommendation of the

Commission: the admission of 100,000 Jews into Palestine.[1]

The Commission presented its report to the two Governments on April 22nd, 1946. Two weeks later, on May 8th, President Truman wrote to the Prime Minister, urging speedy action on the lines recommended by the Commission. On May 16th, after having received two stalling answers from Attlee, Truman sent another more formal note to London. Attlee replied on May 27th, eleven days later. He sent Truman a list of forty-three "subjects" which would have to be settled by British and American experts before the Labour Government could consider the ten recommendations of the Anglo-American Commission. In reply to a further specific question by the President, Attlee replied that the proposed admission of Jews from the camps in Europe could be considered in conjunction with all the other forty-two listed problems. One of these, Attlee had told Parliament, concerned the disbanding of "the illegal Jewish armed units," the Haganah.

We have now reached the point at which it might well be said that the Palestine War really began, still as an Anglo-Jewish conflict; but, unbeknown to the participants, forces that were to bring about the Arab entanglement and the transformation of the conflict into an Arab-Israeli war, were converging on the Palestine problem. For Attlee was disinclined to act on the Commissions' recommendations. His triumvirate of the Imperial General Staff—Montgomery, Tedder and Cunningham—were against the report. It would require another division of British troops in Palestine. It would certainly lead to bloodshed. From Amman, Glubb Pasha, his glory and influence still untarnished, warned "that the Moslem world would go up in flames" if the report was implemented.

Attlee was even more confirmed in his negative indecision when he learnt of the advice given to President Truman by the United States Joint Chiefs of Staff at the end of May 1946[2]. They thought that the implementation of the report would invite repercussions beyond the control of the British troops in the Middle East, but that it would be unwise to send

[1] The British Government's fear that any change in the rate of Jewish immigration would cause violent disturbances throughout the Middle East was explained to the United States Government in a Note dated October 19th, 1945 (Harry Truman *Memoirs*, vol. II (Hodder and Stoughton, 1956), pp. 149–151).

[2] *Ibid.*, p. 159.

United States troops to Palestine. Implementation by force would furthermore prejudice British and United States interests in the Middle East. If that happened, the Joint Chiefs of Staff warned, the Soviet Union might replace the United States in influence and power in the Middle East. They were also concerned about the impact on Western oil supplies should the Arabs be antagonised.

This appreciation was known to the British Government and to the Foreign Office, and, in turn, the over-all picture of the British Government's opposition, supported by their own and by President Truman's military advisers, was also known to Britain's friends among the Arab leaders—especially to the newly-crowned King Abdullah and to the Iraqis. This meant, in fact, that all the Arab leaders were fully in the picture. They knew thus what was expected of them.

As it happened, a conference of Arab rulers was scheduled for June 2nd, 1946, at Inchass, one of King Farouk's country palaces. When it was first arranged the conference was not intended to concern itself primarily with the Palestine question.[1] It was intended to co-ordinate anti-communist measures which the British representative in Cairo had recommended. This had been also the principal topic of the discussions and decision of the "conference of rulers." But this was too convenient an opportunity to miss just at a crucial moment in the Attlee-Truman exchanges. Accordingly the Kings, Regents and Presidents present[2] resolved that the Commission's proposals were unacceptable. They called for an end to all Jewish immigration into Palestine and the prevention of all further sales of land to Jews. Lastly they undertook to support the resistance of the Palestine Arabs "with all the means at our disposal."

Attlee now had the evidence with which he could support his argument with the President, and in Parliament, that immigration must be limited. The Cabinet was already convinced. But with this announcement of policy, the Labour

[1] This information was given me in Amman by King Abdullah a few weeks after the Inchass Conference, on July 20th, 1946—J.K.

[2] They were: King Abdullah (Transjordan), King Farouk (Egypt), the Crown Prince Emir Saud (Saudi Arabia), the Regent Emir Abdul Illah (Iraq), President Beshara el Khoury (Lebanon), President Kuwatly Syria), and Seif el Islam Ahmed (Yemen).

Government had let the *jinn* out of the bottle. They had set a premium on Arab opposition. To the Arab leaders it was clearly a situation that called for maximum political exploitation. A special meeting of the Political Committee of the Arab League was called for June 9th, 1946. The process of Arab entanglement in the conflict between the British Government and the Palestine Jews was under way.

Thus, within a week of the meeting of rulers, the political leaders of the Arab countries arrived at Bludan, a small holiday resort in the hills near Damascus, and the "Bludan Conference" was formally opened on June 9th, 1946, with the customary formalities and platitudes: a speech by the chairman, the Transjordanian Foreign Minister, Shureiqi; a welcome by the leader of the host delegation, Syria's Abdullah al-Jabari; and a short political address by the League's Secretary-General, Abdul Rahman Azzam Pasha of Egypt. But once the pleasantries were over the divergencies began.

There were, in the first place, the genuine interventionists, who made no secret of their intention to march into Palestine on the day the British withdrew—or even earlier, if it were feasible. This group was composed of King Abdullah, the Syrians, and the ex-Mufti, Haj Amin, whose influence had become one of the imponderables of the situation. But even within this grouping the objectives of each of the three members were far from identical. Abdullah wanted to occupy not only the large portion of Palestine which was considered to be the Arab sector, but also certain strategic parts of the country which were considered Jewish, and especially the Haifa port enclave and the largely unoccupied Negev. Having achieved this (and he had been informally assured by both the Foreign Office and the Army that Britain would remain a benevolent neutral) Abdullah was prepared to reach a settlement with the remaining rump of Palestinian Jewry. The Syrians had similar territorial ambitions, but no such political objective. They were concerned in the first place to occupy as much of northern Palestine as they could before Abdullah's Arab Legion got there. They wanted to defeat the Jews, if possible, but they had no intention of reaching any kind of settlement based on co-existence. The ex-Mufti simply wanted the Jews to be driven out of Palestine and his own authority to be re-established there.

The second group of countries might be best described as "pseudo-interventionist." It was made up of Iraq and the Lebanon. Both were, vocally, the most energetic interventionists at all the meetings of the League, starting with this Bludan gathering. But the militant language of both was little more than an unconvincing disguise for their marked disinclination or inability to take effective action against the Jews in Palestine. Neither, therefore, played any serious military part in this unfolding story. But their paper record, as we shall see, could not be bettered. No one throughout these months was more ardent than the representatives of Iraq and the Lebanon to go to war, and no Arab country was less prepared and less willing to do so than either of these two.

Lastly there were the avowed anti-interventionists: Egypt and Saudi Arabia. Neither wanted to get entangled in Palestine. Both had primary domestic interests which were considered to be more important than a conflict with the United States, and a military clash with the Jews of Palestine, with its wholly unpredictable outcome. All through, almost to the end, both Egypt and Saudi Arabia opposed every move designed to lead to official military intervention in Palestine by the armies of the Arab states. But they were unable to prevent it.

For it was precisely this alignment of the Arab countries, this difference of opinion based on national self-interest, which created the actual logic of intervention in Palestine. Abdullah moved to further his own ambition of becoming King of Jerusalem and governing the Arab parts of Palestine, and also to keep the Syrians and the ex-Mufti out of Palestine. The more successful Abdullah appeared to be in furthering his plans, the greater became the ex-Mufti's and the Syrians' pressure on Egypt to counter his ambitions as being a challenge to Egypt's hegemony in the Arab world. It was almost inevitable, when one considers the earlier rivalry, that, in the event, King Farouk and the Egyptian Government should have succumbed to the mixture of fear of a Greater Jordan and the temptation of fruits of victory in Palestine. But the decisive push that brought Egypt into the Palestine War was the desire to counter Abdullah's ambition.

There were two main items on the agenda of the Bludan Conference. The first was to draft an agreed reply to the memoranda sent to the Arab states by the British Government and by President Truman, who wanted to know the Arab position with regard to the report of the Anglo-American Commission on the future of Palestine. The second item assumed that no good would come out of the first; it therefore put before the conference the task of "saving" Palestine. How was this to be done?

In addition to the Arab delegations there were two familiar strangers present at the meeting: Brigadier I. N. Clayton, who was in charge of Arab affairs at the British Embassy in Cairo, and the correspondent of the London *Times* in Damascus. Clayton was more than a friendly "observer". He intervened in the debate to counsel strongly against the proposal to take the Anglo-American report to the Security Council. He advised the Arab leaders not to get the future of Palestine entangled in the United Nations.

But agreement on any of the major issues seemed to be out of the question as one after another of the delegates declared his position.

Makreim Obeid, the Egyptian delegate, said: "If we tell the Palestine Arabs 'to fight with all the arms at your disposal' we shall only be responsible for inflicting heavy casualties on them; for the Jews are much better armed than the Palestine Arabs."

Faris el-Khoury, the veteran Syrian statesman, warned the conference that if it agreed to a proposal to boycott United Kingdom trade "this would ruin the Syrian currency, for our currency has no purchasing power abroad" without British support.

King ibn Saud's special envoy, Sheikh Youssef Yassin, read a memorandum from the King which said that Saudi Arabia would carry out any decision of the League, but it urged that such decisions should be based on a correct assessment of the situation and on a realistic appreciation of what the Arab states could and could not do. The best thing that could be done, King ibn Saud urged, was to get the agreement of the Palestinians to the sending of a delegation on behalf of themselves and the Arab League to Washington and London for further negotiations. They should also exploit all other *political* means at their disposal.

The Transjordanian Foreign Minister, Shureiqi, also proposed that there should be negotiations with the British Government, so as to bring about the establishment of an independent Palestine.

But the Iraqi Government's spokesman, Dr. Fadhil Jamali, differed from all these hesitating proposals. He told the conference that "the time for talking has passed. We have to close our ranks and be practical. The Americans understand only the language of force. We should delay answering the British and American memoranda until we have decided what practical steps the League members propose to take."

Two years later, Dr. Jamali explained the subsequent events of the Bludan meeting to a Parliamentary Enquiry which was set up by the Iraqi Government. Jamali's report recalled that:

> Iraq had shown more concern than any other Arab state for the future of Palestine. After her, came Syria and the Lebanon, but these were still young States and fearful of complications with either Britain or the United States. Egypt had not yet been convinced that she must show more energy; she was content with offers of moral help. But most negative of all was the stand of the Saudi Arabians; they showed how little there was to the report that King ibn Saud and his family were prepared to sacrifice themselves for the sake of the Palestine Arabs. Transjordan and the Yemen showed enthusiastic sympathy for the Iraqi stand, but were too poor to help in any other way.

Thus, after days of discussion, no agreed answer to the two items on the agenda had been reached. The conference therefore agreed on two separate sets of decisions; one set would be published, but the other would remain secret, and be for the guidance of member-state governments.

The published decisions were: to send an answer to the British and American Governments' request for an opinion on the report of the Anglo-American Commission on Palestine; a request to the British Government for negotiations on the future of Palestine under Articles 79 and 80 of the United Nations Charter; two committees were to be set up to deal with the Palestine situation: one, composed of the Arab states, was to sit in Cairo, and the other, composed of the ex-Mufti, Ahmed Hilmi and Tewfic el-Khaledi, was to represent the Palestinian Arabs; Zionist goods were to be boycotted;

a sum of money (unspecified) was to be set aside to help the struggle of the Palestinian Arabs; and, lastly, the sale of Arab land in Palestine to Jews was to be considered as an act of treason.

The secret decisions were more in line with the Iraqi arguments. The first postulated that the Palestine situation was moving towards a major conflict in view of Zionist determination to achieve a Jewish State. This would force the Palestinian Arabs to resort to similar means to defend their interests, which would place the Arab states in a delicate situation, for they would not be able to prevent their citizens from coming to the aid of their brethren in Palestine—with money, arms and volunteers.

The second secret decision was based on the assumption that Anglo-Arab relations would worsen if the recommendations of the Anglo-American Commission's report on Palestine were implemented. In that case the Arab states would grant no further economic concessions to either Britain or the United States; the Arab states would refuse to participate in any international organisation; they would study the possibilities of cancelling all existing concessions; and they would also consider taking the whole Palestine issue to the United Nations.

These then were the public and the secret decisions. For the Arab delegations they were little more than paper to cover up their basic differences. But the concluding speech of the Iraqi representative, Dr. Fadhil Jamali, left little to their imagination, and in an angry closing session the majority decided to strike Jamali's speech from the official protocol of the conference.

Jamali had said:

> The Iraqi delegation leaves Bludan unconvinced of the effectiveness of the resolutions reached at the conference. . . . The Iraqi delegation therefore will recommend to its Government that it should retain its freedom of action with regard to the ways and means of solving the Palestine problem in a manner more effective than expressed in the resolutions of this conference. . . . The Bludan Conference has succeeded in being only one more example of the opposing view-points and the conflicting interests of the Arab countries which are voiced at every conference and find expression in every resolution of the League.

Thus ended the Bludan Conference. It had not been without significance, despite its indecisiveness and Jamali's discontent. For it was the first Arab League conference in which specific proposals had been made to end the Palestine problem with an Arab-inspired solution, and, despite the unwillingness of the majority of those present to think in terms of war, it was the Bludan resolutions that set them on the road to open armed conflict in Palestine less than two years later.

But the conference had yet another, and more immediate, significance. It provided the British Government with the alibi it had sought. It now had the evidence with which to confront President Truman. The recommendations of the Anglo-American Commission could not possibly be implemented without threatening the British and American position in the Middle East. Bludan was the proof, and Brigadier Clayton the witness.

Events now followed in swift succession to prove that the British Government also was prepared to play its part in the development of Anglo-Arab co-operation over the future of Palestine. But the next move did not come as a result of carefully prepared collusion between the British and the Arab leaders; it came instead as a consequence of a colossal miscalculation on the part of the Jewish leaders in Palestine. They had concluded, as had Jamali at Bludan, that the only language to which the British would listen was force. They were therefore going to demonstrate to the British military authorities that without the goodwill of Palestine Jewry the British forces in Palestine might become dangerously isolated. The plan prepared by the Haganah High Command,[1] the semi-legal Jewish Defence headquarters, had been initiated by Moshe Sneh and the Haganah Command, had been co-ordinated with the I.Z.L. and approved by Shertock and the Jewish Agency Executive, and had been submitted (on May 12th) for approval to Ben-Gurion who was in London at the time.

[1] The political head of the Haganah known as RAMA was Moshe Sneh from 1945 until June 1946. He was succeeded by Israel Galili who held the post from June 1946 until it was abolished on May 2nd, 1948. The operational headquarters was made up by Itzhak Sadeh (Chief-of-Staff), Yaacov Dori and Yigal Yadin. Ben-Gurion was the Chairman of the Jewish Agency Executive and Mrs. Golda Myerson was the influential activist General Secretary of the Histadrut, the Federation of Labour.

It was to be at once a warning to the British Mandatory authorities and a demonstration of strength for the benefit of the Jewish population of Palestine. It was to make the power of the Haganah manifest to both, to intimidate the one and to encourage the other. Thus, as the Arab delegations in Bludan were concluding work on their secret resolutions on the night of June 16th, 1946, units of the Haganah moved into action in every part of Palestine, and the I.Z.L. converged on the R.A.F. airfield at Lydda. Four road and four rail bridges were destroyed or damaged, and all movement across the frontiers to or from Palestine was brought to a standstill. Railways and airfields were attacked. Considerable damage was done but great care was taken that there should be no British casualties. The Haganah retired content that it had achieved the demonstrative purpose of the operation: it had shown the British and the Jewish population that the Haganah was a national force which could not be ignored.

But there was another side which had not been calculated by the Jewish leaders. A month after this operation (on July 13th) the Chief Secretary of the Palestine Government, Sir John Shaw, explained privately that when the Haganah launched this attack, the government, in Jerusalem and in London, "heaved a great sigh of relief and went into action." It was just what the British military authorities had been waiting for. It also suited Attlee's book. He had already told Parliament, and the President, that his Government could do nothing until the Haganah had disarmed and disbanded. Here now was first-hand evidence of this need, provided by the Haganah itself. The British authorities in Palestine took energetic measures. The Jewish leaders were arrested on June 30th, 1946. The Jewish Agency was occupied. The British took over complete control of Palestine. The Foreign Office was able to tell the Arab ambassadors of the swift and drastic measures with which the firmness of the Bludan Conference was rewarded. The Anglo-Arab interplay had started. The world was soon convinced that the recommendations of the Anglo-American Committee were so many dead letters.

The possibility of a seemingly pro-Jewish solution sponsored by President Truman, which had loomed large in Arab eyes, had thus been averted. Yet one further inconclusive conference was held with the British Government in London in September 1946.

But this accumulation of diplomatic and political failures did not take place in a vacuum. In Palestine the rate of illegal immigration had reached crisis proportions, and so had the conflict with the Haganah and with the terrorist organisations, the Irgun Zvai Leumi (the I.Z.L.) and the Lehy (the Stern Group). The British, unlike the Egyptians and Saudi Arabians, could not afford to sit on the Palestine problem without doing something about it. So we come to the chain of events already described which led to the handing over of the Palestine question to the United Nations and the announcement in September 1947 of the impending British withdrawal from Palestine. This, in turn, led King Abdullah to a significant reversal of his policy towards Palestine.

In the seven days between March 17th and March 23rd, 1947, Abdullah, who understood the waywardness of British Middle Eastern policy better than any other Arab, or for that matter than most of the Jewish leaders in Palestine, grasped the implications of the British decision. This was a repetition of the 1937 pattern described earlier (on pp. 43–45). Already, at a secret meeting of the Arab League's Political Committee which was held in Cairo on March 17th, 1947, the Transjordanian representative had adopted a cautious and non-committal reserve in the discussion on Arab League policy in Palestine. And when the League reconvened a week later King Abdullah had made up his mind. At this second meeting of the League Committee on March 23rd, 1947, the Transjordanian Premier requested the representatives of the Arab states present to take note that "the Hashemite Government reserves its freedom of action concerning Palestine in order to ensure the maintenance of the Arab character of the country." King Abdullah had taken the plunge.

From then onwards there was even less agreement among the League members about their intentions in Palestine than there had been at any time since 1945.

Before the Arab world could readjust itself to the new situation, there came yet another Palestine Enquiry Commission—under the auspices of the United Nations. The Arab countries boycotted it. Almost ten years to the day after the Royal Commission under Lord Peel had recommended in 1937 the partition of Palestine into an Arab and a Jewish State, the Commission of Enquiry on Palestine reported to the

United Nations. Unlike the Anglo-American Commission of Enquiry, it sought to cut the Gordian knot of the British connection. It recommended the partition of Palestine, with an Arab and a Jewish State and with an internationalised Jerusalem region.

The Arabs were shocked by the report. This was not how they had anticipated the departure of the British from Palestine. Since the secret meeting of the League Council in Cairo in March 1947 they had not considered the new situation which had been created by the placing of the Palestine issue before the United Nations. Now the report, with its drastic recommendations, jolted the Arab world into hasty consultation.

As soon as the contents of the report were known to the Arab governments, the Prime Minister of Iraq, Salah Jabr, sent out invitations for an emergency conference of the Arab League's Political Committee. It was to meet in Sofar, in the Lebanon, on September 16th. It was a measure of the luke-warm position taken by the Egyptian Government that the invitation had come, not from Azzam Pasha and the Egytian-controlled League-Secretariat, but from the Iraqi Government.

The Iraqi Premier also took the chair and presented the conference with its agenda. He proposed that Britain and the United States should be informed immediately that, the published Bludan decisions would be operated if the United Nations were to decide on a Palestine solution which the Arabs considered detrimental to themselves. Furthermore, the conference should take immediate steps to prepare for the execution of the secret measures decided on at Bludan. And, thirdly, Salah Jabr called on all Arab governments to con-tribute to a central fund, which was to assist the Palestine Arabs in their struggle.

But once more, as at Bludan, the Iraqi extremism was countered by Egyptian and Saudi Arabian caution. The Saudi Arabian delegate argued forcibly for the abandoning of the Bludan decisions. He was convinced that the attempt to implement them would lead to failure and would expose the Arabs to the derision of a hostile world. But to this Salah Jabr replied that he was convinced that "Britain and the United States will hesitate to support the proposal to par-tition Palestine, and might even oppose it, if they know that support for the Zionists may cost them their oil concessions in our countries. Neither the British nor the Americans will laugh if we cut off their Middle East oil."

The actual message sent to the British and the United States Governments was more modest. It did not mention the Bludan decisions, it did not talk about cutting off Middle East oil (there was a strong feeling among the Egyptians and Saudi Arabians at the conference that the Iraqis were talking principally for the record rather than for its translation into action). But it said enough to provide the British Government once again with an alibi for rejecting the recommendation of the United Nations, as it had rejected those of the Anglo-American Commission a year earlier, and those of the Peel Commission ten years before. The pattern was becoming almost monotonous. The Note sent by the Sofar Conference to London and Washington said that the establishment of a Jewish State in Palestine (as recommended by the United Nations Committee) would lead to a general outbreak of violence in the Middle East which the Arab governments would not be able to prevent. It was significant that even at this late date the Arab governments were still neither prepared to take, nor even to consider, measures for direct military intervention in Palestine.

The League Committee met again three weeks later, in early October, at Aley, also in the Lebanon. Again the driving force for action was the Iraqi Premier, Salah Jabr. The Committee decided that, despite the discussion at Sofar, the secret Bludan decisions were still valid. It now went further, as it seemed that there might be a majority at the United Nations for the establishment of a Jewish State. A "Military Committee" was set up, consisting of the representatives of Iraq, the Lebanon, Palestine, Syria and Transjordan. Egypt was not represented on it. This decided on the establishment of an Arab General Headquarters and on the mobilisation of the Arab armies on the Palestine border. It also called for the supplying of 10,000 rifles to the Palestinian Arabs, and for steps to acquire fighter planes. The "Military Committee" was kept in being when it was found that there might be some difficulty in establishing an Arab G.H.Q. But here, too, there was still no decision on direct military intervention by the Arab states, though, according to Azzam Pasha, the Secretary-

General of the Arab League, it was first mentioned as a possibility at this conference; but nothing was as yet done about it.

The moving spirits all along had been the Iraqi Prime Minister and the Foreign Minister, Dr. Fadhil Jamali. But there was an air of unreality about the Iraqi activism at these conferences. For the Iraqis alone had no direct territorial contact with Palestine, and their militancy was frankly distrusted or disbelieved by the other Arab delegations. It was known that the Iraqis were in the concluding phase of negotiating a new treaty with Great Britain, and the Government was therefore anxious to reassure public opinion in Iraq by its energetic language on the Palestine issue; this might cover up its concessions to the British in the agreement which was being finalised. But in the last stages of the Aley conference the participants came face to face with the real problem. This was not Iraq's loud talk, but King Abdullah's silence.

The ex-Mufti, Haj Amin, had himself turned up during the closing session and demanded the establishment of a Palestinian Government which would conduct the struggle against the Jews. He was opposed to—and afraid of—direct intervention by the Arab states. In this he was supported by Egypt and Saudi Arabia, but Syria and the Lebanon wavered, and Iraq and Transjordan strongly opposed this plan. The Mufti claimed afterwards that the conference had supported him, but before it adjourned the delegates were overcome by a sudden need for a realistic appreciation of the situation. Their decisions, they realised, would either stand or fall by the policy which King Abdullah would pursue, not by their debates in Aley. For he alone had the armed forces that could be the decisive factor.

Accordingly, the delegations did not disperse after the conference but proceeded in a body to Amman, in order to confer with King Abdullah and to sound him on his intentions. For suspended over all their decisions was the ominous statement which the Transjordanian Prime Minister had made at the secret meeting in Cairo in March: that Transjordan would henceforth reserve her freedom of action in Palestine, no matter what decisions the Arab League might take.

Abdullah was adamant on all counts. He would not hear

of a Palestinian Government, with or without Haj Amin. Azzam Pasha especially tried to get Abdullah to change his attitude, but he had no success. Abdullah also opposed the proposed arming of the Palestinian Arabs for operations against the Jews. The Jews were much better armed, he argued. But on the second issue which the Aley delegations had raised they found the King surprisingly co-operative. They asked Abdullah to abandon his project for a Greater Syrian state, embracing Syria, Transjordan and the Arab part of Palestine (a dream which he had cherished, as far as they knew, since early 1946). The King agreed without debate. The delegations were delighted. They ought to have been suspicious. For Abdullah's mind was already made up; he was now interested in a Greater Transjordan, not a greater Syria.[1] Perhaps alone among all the many contestants for the future control of Palestine he knew precisely what he wanted. He explained this to a close friend, a Palestinian Arab, in a conversation on October 1st, 1947, almost a fortnight before the arrival of the Arab delegations from Aley. This is how the Palestinian subsequently recorded the King's words:

The English have agreed to my requests, the most important of which was to increase the supply of arms, including armour and ammunition. . . . I will not let others precede me in the capture of the strategic positions in Palestine, but that does not mean that I intend to act all alone.

The Mufti and Kuwatly want to set up an independent Arab state in Palestine with the Mufti at its head. If that were to happen I would be encircled on almost all sides by enemies. This compels me to take measures to anticipate their plans. My forces will therefore occupy every place evacuated by the British.

I will not begin the attack on the Jews, and I will only attack them if they first attack my forces. I will not allow massacres in Palestine. Only after quiet and order have been established will it be possible to reach an understanding with the Jews.

In another talk a few days later Abdullah explained that his military advisers had said that they must let the Syrians and Lebanese occupy a narrow strip of northern Palestine, but

[1] Bevin had told Abdullah during his talks in London in February 1946 that the British Government could not support his aspirations for a Greater Syria, and told Abdullah to drop it. It was part of the price which the Emir Abdullah had to pay for his crown.

that he, Abdullah, would occupy Acre and would see to it that
the Syrian and Lebanese occupation zone was not in any way
extended.

A few weeks later, in November 1947, Abdullah secretly
received Mrs. Golda Myerson[1] as the representative of the
Jewish Agency. They discussed the prospects of the resolution
to partition Palestine which was then before the United
Nations. The King told Mrs. Myerson that he would take over
the Arab part of Palestine, for he would not permit another
Arab state to be set up; he would then conclude a treaty with
the Jewish State. Abdullah foresaw no exceptional difficulties
in the way. But, he added, "we both have a common enemy
who will obstruct our plans—the Mufti."

These conversations, and the evidence of his military and
political advisers, especially Glubb and Kirkbride, make it
clear that Abdullah was not acting as a pawn for the British.
If anything, he was setting the pace and taking the initiative
for his own ends. But his ends also suited the British and he
was not obstructed by them. In fact, it would be safe to
conclude that he received a good deal of encouragement—at
least unofficially—as well as quite official military and
economic aid. There was only one firm condition which the
British Foreign Secretary, Ernest Bevin, attached to all
relations with King Abdullah: whatever he proposed to do, he
was to hold his hand until the British had formally left
Palestine.

Thus the Amman talks did not change anything. The
ex-Mufti, supported by Syria and the Lebanon, proceeded to
organise arms and volunteers for the Palestinian Arabs; King
Abdullah retained his freedom of action; and the Iraqi
leaders continued to act as go-between with the British while
breathing brimstone for home-consumption. But as the
delegations left Amman there were still two all-important but
unanswered questions:

   (1) What was going to happen in New York at the
       United Nations Assembly?
   (2) What did Abdullah really mean by his "freedom of
       action"? Would he try to occupy the whole of
       Palestine, or only those parts which the United
       Nations would allot to the Palestinian Arab State?

[1] Later Mrs. Meir, the Israel Foreign Minister.

Both questions were to receive their answer. The first was settled on November 29th, 1947, when the United Nations Assembly voted the partition of Palestine by 33 votes to 13. But the answer to the second question remained open for another six months, until May 15th, 1948, when the King would be prepared to show his hand.

Meanwhile, how did the Jews in Palestine approach their supreme test? We must turn now to the other side of the hill, where the Jewish leaders were in the process of shedding their pet illusion: that all might yet be settled peaceably.

3

HOW THE WAR CAME TO ISRAEL: THE ILLUSION OF A SETTLEMENT

I т was a faith that did not die easily. The Jewish leaders in Palestine—with some significant exceptions—had fallen victim to that most dangerous infection of political warfare: they had come to believe their own propaganda. Thus, in the summer of 1947 the whole of the Jewish underground and para-military organisation was geared to the struggle against the British mandatory power: arms, military formations, intelligence and propaganda were organised on the assumption that they would have to be operated against the British.

None of the Jewish leaders believed that the British were in earnest in their declared intention to give up the Mandate and withdraw from Palestine. And this conviction was backed up by its corollary that the Arabs would not seriously oppose a United Nations decision, and that therefore there was no real danger of a major war with either the Palestinian Arabs or the Arab neighbours of Palestine.

From this conclusion there was only one major dissentient among the Jewish leaders in the summer of 1947—Ben-Gurion. He was the over-all director of the Jewish Agency's security policy.[1] He was probably the only one who had calculated the real military cost of partition. But few of his colleagues shared his conclusions. Therefore nothing could be done about it.

Ben-Gurion also did not press the issue. For he did not then believe that the British were really determined in their decision to leave Palestine. Perhaps he was not so wrong at the time.

But the upshot of this thinking was that the Jewish leaders

[1] He had been appointed to this position at the Zionist Congress in Basle in December 1946.

concentrated all their energies on the political struggle for the support of the United Nations Commission of Enquiry, and in the underground battle against the British, principally by bringing "illegal" Jewish immigrants into Palestine. The prospect of facing an all-out war waged against them by the Arab States thus receded in their reckoning into the background of time and urgency. The underground military forces were not reorganised. No special effort was made to obtain more and heavier arms from abroad. And the intelligence service behind Arab lines was still taking second place to that which operated against the British.

The Jewish leaders, admittedly, argued that first they had to win the political victory at the United Nations. On the other hand, their vision of what lay beyond such a victory was generally blurred—except in the case of Ben-Gurion. The Jewish defence forces in Palestine were, in fact, much weaker in the summer of 1947 than the world believed and than most Jewish leaders realised.

But concern about this situation was for the time being set aside while all attention was focussed, first, on obtaining a United Nations report favourable to the establishment of a Jewish State in a partitioned Palestine, and, secondly, on winning the necessary two-thirds majority in the United Nations Assembly. It was, furthermore, the considered view of the Jewish leaders that while the Arab peoples would not recognise processes in history, they would accept an established fact. Therefore, once the United Nations had approved the formation of a Jewish State, it would also be accepted by the Arab countries.

The warnings to the contrary by the Arab leaders were not taken seriously either by Palestinian Jewry or by World Zionists. Both argued that the Arab warnings were designed only to intimidate the Jews, the Commission of Enquiry and the United Nations Assembly. In a sense, they were right, as can be seen from the record of Arab League meetings in the previous chapter. But in another sense the Jewish leaders were mistaken. They underrated the strength of Arab national feeling, and, above all, they mistook the intentions of King Abdullah.

On his way to New York for the critical meeting of the United Nations Assembly, the Secretary-General of the Arab

League, Abdul Rahman Azzam, sought to dispel these Jewish
illusions. At a Press conference in London on September 15th,
1947, he gave "a solemn warning that any attempt to impose
the committee's recommendations, or any similar scheme,
would be implacably resisted by the Arabs. . . . Let there be
no doubt that the Arabs, if compelled, would fight for
Palestine."

Some days later Azzam repeated the warning personally
with convincing persuasiveness to the two principal advisers
of Moshe Shertock: Aubrey Eban, then spokesman for the
Jewish Agency at the United Nations, and David Horowitz.

There was an irresistible logic in Azzam's warning. The
moderates among the Arab leaders could not prevent a war.
The Arab mood was created by the young men who burnt
trams in the streets of Cairo. There was not one Arab statesman who could stand up to the power and terror of "the
street" and live. But the Jewish leaders could not bring
themselves to accept the inevitability of Azzam's conclusion.
They were prepared to agree that the Arab leadership had been
intimidated by this fear of "the street," but they would not
believe that either the British or the Americans would allow
this type of mob-rule to dictate to them their policy in the
Middle East.

This Jewish scepticism of the Arab warning, that the Arabs
would not submit without a struggle, was greatly increased
when on October 13th, 1947, the Soviet Union declared its
support for a Jewish State in a partitioned Palestine. After
this it seemed to most Jewish civilian leaders either unrealistic or unnecessarily alarmist to assume that the Arabs
would be so foolhardy as to challenge the combined authority
of the United Nations, the United States and the Soviet
Union, both these powers now being in favour of partition
for Palestine. The key to Jewish independence was therefore to be found in the Assembly and in friendly relations
with the United States and the Soviet Union—this unique
coalition of the two world powers who seemed to differ on
everything except the need for the establishment of a Jewish
State in Palestine. A corollary to this reading of the situation
was the equally strongly grounded conviction among the
Jewish Agency leaders in Palestine, London and ·New York

that, in the face of this world coalition, not even the British Government would be able to prevent the implementation of a United Nations decision. To get this decision was therefore the supreme objective of the Jewish effort.

The disinclination of the Jewish leaders to treat seriously the prospect of an all-out Arab attack was encouraged also by the reports prepared by the Political Department of the Jewish Agency. Its Arab section was in constant contact with some of the foremost Arab representatives; among them were King Abdullah, the Lebanese Premier, Riad-es-Solh, and leading Syrian and Egyptian politicians. From these private reports and contacts the head of the Middle East Department of the Jewish Agency, Eliahu Sasson, concluded that the Arab leaders had no real desire to go to war.

But in Palestine there was a dissident who did not share these assumptions, who looked upon the importance of the United Nations as secondary to the requirements for Jewish self-help, and who regarded the risk of the British determination to frustrate any United Nations decisions as much greater than most of the Jewish political leaders were prepared to accept. This was essentially the position of Ben-Gurion among the political leaders. But he was supported in the Haganah High Command by most of the senior officers, if one can use such a term for amateur soldiers who were in many cases still in their twenties or early thirties. They had been discussing since the beginning of 1947 the new aspects of the problem facing this Jewish underground army.

At this time the Haganah High Command was made up as follows—and it remained so until May 2nd, 1948:

Head of the command (RAMA) was Israel Galili; the Mapai party was represented by Yosef Israeli and Ze'ev Finestein; Hashomer Hatzair by Baruch Rabinov; the Mizrahi by Shimom Wasserman; the Right Wing groups by Selig Russetzky, Gad Machness, Issachar Sitkov and Yosef Jakobson. Of these only three took part in the work of the operational executive, known as Makhlekat "Bet",—namely, Galili, Israeli and Jakobson. The Chief of Staff was Yaakov Dori; Yitzhak Sadeh was his assistant, Alon, and Eshkol acted as Ben-Gurion's assistant, before taking charge of all financial matters. Yigal Yadin fully emerged among the military leaders only after Dori fell out because of illness.

The Haganah leaders had now become convinced, like Ben-Gurion, that there would be fighting with the Palestinian Arabs, and possibly with Arab volunteers from some neighbouring countries. But they did not consider that it would be possible for the Arab countries to mount a regular invasion of Palestine with the United Nations, the United States and the Soviet Union aligned against them. The effective Haganah leadership at that time therefore urged greater military preparedness, more training, more arms (principally rifles and machine-guns) and better organisation. But the shape of the war to come which they visualised was essentially an improvement of the Arab guerilla uprising of 1936, and the military measures proposed were designed to meet that kind of situation. The largest operational unit of the Haganah which was visualised at this time (the late summer and autumn of 1947) was a Palmach battalion of about 600 men.

Ben-Gurion disagreed. He wanted a properly organised army. He wanted heavy equipment, artillery, fighter planes and bombers. As far back as June 1945, during a visit to the United States, he had urged American Jewish leaders to help in the establishment of a military industry in Palestine.[1] But, quite apart from the financial problems involved, his military advisers could not see how they could get heavy equipment into the country through the strict British supervision, or how they could train an army when it had to be done without risking British interference. Ben-Gurion, however, did not accept this military argument, advanced with special force by Israel Galili and Yigal Yadin. Somehow he was sure that the traditional Haganah pattern would be inadequate for the coming struggle with the Arab armies—or, as seemed the more likely task, to force the British out of Palestine. For at this time Ben-Gurion was still convinced that the British were not really intending to withdraw their troops from Palestine. It was his conviction that before the military showdown with the Arabs there would have to be a

[1] For this purpose, a group of twenty specially chosen American Zionists were assembled in New York. Within a short time this group raised several million dollars and acquired the heavy machinery necessary for starting an arms industry. Haim Slavin, who was in charge of the operation, successfully evaded British control and brought the equipment to Palestine, but it could be used only after the British departure.

political showdown between the Jews in Palestine and the British occupying forces.

Yet Ben-Gurion was also increasingly conscious of the possibility of a major clash with the Arabs, once the British were forced to withdraw. The Jewish leadership would therefore have to pursue two parallel lines of action: a political campaign aimed at forcing the British withdrawal from Palestine coupled with a supreme effort to get the Haganah into a state of maximum possible preparedness with the greatest possible urgency. It was not a very precise situation, there were too many unknown factors and political imponderables.

But Ben-Gurion was virtually alone in the political leadership of the Jewish Agency in appreciating this need for urgency. When, in August 1946, he assembled members of the Jewish Agency Executive in his room at the Hotel Royal Monceau in Paris (other than those who had been arrested in Palestine), he asked for an allocation of five million dollars for arms. His colleagues thought he was joking. It was only after protracted discussion that he received a promise of $3 million—but it was not until much later that the money was actually made available.

This conflict inside the Jewish Agency and the Haganah High Command continued right through the summer and extended into the autumn as the hour of decision approached. On the one hand, it was impossible for the military men (including Ben-Gurion) to obtain the approval of the Jewish Agency leaders and of the political leaders in Palestine for a substantial increase in the arms budget—or even to achieve the psychological switch required before the new arms requirements were seriously considered. Arms were purchased by an organisation in Europe which acquired a dozen rifles here, fifty there and three machine-guns elsewhere. Ben-Gurion wanted them to think in thousands. But it was not until November 1947 that Ehud Ueberall (Avriel), Yehuda Arazi, Munia Marder and Eliahu Sacharoff left for Europe and Canada on the first large-scale assignment.

Similarly, it required long arguments with the political leaders before the Vaad Leumi, the National Council of Palestine, agreed to a plan for a general mobilisation of Jewish manpower in Palestine. It was not until October 1947 that the

Haganah received the approval for this step to be taken.

The Jewish leaders had found it desirable to build up the image of a massively armed and fully trained Jewish community in Palestine which was quite capable of looking after itself. Politically, this image was to make a profound impact on the world; psychologically, it also strengthened the confidence of the Jews in Palestine; but realistically, the picture—as it presented itself to the inner circle of Haganah leaders during these last crucial days of the Assembly debate— was very different. The only fully trained and organised force immediately available in case of need was the Palmach, the special striking force of the Haganah. Its establishment in November 1947, as will be seen in Chapter Four, was 3,000. Of these about 1,000 were girls.

In addition, several units of the Hish[1] could be mobilised within twenty-four hours. But these were in reality a kind of territorial home guard. Neither the Palmach nor the Hish had been trained to operate at anything larger than small battalion strength. It would have been virtually impossible to do so in view of the ubiquitous presence of the British.

As Ben-Gurion surveyed these puny Jewish forces, which were to face not only the British occupying troops (as he believed) but also the Palestinian Arabs, backed by volunteers and possibly even the armies of Egypt, Syria and Transjordan, he felt that with such a "partisan" force and organisation the Haganah would not be able to match the occasion. He began to insist on the need for laying the groundwork for a regular army on the British pattern. His Haganah chiefs, especially Galili and Yadin, did not agree. Ben-Gurion therefore began to think of setting up a regular army command side-by-side with the Haganah. He named a number of officers who had served with the British forces for this projected headquarters. Among them were Sacharoff, Barnea, Laskov, Shamir and Yohanan Rattner (who had not served with the British) but who was to be the Commander-in-Chief. But the Haganah leaders were convinced that Ben-Gurion's idea

---

[1] "Hish" is an abbreviation of the two Hebrew words Heyl Sadeh, meaning Field Army. These were the infantry units of the Haganah. There were also units of "Him," or "Heyl Matzav"—the static units. These were made up of second-line troops who were used for the static defence of settlements and towns.

was wrong and could not work. When the crisis came Ben-Gurion himself did not press his proposal for a "regular army" any longer. But he did not abandon it. Six months later when circumstances had changed he returned to it, and then he had the support of most Haganah commanders.

Palestinian Jewry therefore approached the crisis of November 29th, 1947, with all hands on deck fighting the political battle, but sorely unprepared for the real war that lay ahead. While most of the Jews—fortunately for them—remained blissfully unaware of the real state of affairs, it seemed that, apart from Ben-Gurion and his closest confidants, only the British had some idea of the actual situation, although they in turn harboured their own pet illusion about the course which events would take at the United Nations.

Like the Jewish leaders in Palestine, the British continued to believe that they would have the last word in Palestine because of the inevitable deadlock at the United Nations. "Why did you agree to let the Palestine question go to the U.N.," Bevin's adviser on Palestinian affairs, Harold Beeley, asked David Horowitz, "where you can get a decision only if the United States and the Soviet Union agree?" The Foreign Office had excluded this hypothesis from its list of possibilities. Thus, nine days before this unthought-of assumption became a fact, the Foreign Office in London explained that it was still assumed in Whitehall that the key to a Palestine settlement remained with the British Government. Bevin would try to make the Jews, the Americans and the Russians face up to the real issue: the enforcement of the United Nations decisions. Since neither America nor Russia would be prepared to enforce the decision, and since the Jews could not do so alone, the onus would again fall on the British. And they would not enforce partition unless both Jews and Arabs agreed. But what would happen if this situation actually arose?

On this question the Foreign Office declared itself both before the United Nations decision was taken and again afterwards in December: "The British Government was not concerned with the danger, or even the remote likelihood," it said, "of the regular Arab armies marching into Palestine." That was the opinion on November 20th, 1947. And a month later the Foreign Office explained that the British Government's military advisers "felt strongly that there was no

danger of the combined Arab armies moving into Palestine
other than the occupation of certain parts of the Palestine
Arab state by token forces." That was on December 20th.

Could it be that the shadow of Abdullah was beginning to
fall across the set pattern of British policy in Palestine?
Thus, as the Palestinian Jews watched with happiness and joy
as the United Nations voted, and with mounting concern as
the Arab reactions became apparent in the burning business
centre of Jerusalem and in attacks on Jewish buses passing
through the Arab towns of Ramle and Lydda, Ben-Gurion
called in Ehud Avriel and Yehudu Arazi. He gave them instructions to go to Europe and somehow get 10,000 rifles and
450 machine-guns, and to look out for aeroplanes and artillery.
Avriel was given a credit of $750,000. But, apart from Ben-
Gurion, no one had much faith in this mission. Some thought
it wishful thinking; others sheer madness. As it turned out, it
was the first step away from the world of make-believe with
which the passing of the United Nations decision to partition
Palestine was surrounded. The harsh realities of the situation
began to assert themselves. How this happened we can see
as we turn to the aftermath of the partition vote.

PART TWO

The Unofficial War

4

THE JEWS AND THE ARABS PREPARE FOR WAR: EARLY HOSTILITIES

THERE was not much time for the outburst of rejoicing and fraternising between the Jews and the British troops in Palestine over the outcome of the partition vote at the United Nations and the subsequent British decision to withdraw the Administration by May 15th and the troops by August 1st. With the dawn of November 30th, 1947, there came also the first shots in Jerusalem and the other "mixed" towns, and along the highways. This was the Arab answer to the assumption of the Jewish leaders that all might yet be settled without undue violence. The optimists among the Jewish politicians now had their reply; and the Haganah took command of Palestinian Jewry. But, as we have already explained, the Haganah was not the kind of force it was made out to be. Military correspondents of British and American newspapers had written of a militia of 80,000 men being ready to take up arms; other published reports referred to secret stores of artillery, and even to "Haganah tanks." The Arab military leaders estimated the Haganah establishment in similar terms (see p. 79). The actual state of affairs was somewhat different.

The Haganah had been founded in the nineteen-twenties to serve as the defence organisation of the Jewish community in Palestine—the Yishuv, as it was commonly called. Its existence was illegal and its training clandestine; its weapons had to be secretly brought into the country or illicitly purchased from British troops. The Haganah members were not formally mobilised but were called up every month for rudimentary training in field-craft and in the use of firearms—mainly pistols and second-hand revolvers, and, occasionally, locally produced

Sten guns and hand-grenades. This training took place "after hours" in schools, in hospitals and even in synagogues. An elaborate alarm system had been established to give timely warning of the approach of British troops or police. It was not unusual for police squads to be rushed to a school or to a first-aid station, after having received information that Haganah training was in progress there, only to find an evening class hard at work, or a nurse attending to a group of suspiciously healthy-looking out-patients. These training centres were frequently switched from place to place, and the times of attendance were similarly changed, so as to avoid the traps and ambushes which the Mandatory forces had set for them.

The more serious training, such as the special courses for squad and platoon commanders, took place in settlements and remote villages. Ben Shemen, Mishmar Ha'emek and others were regular hosts to the Haganah. Even there, training courses had often to be broken off, or at least temporarily interrupted, because of the sudden arrival of a British search-party. All this was naturally not conducive to either intensive or really effective training. These searches continued even after the partition decision of the United Nations. The British had decided to withdraw from Palestine, but they refused to agree to the setting up of local militia in those areas allotted to the Jews and the Arabs by the United Nations' resolution. The Mandate would be given up as a whole on May 15th, and until that date the British authorities would be responsible for law and order. To the Haganah it seemed that this responsibility was exercised in a somewhat one-sided manner, for they were forced to continue the clandestine nature of their organisation and be subjected to searches long after the Arab Liberation Army had openly deployed and organised themselves in the Arab areas of Palestine, often not more than a mile or two from British army camps. But in a sense all these many difficulties helped to familiarise the future Palmach commanders with the terrain over which they would have to fight.

When it came to weapons and equipment generally the Haganah also fell grimly short of the British and Arab estimates of its potential. The weapons which had been purchased by the Haganah emissaries abroad, had come from a very limited budget. They had been able to bring together a motley collection of firearms, ranging from Austro-Hungarian Steyer pistols to Finnish tommy-guns, and from Russian "Nagans" to a few prized Bren, Lewis and Hotchkiss machine-guns. In addition, a few underground workshops in Palestine manufactured a small number of grenades, Sten guns and mortars. But a good many were obtained in the Middle East after el Alamein and after the French withdrawal from Syria.

One of the most capable of the Haganah emissaries was Ehud Avriel, whom Ben-Gurion had sent to Europe with the order to buy 10,000 rifles and 450 machine-guns. Avriel was no novice at such an assignment; he had won his laurels—and gained his experience—as one of the ablest workers of the Mossad le Aliyah Bet, the underground movement which had been responsible for the organisation of "illegal" immigration of Jews into Palestine during the Mandatory period. Also "on mission" were other experts in this field: Slavin in the United States and Yehuda Arazi in Canada and later in France where he acquired the first six pieces of artillery for the Haganah which played an almost decisive role in the encounters on the day of the invasion.

Avriel arrived in Paris at the beginning of December 1947 and immediately contacted the many connections he had from the days of the Mossad. It was not long before he began receiving intriguing offers of arms for sale, and he soon found that most of them emanated from Prague. An English friend told him the official purchase papers of a certain South American country could be bought for the price of a ten per cent commission on every deal. It was expensive, but there was no alternative. Avriel was interested. He knew that the Czechs were willing to export arms to South America. He began to work on a variation of the scheme. He still had official papers of a certain country hidden away, dating from the days of his "illegal" work. In these papers it was stated that Mr. Ueberall (Avriel) was the official representative of the Head of that State and was entitled to purchase military equipment in his name. Armed with these documents, he left for Prague, after other Haganah emissaries, Pino Ginsburg and Uriel Doron, had prepared the ground.

With this fortuitous help and Avriel's not too genuine

papers, the two began putting out feelers at the Czechoslovak
Ministries of Defence and Supply. They found the Czechs
unexpectedly co-operative and friendly. They were keen to
the point of enthusiasm to help a small nation fight for its
independence—especially against the British.[1] Moreover, they
were badly in need of dollars, and they sold, in the main, only
surplus weapons.

But it was not until after protracted discussions between
Moshe Shertock and Andrei Gromyko in New York had been
concluded in January 1948, and after the Russians had given
their approval, that the Czechs finally agreed to sell arms.
From then on, however, they were quite willing to accept
Avriel's documents at their face value: the British Notes of
Protest which began to arrive in Prague only caused them
amusement and made them even more demonstratively
friendly towards the Haganah representatives. By the end of
January the first arms puchase from Czechoslovakia had been
completed. But the arms had now to be got to Palestine
undetected past the strict British blockade at sea and the
mandatory surveillance on land. For although the British
withdrawal was by then well under way, the British still
maintained the blockade of the Palestine coast. To get the
arms through, another veteran of the Mossad le Aliyah Bet,
Yehuda Arazi, was called upon for his experienced assistance.
Operating from Italy, he successfully transferred the arms
concealed inside tractors, cases of foodstuffs, and many other
devious hiding-places. The successes of Avriel and Arazi
came only just in time to save the situation. For the arms at
the Haganah's disposal at the beginning of the fighting were
hardly sufficient for static defence against guerilla bands,
and were wholly inadequate against the Arab regular armies.
When Ben-Gurion checked the armouries of the Haganah
in April 1947 he found its stock of weapons to be as follows:

> 10,073 rifles (of these only 1,353 were stored in the
> central armouries or were in the hands of the Haganah
> or Palmach units—the remaining 8,720 were scattered
> in "penny packets" under control of the settlements
> and kept there for local defence);

[1] They were equally willing, however, to sell arms to the Arabs (see
Chapter Ten, pp. 205/6.

1,900 sub-machine-guns;
444 light machine-guns;
186 medium machine-guns;[1]
672 2-inch mortars, and
96 3-inch mortars.[2]

There were no heavy machine-guns, no artillery, no anti-tank or anti-aircraft weapons, no real armoured cars nor any vestige of air or naval strength.

Only the special commando groups of the Haganah, the Palmach, were permanently mobilised. The principal units of the Palmach were dispersed among the collective settlements, where they alternated two weeks' training with two weeks' work to pay for their keep. When fighting started on November 30th, 1947, the Palmach establishment was 3,000; of these about 1,000 were girls. But the existence of a partly-trained reserve of nearly 3,000 enabled the Palmach to mobilise quickly a total of five battalions numbering about 5,000—1,200 of these were girls. Although the Palmach was officially a part of the Haganah (it also had a nucleus of the air force and of the navy), it operated under a separate head-quarters, which acted as intermediary between the Palmach units and the Haganah High Command. It led a largely separate existence from the rest of the Haganah units, and on the tactical level enjoyed virtually complete independence. Its first company commanders, back in 1941, were two young men in their early twenties, Moshe Dayan and Yigal Alon.

The Haganah mobilised its largest battalions—the Hish, or field units—immediately after the first outbreak of violence which followed the partition vote of November 29th. But this was no twenty-four hour mobilisation. The call-up was leisurely, and it was mid-January before the general mobilisation of all Haganah members was proclaimed: able-bodied citizens who were not already serving in the Haganah were not called to arms until March. The Jewish Agency leaders still failed to appreciate the real urgency of the situation. They

[1] Of the above weapons, only 636 rifles, 130 sub-machineguns, 33 light machineguns and 5 medium machineguns were, at that time, in the possession of the Palmach.

[2] These figures were given by Ben-Gurion in a talk to Jewish leaders in Israel in July 1948.

had been asked by the Haganah Commander, Israel Galili, to call up married men over the age of twenty-five. Galili's request was turned down five times by the Committee of sixteen Jewish Agency and Vaad Leumi (Representative Council) leaders, who had the last word in all matters affecting mobilisation. When he made the same request for the sixth time, it was conceded, but by then the grim facts of the situation were too apparent to call for further argument.

Throughout the first months of conflict hostilities were largely confined to isolated attacks on the mixed Arab-Jewish cities of Jerusalem and Haifa, and on the quarters with mixed populations which divided Tel Aviv and Jaffa. The British troops who were still stationed in these cities, and in particular in Jerusalem, did nothing to stop these skirmishes. When the Arab mob set fire to the Jewish Commercial Centre in Jerusalem at the outbreak of hostilities, British troops in armoured cars stood by, taking photographs of the scene. When Haganah forces were rushed up to prevent the pillage the armoured cars were moved against them, preventing them from reaching the conflagration. Later, during the nightly attacks on the isolated Jewish quarters in Jerusalem, the British would content themselves with an occasional search party, usually to search the Haganah defenders. During the first weeks of hostilities in Jerusalem the Haganah forces were far more wary of the British then they were of the Arabs, and this feeling was exacerbated when once a British patrol disarmed some Haganah men, took them to the Arab lines in the Old City and set them free. They were immediately killed by the Arabs. To prevent another such experience (it was a singular but long remembered exception), Haganah men would go out on patrol dressed in the long black coats and the wide-brimmed hats of the ultra-orthodox Jews of the Mea Shearim, or they would go arm-in-arm with girls, who would hide their guns for them in case of sudden British searches.

But throughout December, January and February the incidents remained largely isolated. There was sniping, and buildings were blown up; bombs were thrown by Arabs in the Jewish quarters and by Jews in the Arab quarters, by way of retaliation. These Jewish reprisals were often carried out by the two dissident organisations: the Irgun Zvai Leumi (the I.Z.L.) and the Lehy (the Stern Group). But in the chain

of events it soon became difficult to tell which were the attacks
and which were the acts of retaliation. But they all stemmed
from the Arab decision to set aside the U.N. vote by the use of
force in Palestine.

We must now turn to the other side, and see how the
Arab leaders faced the new situation. The partitioning of
Palestine was about to begin. What did they propose to do
about it? Two weeks after the United Nations vote which
decreed partition the Arab premiers met in Cairo on December
12th, 1947. Again the initiative had come from the Iraqi
Prime Minister, Salah Jabr. The minutes of the meeting show
that the old differences had not been resolved; if anything,
they had become more pronounced in the face of the
inevitability of a conflict in Palestine.

The Iraqi Premier proposed that the secret decisions of the
Bludan Conference should be put into immediate effect, and
that the Arab countries should proceed to intervene militarily
in Palestine on the lines proposed by the Chairman of the
Arab League's Military Committee, the Iraqi General, Sir
Ismail Safwat Pasha. In his report to the Premiers' conference,
General Safwat estimated that the Jews in Palestine had
organised armed forces totalling 50,000 men, not including
reserves; the Jews, furthermore, had adequate supplies of
light arms and large quantities of artillery and armour and a
sizeable air force. From this estimate of Jewish strength,
Safwat concluded that the Palestinian Arabs alone could not
stand up to them, and that it would therefore be necessary to
send the best arms possible to the Palestinians, to reinforce
them with volunteers, and to concentrate the regular Arab
armies on the borders of Palestine. Some of these would have
to intervene in the fighting.

The subsequent debate was confused but revealing. The
Saudi Arabian Premier was against putting the secret Bludan
decisions into operation. He was against arming the Palestinian Arabs and against using threats against British and
United States oil interests, and he was still more opposed to
the intervention of the regular Arab armies in Palestine.
The Egyptian Premier was also against any intervention by
regular armies, but he was prepared to support a move to
strengthen the volunteers fighting in Palestine. A memorandum

which had been submitted by Haj Amin, the former Mufti, also argued along these lines. The Mufti wanted no regular armies intervening in Palestine—for this meant intervention by King Abdullah—but he wanted the mobilisation and arming of the Palestinian Arabs. The same reasons which led the Egyptians and the ex-Mufti to adopt this attitude induced King Abdullah to oppose it. He wanted no arming of the Palestinian supporters of the ex-Mufti; he urged intervention by the regular Arab forces (meaning the Arab Legion), but not before the British had officially withdrawn on May 15th, 1948.

Faced by these irreconcilable differences, the Premiers agreed on generalities: they would do all in their power to frustrate the partition plan; they would supply the Arab League's Military Committee with 10,000 rifles, other light weapons and ammunition; they would arrange for the passage of 3,000 Arab volunteers through Syria into Palestine; they would give £1 million towards the cost of the "defence of Palestine"; and they would set up a technical committee to organise, train and equip the volunteers. General Safwat would be the Commander-in-Chief of these forces.

The Iraqi and Transjordanian delegations were satisfied with the decisions. They left Cairo and adjourned to Amman for further talks with King Abdullah. He assured them that they alone could carry out Safwat's project; Syria and Egypt did not count when it came to really effective intervention. The Iraqis returned to Baghdad and reported on their successful mission. The results of the Cairo and Amman deliberations were also relayed to Iraq's elder statesman, Nuri Said, who happened to be in London. On January 16th, 1948, Nuri had a private meeting with Ernest Bevin. Nuri told him fully what had been happening and what the Arab leaders had in mind. Bevin's reply was encouraging. "It became clear to us," Nuri wrote in a subsequent report on his mission,[1] "that Britain viewed with favour the Arab aims regarding Palestine. Talks about arms for the Iraqi army were most satisfactory."

There was another League meeting in Cairo on February 2nd, 1948. General Safwat reported on the poor response to the decisions of the December meeting and demanded that the

[1] Presented to the Iraqi Parliament.

Arab states implement the steps on which they had decided two months earlier. He wanted a joint meeting at once of all the Arab commanders (it took six weeks to arrange). The League also decided to grant no further oil concessions or permits for new pipe-lines; but these brave words fell a long way short of the threatening posture of oil boycott which had been the gist of the secret decisions of the Bludan Conference. But no sooner had Safwat returned to Baghdad than there began a grave government crisis. This was brought about by disturbances in the country in protest against the signing of a new Anglo-Iraqi Treaty in Portsmouth on February 15th, 1948. The Regent, the Emir Abdul Illah, was compelled to dismiss the Salah Jabr government and denounce the new treaty. Neither the Prime Minister nor General Nuri felt safe to return to Iraq for the time being, and the Foreign Minister, Dr. Jamali, was placed under house arrest. The British Government thereupon did not consider it necessary or wise to carry through the arms procurement which had been arranged by Nuri with Bevin. For the time being the Iraqis were in any case compelled to look after their home affairs. In the decisive months ahead Iraq ceased to be a serious factor in the Palestine situation.

The Iraqi crisis did not effectively diminish the Arab superiority in men and arms. But the Arab leaders were in no hurry to take advantage of this superiority. From the first, despite their own reports of Jewish strength, they believed that the isolated Jewish settlements scattered in Arab districts would fall to them without undue exertion on their part, and that the rest of Jewish Palestine could be dealt with at leisure once the British had departed. In this comforting belief they were frequently supported and even encouraged by local British officials, and by some of the commanders among the British officers. Moreover, the local Arabs, who had only the haziest of notions concerning the strength of the Jews, knew even less about the nature of their own forces. They had heard and believed the reports of Arab League resolutions urging that more money, more arms and more volunteers should be sent to the Palestinian Arabs. They accepted them as accomplished facts. No one told the Palestinian Arabs in their villages—until it was too late—that the Arab countries were not fulfilling all they had promised and that many of the weapons which they had sent were old, decrepit and useless.[1]

But essentially, Arab planning, even on the local level, suffered from the total absence of co-operation among the Arab leaders. The differences between the Husseinis, the followers of the ex-Mufti, and the anti-Husseinis, led by prominent families such as the Nashashibis, frequently produced chaotic conditions. In Jaffa, two independent commanders were installed, each giving separate and often contradictory orders; in Haifa, the rivalry among the Arab factions led to one group often commandeering arms and ammunition destined for the other group; in Lydda, there were open clashes between the opposing factions among the Arab bands.

Then, in the first month of 1948, a new factor made its appearance on the Arab scene in Palestine. On January 20th the first battalion of Arab volunteers moved across the border of Transjordan into Palestine and camped in the vicinity of Nablus. It was soon followed by other battalions. The "Arab Liberation Army," commanded by the Lebanese, Fawzi-el-Kaukji, had begun operations.

The Arab governments had started to organise and train volunteers for Palestine during December 1947. The operation was supervised by the Military Advisory Committee of the Arab League. Ismail Safwat, its Commander-in-Chief, set up his headquarters at el-Qudsieh, on the outskirts of Damascus, and took possession of the Syrian army's training camp at el-Qatana. This was to be the base for the training, equipping and launching of the volunteer army into Palestine.

Already during September, the first minor skirmishes had developed in northern Palestine. Safed in particular was troublesome to the British authorities because of continuous sniping between the Jews and Arabs. There were also more frequent incidents in the Huleh valley. This led the Haganah

[1] According to a report prepared for the Arab League Council by the Arab League's military Committee on February 8th, 1948, the Committee had by that date handed over to the Palestinian Arabs 1,700 rifles, half a million rounds of ammunition and a small number of pistols and grenades. In addition, the Egyptian Government had sent to the ex-Mufti, for distribution to his supporters, 1,200 rifles and 700,000 rounds. Shortly after the preparation of this report the Iraqi Government sent a further 1,000 rifles, and the Syrian authorities another 78 machine-guns, 8 mortars and 645 rifles.

to practise a new form of retaliation in order to impress and intimidate the Arab villagers by demonstrating to them that the Haganah's long arm could reach out even into the remotest Arab districts and hit back. But before this was fully developed, it was preceeded by the now customary theoretical debate. During the first phase of these actions, retaliation was directed only against "guilty" Arabs, against proven perpetrators of outrages against Jews, demonstrating as it were the long arm of the Haganah's justice. The Jews, it was argued, should do nothing that "would spread the fire." Indiscriminate retaliation, it was thought, would have just that result. One such retaliatory action took place on December 18th in the Arab village of Khissas, near the Syrian frontier. A small party of Haganah men penetrated into the village at night, killed ten Arabs and wounded five with grenades and machine-gun fire. They withdrew without casualties, after leaving pamphlets which said that the attack was carried out as an act of reprisal for the casualties suffered in Safed, and for an incident which had taken place near Khissas in which a Jew had been killed. In this attack, two Lebanese and two Syrians, visitors to the village were among those killed. It was claimed afterwards that this contributed to the subsequent invasion of the Arab Liberation Army, but it would be more correct to say that the Khissas incident was only one link in a very long and complicated chain of events, which, with the arrival of the Liberation Army, now enter a fresh phase. The Arabs had launched their attack, but now the Haganah began to hit back systematically, no matter whether it was in the north or south, or on the road to Jerusalem.

But there was increasing pressure from the field commanders, and also from Ben-Gurion and Galili, against the limitations on the retaliatory actions. They argued that the fears and scruples of the supporters of restricted retaliation were both unreal. It was becoming increasingly difficult, if not altogether impossible to pin-point the "guilty" Arabs. It was putting a degree of risk on the already overburdened Palmach which was no longer justified. Retaliation had become a national issue; it was no longer a purely personal matter. Its purpose now, was rather to warn and intimidate rather than punish. Typical of the new policy was the raid on

Sassa on February 15th, 1948,[1] an almost inaccessible village in Central Galilee, some 12 miles from the nearest Jewish settlement. If any Arab village was known to feel safe in the heart of Palestine Arab territory it was Sassa. But on that night a Palmach column of sixty under Moshe Kelman moved across country through the gluey Galilean winter mud, reached Sassa, blew up twenty houses, and withdrew again 12 miles through "enemy territory." It was meant to demonstrate that no Arab village was beyond the long arm of the Haganah. And to make doubly sure, a number of other operations of the same kind were executed that night against Arab villages and road bridges according to a carefully calculated scheme. It did convince many of the Arab villagers if not their leaders.

[1] On the same night as the Arab Liberation Army launched its first attack on the Jewish Settlement of Tirat Zvi.

5

JANUARY—APRIL 1948: THE FIRST CONCEN-TRATED ARAB ATTACKS: THE JEWS GAIN THE INITIATIVE

THE first larger attack by Arab irregulars from across the border was carried out on January 9th, 1948, against the northernmost Jewish settlements in Palestine, Dan and Kfar Szold. They were attacked by two groups of Arabs, each numbering about 150. The shooting attracted a troop of British armoured cars, which began to engage the Arabs, and after a fairly prolonged engagement forced them to withdraw. But this was still not the real thing. The Arab Liberation Army under Kaukji had not as yet been committed. In fact, the Arab leaders were trying to impress on the villagers that these local attacks were not the opening of the Arab offensive against the Jews. They wanted to prevent a premature uprising so long as the British were still in Palestine and able to intervene. They did not want to court British intervention in their all-out attack on the Jews. They were sure they could afford to wait until the last of the British had pulled out.

But as the days lengthened the Liberation Army movement across the border became increasingly bolder. On February 4th one of its units ambushed some army vehicles, thinking they were Jewish; in fact they were a party of Irish Guards. In the subsequent engagement the main body of the Arabs managed to withdraw. Six, however, were taken prisoner by the Guards and found by them to be first-class Arab troops. They were Syrians and described themselves as soldiers of honour. From their interrogation, the British authorities concluded that if these were typical of the Arab Liberation Army soldiers, "the Jews had a difficult time ahead."[1]

[1] Major R. D. Wilson in his history of the 6th Airborne Division in Palestine, *Cordon and Search*, p. 166.

A somewhat extraordinary situation was now unfolding. The Arab governments were still cautiously watching White-hall for any hostile reaction to their open intervention in Palestine. Some of the more adventurous Arab leaders urged them not to worry and not to hesitate. Even so, the Liberation Army moved only gingerly into Palestine, feeling its way, anxiously watching for the British reaction to this open invasion of British-controlled territory. After the first attack on Jewish settlements on January 9th, the British Government protested to Syria. The Syrians ignored the protest, and waited awhile. But when there was no further sign of British displeasure the movement of the Liberation Army was resumed and stepped up; its headquarters at Tubas in Central Palestine (not twenty miles from the British headquarters) was consolidated and it was decided to move the whole of the Arab Liberation Army, numbering 8,000 men, into Palestine and prepare for action.

The British G.O.C. Palestine, General Sir Gordon Macmillan, still had about 50,000 British troops in Palestine, including such expert units as the 6th Airborne Division, which was located in the assembly region of the Arab Liberation Army. Had Macmillan been authorised to take action against the Liberation Army infiltration or against its commander, the Lebanese Fawzi el-Kaukji, he could have cleared them out of Palestine within forty-eight hours, but Macmillan had strict directives from London, signed by the Secretary of State for War, Emanuel Shinwell. These ordered Macmillan to refrain from becoming involved in any military encounter with either Arabs or Jews unless their actions interfered with the smooth flow of the British withdrawal (see Chapter Six, p. 114). In fact, Macmillan was forced into the humiliating position of negotiating a live-and-let-live understanding with Kaukji, which assured Kaukji of British non-intervention so long as the Liberation Army kept quiet.

Kaukji, however, was a man of parts. He not only made an agreement with the British, but also with the under-cover representatives of the Jewish Agency. He was visited at his Tubas headquarters first by Macmillan's representative, Labouchère, and then secretly by Joshua Palmon of the Arab Affairs Bureau of the Jewish Agency. Kaukji told Palmon that he would not launch any attacks against the

Jews, and would not go to the aid of the ex-Mufti-controlled bands in the Jerusalem and Jaffa regions if called upon to do so by Abd el-Kader, who commanded the Jerusalem irregulars.

But most—if not all—of the Arab activist leaders remained unaware of these secret negotiations and arrangements. What they did see and note was the apparent connivance of the British Government in the planned Arab intervention by means of the Liberation Army. As they watched for the British reaction to the challenge of organised mass infiltration into Palestine, they received a chain of open and unmistakable signs of where the British Government stood. In retrospect it would be fair to say that these "signs" by the Labour Government were not intended to be understood in this manner, but the Government and the Foreign Office could hardly blame the Arabs for so misunderstanding British actions and misreading British intentions.

For as the Liberation Army began to move into Palestine, and as the Arabs watched, the British Government concluded a generous agreement for the release of Egypt's blocked sterling. That was on January 5th, 1948. On January 10th an agreement was concluded with Iraq promising immediate massive military assistance (see Chapter Four, p. 81).[1] On the previous day the first organised Liberation Army formations had crossed into Palestine. On January 12th the Foreign Office spokesman in London confirmed that the British Government would continue the supply of arms to Egypt, Iraq and Transjordan, in accordance with the Treaties of Alliance with these countries. On January 21st the British representative at the United Nations, Sir Alexander Cadogan, informed the United Nations Palestine Commission that it was "not possible" for the British Government to accept the Commission's recommendation to open, on February 1st, a major seaport in Palestine to facilitate substantial Jewish immigration. While Sir Alexander was speaking in New York, a mobile unit of the Liberation Army, some 700 men under Safr Bek, a Syrian officer, drove across the border into Palestine in twenty trucks with Syrian number-plates. They

[1] It was not the fault of the British Government that Iraqi public opinion subsequently rejected the treaty—and so lost the supplies of British arms which were to be delivered under the new agreement.

were armed with rifles and mortars and they were equipped with a mobile radio transmitter.

Nothing happened. No one objected. No one interfered. Four days later Fawzi el-Kaukji felt himself safe enough to to take charge of the Arab Liberation Army in person. On January 25th he moved to Tubas. But the ease with which the Liberation Army had moved into Palestine, and the striking absence of British intervention, began to produce unexpected consequences. The activists in the Liberation Army were greatly encouraged in their conviction that the British army would not or could not intervene. They pressed for more aggressive action by Kaukji. He had to give way.

During the night of February 15th, came the first major Liberation Army attack. Rather more than 500 soldiers of the A.L.A., supported by local irregulars, launched a clumsy assault against the religious settlement of Tirat Zvi, south of Beisan in the Jordan valley. The settlers managed to fight off the frontal attacks and to signal for help. During the morning a British force left Beisan for Tirat Zvi. They had some minor encounters with Arabs on the way, but when they reached the scene of the battle they found the Arabs had broken off the attack. Forty Arabs were reported dead and about the same number were wounded. The Jewish casualties were one dead and two wounded.

The encounter must have greatly strengthened Kaukji's hand against the activists. They had been badly shaken by this unexpected set-back. But for the Arab public at large, in Palestine and in the neighbouring countries, Tirat Zvi was presented as an impressive Arab victory. So were a number of other, largely imaginary, encounters with the Jews.

Despite the failure at Tirat Zvi, the infiltration of Arab volunteers continued. By March their number exceeded 4,000 men of the A.L.A., with a fluctuating addition of some thousands of Palestinian irregulars. Together they covered the country.

The northern sector, reaching down to a line running westwards from Qalqilya, numbered 7,000 men.[1] It was under the personal command of Kaukji and of Adib Shishekli.

The central sector, from Qalqilya in the north to Gaza and

[1] According to the Iraqi General Taha Hashemi, in his book *Diary of the War* (in Arabic).

Beersheba in the south, was held by 5,000 men, virtually all irregulars. This front was commanded by Abd el-Kader el-Husseini in the Jerusalem-Ramallah sector, and by Hassan Salame in the Ramleh-Lydda-Jaffa sector. Both commanders were staunch supporters of the ex-Mufti and both were later killed in action.

The southern front, comprising the entire Negev, was given over to a fluctuating number of volunteers of the Egyptian Moslem Brotherhood, ranging from a few hundred to some two thousand; in the Negev (including Beersheba) there were over 100,000 local Arabs, as against 1,000 Jewish settlers, who were sent one mobile Palmach battalion under Moshe Netzer. Later, Sarig joined them as area commander.

A small number of Palestinian Arabs had received training in their two para-military organisations, the Nejada and the Futuwa. But most Arabs knew how to handle firearms and were experienced in field-craft. Most villages had hidden supplies of some kind of weapon, and their inhabitants joined the affrays with increasing enthusiasm as the tide of victory seemed to flow their way.

With the mounting number of Arab combatants, the isolated incidents which had marked the outbreak of hostilities in December and January began to develop into more systematic attacks. Concentrated assaults were launched against the Jewish quarters in the cities with mixed populations— especially in Jerusalem, where some Jewish quarters were sandwiched between the Arab parts of the city. From now on the Jewish districts of Shimon Hatzadik, Yemin Moshe, Mekor Haim and the Jewish Quarter of the Old City were subject to almost continuous attacks. At the same time, isolated settlements in all parts of the country were besieged and attacked, in a manner which recalled the Tirat Zvi foray.

One of the more formidable of these assaults was launched on January 15th against Kfar Etzion, a collective settlement situated, together with three other settlements, in the Hebron Hills, near Bethlehem, in the heart of an area fairly thickly populated by Arab villages, and on the road from Egypt and Beersheba to Hebron, Jericho and Transjordan. The attack was led by the ablest of the guerilla commanders, Abd el-Kader el-Husseini. It was supported by his bands and by many hundreds of local villagers. Abd el-Kader succeeded in breaking through the outer defences of the settlement; but, with victory almost within his grasp, the attacking Arabs began to retreat when a platoon of Palmach coming from one of the neighbouring two settlements launched an unexpected counter-attack on his flank. The Arabs left 120 dead on the fields of Kfar Etzion. The following day the Arab villagers avenged their defeat when they ambushed a platoon of thirty-five Haganah men in the Hebron Hills, nearly all Hebrew University students. They had been sent as reinforcements from Jerusalem to besieged Kfar Etzion. All thirty-five men were killed.

News of this disaster shook the Jewish community—especially in Jerusalem—more than anything that had yet happened. For there was no unknown soldier in the Haganah; one or the other of the thirty-five families who were bereaved was known to everyone among the Jews of Palestine. It created something akin to a moral crisis in the Yishuu; its self-confidence waned as it had never done before—or since. It took some weeks before it fully recovered, very critical weeks.

The principal objectives of the Arab attacks during this initial phase were the lines of communication of the Jews. Road blocks were erected; cars, buses and trucks were ambushed. The roads from Tel Aviv to Jerusalem, from Haifa to the settlements of the Western Galilee, from Tiberias to the Eastern Galilee, and from Afuleh to the Beisan Valley became almost unusable for Jews. The settlements in the Negev and in the Hebron Hills, and the lonely settlement of Bet Ha-Arava on the northern tip of the Dead Sea, were effectively cut off from the rest of Jewish Palestine.

This was now the Achilles Heel of the Jewish position. The grim home truth—that the master of the communication lines would also be the victor in battle—was impressed on the Jewish leaders as convoy after convoy was shot up, casualties mounted, and the position of the besieged settlements—and, above all, of Jerusalem itself—became increasingly critical. The Arab leaders also understood that this was the way to victory. They changed their tactics. Instead of sporadic and haphazard ambushing of Jewish convoys, they began a systematic movement to occupy and dominate the high ground overlooking all the main roads in the country, and in particular the key to Jerusalem: the highway from Tel Aviv.

The Jewish leaders recognised the extent of their predicament. But during these first four months of fighting there
was nothing much they could do about it. The initiative rested
entirely in the hands of the Arab forces in Palestine. The Jews
were engaged in purely defensive fighting, or, at best, in local
offensive forays as part of a general defensive strategy.
For the strategy of the Haganah leadership during this phase
was based on two main considerations.

The first was purely political and was designed to counter
the Arab assertions, supported unofficially by British spokesmen, that the United Nations partition resolution was impossible to implement. In order to demonstrate that this was a
false assumption, the Jewish leaders decided to show the world
that the Arabs could not capture even a single Jewish village,
and that the Jews were able to defend themselves and their
territory. It was, therefore, vital to defend every single settlement in the country, even the most isolated among them.
This was Ben-Gurion's and also Galili's view, which both had
to maintain against many of their military colleagues. Thus
emerged the policy of no retreat, of fighting to the last for
every village and suburb, no matter how untenable the position might be by purely military calculations. This policy
meant, however, that the small organised force of the Palmach
and the Haganah fighters was dispersed in small packets
throughout the country. It prevented any concentration in
strength and compelled them to practise a policy of static
defence. Furthermore, this policy of holding every position at
all costs compelled the Haganah to send supplies to these
isolated settlements through the Arab-held territory. This
provided the Arab bands with repeated opportunities to
ambush Jewish convoys on the road to the settlements of
Nevei Yaakov, Atarot, Kfar Etzion, Yehiam, Ben Shemen and
many others. It turned out to be a militarily costly but
politically wise decision. It was in the last analysis made
possible by the determination of most of the Kibbutzim—
even the most exposed—to stay put and fight for their settlements.

The second consideration which governed Haganah strategy
was purely military. The High Command realised that until
the mobilisation of the Haganah could be completed, and until

sizeable arms consignments reached them, there could be no thought of offensive action on any scale. All available troops were committed to defending the settlements, or to convoy escort duty, in accordance with the declared policy of "no retreat." Moreover, the Haganah still suffered from a severe lack of arms. The first Hish infantry unit (the 2nd Carmeli Brigade), which was assembled in the latter part of January, had weapons for only about a third of its combat troops.

Thus, while the 3,000 Palmach shock troops, and another 3,000 men of the Hish infantry units which had been mobilised at the beginning of the fighting, remained fully engaged in continuous holding actions in the execution of this policy, the High Command endeavoured to mobilise, organise and train additional brigades of Hish infantry. At the same time, far from the actual firing line in Palestine, Haganah emissaries in Europe and in the United States were ordered to spare no guile in their attempts to acquire weapons to arm these Hish brigades.

During this period of general preparation, the Haganah began to plan for the day when it would be sufficiently numerous and well-armed to take over the initiative from the Arabs. Ben-Gurion, Galili, Yadin and the other Haganah strategists assumed that the main aim of the Arabs would be to isolate and, if possible, capture the Negev and Eastern Galilee, to penetrate the Sharon and Hefer valleys from Qalqilya in the direction of Natanya and Herzlia, to isolate the three large cities—Jerusalem, Tel Aviv and Haifa—and to interrupt the essential services throughout the country— water, electricity and, particularly, petrol supplies.

To meet this situation, they evolved a new plan of action for the Haganah, known as "Plan Dalet." It called on the new Hish brigades and the Palmach forces to regain the initiative from the Arabs. Their aim was to be twofold: to capture strategic heights dominating the most likely lines of advance of the invading Arab armies, and to fill in the vacuum left by the departing British forces in such a way as to create a contiguous Jewish-held area extending from the north to the south. New objectives were assigned to the Palmach and Hish units: which defence positions they were to hold, which police fortress or village they had to capture, what raids into Arab-held territory they were to carry out. Orders for the implementing of Plan Dalet, however, would be given only after the two pre-requisites needed for a Jewish offensive —full mobilisation and additional arms—had materialised.

There was, however, a third factor which the Haganah planners were forced to take into account. The British were the great unknown factor on which everything depended. The Jewish leaders watched and waited anxiously through these first months of 1948; they were still not sure whether the British really meant to leave Palestine. Until the Haganah Command knew the answer they could not implement Plan Dalet. For the presence of the British administration and of British troops greatly impeded the Haganah's war preparations. Because of the continuous searches, arrests and confiscation of arms by the British, the Haganah had to maintain its underground character long after the Arabs had openly assembled the units of the Liberation Army in British Mandatory Palestine. The British, in the eyes of the Jews at any rate, construed the laws of impartiality in such a way as to favour the Arabs in every manner possible. This "weighted" impartiality was felt by the Jews in many ways: the continued searching of Jewish convoys for arms, despite the fact that convoys were being ambushed and shot up on every road in Palestine; the British refusal to let the Haganah operate, and the arrest of Haganah men in Jerusalem, Haifa and Tiberias despite the constant Arab attacks on the Jewish quarters; the refusal to allow Jewish immigrants to enter the country despite the fact that hundreds of Arabs were daily crossing the land frontiers of Palestine. But in the Haganah leadership this British attitude induced more than bitterness; it produced a state of military thinking which remained more pre-occupied by the threat of British intervention than by the menace of Arab invasion. For example, when on April 15th, 1948, a British military patrol appeared near the Palmach strongpoint of Mount Canaan, the immediate reaction of the Palmach unit (which was surrounded by Arab-held territory) was to bury and hide its weapons.

The bitterness generated among the Jews by this attitude was exacerbated by numerous hostile acts carried out by individual members of the British security services. Most extreme among these incidents was the planting of a lorryload of explosives by men dressed in the uniform of the

Palestine Police in one of the main Jewish streets of Jerusalem, an act which caused the loss of some sixty lives. The Jews could not understand that in these acts they were reaping the retribution for the incessant terrorist activities of the two dissident organisations: the Irgun and the Stern group.

Thus, as long as this strict British supervision of the Jewish war preparations continued, no large-scale Haganah offensive was practicable. But as the winter drew to a close, and the British evacuation programme gained momentum, the Jews and the Arabs were left increasingly on their own. The hour for implementing Plan Dalet was now fast approaching. By the end of March, the first consignments of Czech arms arrived and were safely delivered to the Haganah. And now the six new Hish brigades were at last ready for action—but even so they were not at full strength, not yet adequately trained or equipped.

But before the Jews could complete their preparations something happened to upset all their calculations, and threaten the whole policy of "no retreat." The Arabs had beaten the Jews to it; the holding action of the Haganah had cracked. Within a matter of weeks, in every part of the country, the Arabs scored a series of major successes against Jewish transports which threatened the entire network of communications in the Jewish-held areas. Within one week, a convoy in Galilee on its way to the isolated settlement of Yehiam, on the site of the Mameluke castle of Kalaat Gidin, was ambushed and forty of its defenders were killed; another convoy returning to Jerusalem from Kfar Etzion was surrounded at Nebi Daniel, and, after a battle with heavy casualties on both sides, the Jews were saved from complete annihilation only by British intervention. All the armoured cars and equipment of the convoy, however, fell into Arab hands. Two other convoys attempting to reach Jerusalem during the same week were ambushed and badly mauled. As a result of these actions nearly all of the locally manufactured Jewish armoured cars were put out of use, and the whole Haganah system of convoys was in danger of collapse.

Furthermore, these Arab successes not only threatened the Haganah policy of holding on to even the most isolated of the settlements, but, to a far greater extent, they endangered the heart of the Jewish position in Jerusalem. For Jerusalem was the most vulnerable of all the Jewish positions, and, in Ben-Gurion's eyes, also the most important from the political standpoint. It was, therefore, around Jerusalem that the most severe and most bitter fighting took place.

The position of the Jews in Jerusalem looked fairly hopeless

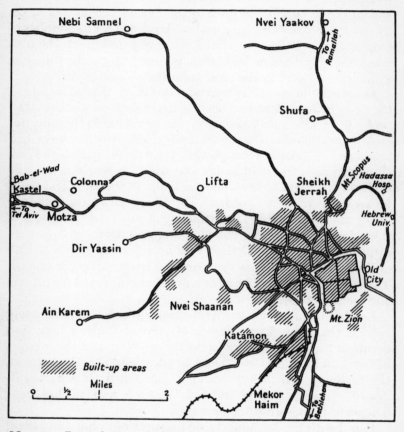

Map 2. Jerusalem and its surroundings at the beginning of May 1948.

during these first months of 1948. The Arabs held the topographical keys; they occupied the dominating hills surrounding the city, with the single exception of Mount Scopus, where the buildings of the Hebrew University and the Hadassa hospital stood in splendid and literal isolation. Even more dangerous for the Jews was the Arab hold on the three main roads leading from Jerusalem: to the north, on the road to Ramallah and Nablus, were the two isolated Jewish villages, Nvei Yaakov and Atarot, which lay besieged and in mounting danger of capture; to the south, on the road to Bethlehem, Hebron and Beersheba, lay the four Jewish settlements of the Kfar Etzion group under constant attack; and to the west was the road to the Jewish coastal plain. On this western road Jewish Jerusalem depended for its supplies of food and munitions for the Jewish population of 100,000. Even the city's water had to be pumped up by the pipe-line which ran parallel to the road from the coastal plain.

The situation was clear to Arabs and Jews alike. The fate of the Jews in Jerusalem had become dependent on whether they could keep this one road open for supplies. It became increasingly difficult. During February only two convoys had succeeded in getting through the rocky defile of Bab el-Wad, through which the road twists and winds as it makes its way up from the plain to the Judaean Hills. It was the ideal scene for an ambush: steep, wooded hills, strewn with loose boulders, tower above the road. The attacking Arabs made the most of this advantage. Three great food and munition convoys were attacked as they wound their way up the steep slopes of Bab el-Wad towards Jerusalem: scores of trucks were destroyed. The road to Jerusalem became a dreaded graveyard for drivers and their vehicles.

By the end of March, the Arabs had succeeded in completely closing the road. Large forces of Abd el-Kader's men had occupied the heights overlooking Bab el-Wad, and the villages of Saris, Suba and Qastel, close to the road. They had strewn the highway with heavy boulders and felled trees across it. Jewish Jerusalem was isolated, starved and in apparent danger of falling into Arab hands.

Faced with the uncomfortable prospect of losing Jerusalem, the Haganah High Command had to make fresh plans before they could execute the proposed counter-offensive which was to come into operation as soon as the Haganah brigades were sufficiently strong in numbers and weapons. The initiative had been left to the local commanders, but in Jerusalem Colonel Shaltiel had decided that it was not possible to launch any kind of offensive with the forces and arms at his disposal.

But now there was really no choice; Jerusalem was in danger. The offensive had to be mounted somehow, even though the expected arms had not yet arrived in adequate quantities. On the last day of March Ben-Gurion cabled Haganah headquarters in Prague. He ordered Doron and Avriel to load as many rifles and machine-guns as could be transported in a Dakota and fly them to Palestine immediately. The weapons were needed to add bite and as a morale booster for "Operation Nahshon," which was the code name given for the "save Jerusalem" action on which he had decided. For this operation units of the seasoned Palmach "Harel" Brigade were chosen, together with a battalion of the newly formed "Givati" Brigade, some units of Kiriyati and a company of the more seasoned "Etzioni" troops from Jerusalem.

The Givati troops were to attack the Latrun foothills from the west; the others were to strike across from Jerusalem to the dominating villages of Qastel, Saris, Colonna and Suba. With forty-eight hours to go before the attack, the aeroplane from Prague arrived. The weapons, still in their original Czech packing, were rushed to the Givati troops, who had assembled, largely unarmed, in a transit camp near Tel Aviv. The troops were allowed one firing practice to get the feel of the new rifles, and then left for Na'an, where Colonel Shimon Avidan, commander of the Givati Brigade and of Operation Nahshon, had set up his H.Q.

The offensive opened on March 31st, with a Palmach attack on Qastel, five miles to the west of Jerusalem. Qastel was the key to the battle, rising as it did to more than 2,500 feet above sea-level. It dominated the surrounding countryside, and in particular the Jerusalem road, which wound its way up the Qastel slope for more than three miles. The village of Qastel itself was perched at the top of this promontory. Its stone houses had been converted into strong points, and from them the defenders commanded an excellent view of the long, steep, rock-strewn gradient which led to the village. For the possession of this hill and its village, Jews and Arabs contended in some of the most determined fighting of the war. It was a ding-dong battle. The Palmach captured the village, only to be dislodged by a determined counter-attack by the villagers. A second attack once more gave the Palmach possession. This time a company of Etzioni troops from Jerusalem moved in to hold the village. But it was ejected again in a series of encounters during which a large part of the company was killed. The remainder retreated under the covering fire of a company of Palmach reinforcements. But the Palmach company was also forced to retreat. It did so after its commander had given the order: "All privates to retreat immediately towards Nahlat-Yitzhak. Platoon- and section commanders will remain to give covering fire." Only one N.C.O. managed to get out of Qastel. The company-commander who had given the order to the privates to retreat was found dead at his machine-gun post. The battle for Qastel continued for six days, with heavy casualties on both sides. On April 9th the battle turned into intense hand-to-hand fighting on the hill-top. In this engagement Abd el-Kader el-Husseini, the commander of the Arab forces of the Jerusalem area, was killed while leading the charge; the Arabs, on seeing their leader fall, made one last valiant effort to avenge his death and recapture the hill-top. When this attack also failed they lost heart. The hill was left in Jewish hands. One of the decisive battles of the Palestine War had ended. The Arabs had lost not only a dominating height but also a dominating personality, their bravest and most aggressive leader.

Simultaneously with the assault on Qastel, on April 4th, the western half of the Jewish task force had advanced on Deir Muheisin, in the foothills of Bab el-Wad, close to Latrun. But they were forced to withdraw by a British armoured car unit, whose commander claimed he needed the road to be kept open—a claim received somewhat sardonically by the Jews in view of the fact that the road had been blocked for the past month by Arab forces. The Givati force turned away to attack the villages overlooking Bab el-Wad itself, and captured Dir Muheisin and other heights. Meanwhile, the Palmach force, having consolidated the Haganah position at Qastel, captured the village heights of Colonna, Liftah and Saris. It failed, however, to take Suba, which, like Qastel, was perched on top of a steep hill and had been strongly fortified. With that, Operation Nahshon came to a halt. It had achieved its principal objective—but only temporarily.

Three large convoys, one of more than 250 vehicles, had passed through the blockaded road to bring food and munitions to beleaguered Jerusalem. The city inhabitants welcomed the convoys with almost hysterical joy, for food supplies in the city had become alarmingly low. On April 20th another convoy of 294 vehicles attempted to get through. But this time, the Arabs were ready for it. They had recaptured some of the heights overlooking Bab el-Wad, and the convoy suffered great damage before it reached Jerusalem. Operation Nahshon had given a much-needed respite to the defenders of Jerusalem; it had brought essential food and munitions to the city. But the Haganah failed to keep the lifeline open or to make the most of it while it was open, and by the end of April the Arabs were able to reimpose their stranglehold on Jerusalem.

This was partly the fault of the High Command. It had failed to exploit sufficiently the Haganah successes in Operation Nahshon. Even a scratch force stationed between Nvei Ilan and Hulda, and at Latrun, would have been sufficient to keep the western road open. But in the face of the other demands made on their available manpower, the Haganah leaders decided against this holding action.

Thus the outcome of Operation Nahshon was that the Jews had not wrested the initiative from the Arabs. The campaign had served only the limited objective of preventing the collapse of the Jerusalem defence. And, with all the Jewish reserves concentrated in the Judaean Hills for the Nahshon battle, the Liberation Army, under the command of Fawzi el-Kaukji, had taken the opportunity to begin an offensive of its own, in Lower Galilee. But, significantly, it had made no attempt to come to the aid of Abd el-Kader on the Jerusalem front.

On the night of April 4th, the same night that the Haganah troops began their Nahshon advance on Bab el-Wad, Kaukji massed a force of about 1,000 men, with a battery of six 75 mm. guns, in the hills overlooking the settlement of Mishmar Ha'emek. This stands at the gateway to Haifa Bay; it guards the Wadi al Milh route which leads to the coastal plain, and it stands astride the road from Jenin into the wide Jezreel Valley; it also constituted a threat to the Arab lines of communication from Haifa and Acre to Jenin. This was Kaukji's objective for his first major offensive: the capture of Mishmar Ha'emek would enable him to pass through Wadi al Milh and attack the vital Tel-Aviv—Haifa highway from the flank, or

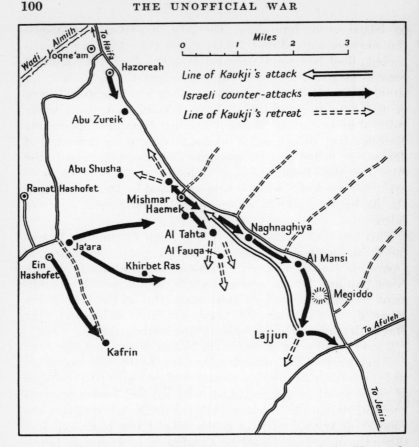

Map 3. Kaukji's attack on Mishmar Ha'emek and the Haganah
counter-attack, April 4th–12th, 1948.

to turn eastwards and invade the prosperous Jewish agricul-
tural settlements in Jezreel Valley. He would show the critics
at home that he was not playing at war.

Thus, on the night of April 4th Kaukji opened his attack
with a bombardment of the settlement with his 75-mm. guns
which took the settlers and also the Haganah command by
surprise. The defenders had only one machine-gun, and not
enough rifles for all the male settlers. Had Kaukji charged at
dawn on the 5th he might well have swamped the settlement
with his superior numbers, for the settlers were stunned by
the bombardment and by their casualties. But Kaukji

preferred to continue with his artillery, confident that this would bring about the surrender of the settlers.

The Haganah High Command quickly appreciated the hazardous position of the settlement. The use of artillery by Kaukji had come as a surprise; furthermore, the tactics of the Liberation Army had greatly improved over those used two months previously against Tirat Zvi. Mishmar Ha'emek, they feared, would not be able to hold out on its own against such odds. The order was therefore given to Palmach and Hish units in the area to denude the defences of other settlements and to rush reinforcements to Mishmar Ha'emek. A battalion of the Palmach under the command of Dan Laner and two companies of Hish were hastily assembled. Kaukji also brought reinforcements from Jenin. All was set for a showdown between the two forces.

But before the battle was fully engaged there occurred one of those incidents about which only contradictory accounts are available. On April 5th—the day after the initial attack— a troop of the 3rd Hussars, who were the nearest British troops to the scene of fighting, came to investigate. They concluded that they had neither the force nor the authority to turn back Kaukji and his men. Instead they found one of Kaukji's deputies. After some negotiations the British unit returned to its base at Ramat David and reported that the Arabs had refused to withdraw but had undertaken not to resume the attack. On the following afternoon the Arab assault was resumed with heavy gunfire, and on the morning of the 7th the commanding officer of the Hussar regiment, Lieutenant-Colonel Peel, arrived in Mishmar Ha'emak. The Arab commanders blamed the defenders for the resumed attack. The Jews had razed the neighbouring village of Rubaya during the previous day's lull. Peel then asked the settlers whether they would respect a truce. At first they would not commit themselves, but on Peel's suggestion agreed to a twenty-four-hour truce so that the women and children could be evacuated from the settlement. This was done and hailed as a great victory by Kaukji's men.

On the next day Peel tried to get agreement on an extension of the truce. He was shocked when the settlers told him that they had no authority to negotiate but that the British presence had given them time to bring up reinforcements.

This was not cricket, and he told the Jews that they were in effect breaking the truce. When the colonel saw that the Haganah had actually brought in reinforcements and had begun operations, he gave up and withdrew, still failing to appreciate that in this absurd war the Jews were fighting for survival, and not knocking up a cricket score. But even so, most historians now skip this humane intervention or attribute quite unjustified intentions to it. It was a typical, well-intentioned, ill-considered and ineffective step which did, however, enable the women and children of Mishmar Ha'emek to be moved out of the settlement before the battle was joined in earnest.

Kaukji had placed his guns in the hills above the two Arab villages of Upper and Lower Rubaya from there they commanded an excellent field of fire in Mishmar Ha'emek, which they shelled intermittently for four days. He put his forces in the two villages and in the surrounding hills with the intention of moving through the wooded hillside above the settlement and assaulting Mishmar Ha'emek itself after resistance had been broken by his artillery. When Laner's relief force appeared it was first deployed against the two Arab villages, which soon fell to the Jews. But the Hish company in Rubaya was almost immediately subjected to a heavy counter-attack, which continued all through April 9th. Kaukji understood that during the hours of daylight he had all the advantages of superior numbers and heavier weapons; the nights, however, were exploited by the Jews, who had discovered that the Arabs did not like fighting at night. By nightfall on April 9th the Jewish positions were on the verge of collapse: the Jews' ammunition was almost exhausted; their troops had been in action throughout the day with neither food nor water; their casualties were relatively high. As night fell the Arab bombardment reached a new peak; it seemed to Laner that this was the prelude to the decisive assault. But the heavy bombardment turned out to be a cover for the retreat of Kaukji's forces. The Haganah leaders were greatly relieved, and also puzzled by Kaukji's failure to exploit his tactical advantage. The excuse that he had exhausted his ammunition supply seemed to be neither true nor convincing.

But the battle was not yet over. Kaukji brought up fresh reinforcements. He was still determined to capture Mishmar

Ha'emek, and he now changed his strategy. Instead of making a frontal assault, he moved into wooded hillsides overlooking the settlement. On April 14th he resumed his advance, with about a thousand soldiers of the Liberation Army infiltrating through the wood, dragging with them their battery of guns. But Laner had anticipated his move, and occupied Khirbet Beit Ras, a dominating position in Kaukji's rear, with a company of Palmach and with two more companies in reserve. They waited until Kaukji's forces had come within three hundred yards. Then they opened fire. The surprise, and the fire-power concentrated on them, were too much for the Arabs. They withdrew in confusion, with the Palmach in keen pursuit. Before Kaukji succeeded in breaking off the engagement most of the surrounding territory had fallen into Jewish hands, including the villages of Abu Shusha, Naghnaghiya, Mansi and Lajjun. As at Qastel, the Jews remained in occupation. But Kaukji had the last word. He issued a communique proclaiming a great victory at Mishmar Ha'emek. Hundreds of Jews were dead. The settlement had been razed and flew the Arab flag.

Meanwhile, in response to an appeal from Kaukji, the Commander of the Druze battalion of the Arab Liberation Army, the Druze Shakhib Wahab, led a force against the settlement of Ramat Yohanan, to the south-east of Haifa. This lay near the main diversionary route for Jewish traffic from Tel Aviv to Haifa; it was of vital importance to Jewish communications. Here also the Jews beat back the attack and gained possession of two Arab villages strategically placed to help guard the settlement. They held on to the captured villages; the days of hit-and-run raiding were now over.

Nahshon, Mishmar Ha'emek and Ramat Yohanan marked the transition to a new phase in the war, in which (except in Jerusalem) the initiative in the fighting passed to the Jews, and in which the Plan Dalet offensive could now be put into operation. But what decided the Jewish leaders to launch Plan Dalet was not the fulfilment of the preliminary conditions which they had laid down; it was their growing certainty that the British really intended to evacuate Palestine.

Until April, many members of the High Command were by no means convinced that the British were in earnest. In

104 THE UNOFFICIAL WAR

fact, to Jews and Arabs alike it was as vital as it was difficult to assess correctly the intentions of the British during the period between the partition vote at the United Nations and the terminating of the Mandate on May 15th. We must now look at British policy during this period and the best way to understand it is to consider the one factor which bore strongly upon it: King Abdullah's ambitions in Palestine.

6

ABDULLAH'S AMBITIONS IN PALESTINE: BRITISH POLICY FOLLOWING THE PARTITION VOTE

DURING these early months of 1948 in Palestine, a situation was developing which was very near to what King Abdullah had foreseen in his meeting with Mrs. Golda Myerson, the Jewish Agency representative, in November 1947, when he said to her that "we both have a common enemy—the Mufti."[1]

Apart from the Palestinian Jews, there were only two contestants for position in Palestine: the ex-Mufti with his irregulars, and King Abdullah with the Arab Legion. The Syrian-Lebanese sponsored "Liberation Army" of Fawzi el-Kaukji soon ceased to rate as a political factor, although numerically it was the largest single force operating in Palestine, larger than the Arab Legion and more numerous than the Palmach. In order to forestall the ex-Mufti, King Abdullah now made up his mind. He instructed his Prime Minister, Tewfic Abul Huda, who had been in London negotiating some revisions to the Anglo-Transjordanian Treaty, to seek an interview with Bevin and to put all his cards on the table.

Tewfic Abul Huda, with General Glubb acting as interpreter, called on Bevin late in February 1948. Tewfic Pasha explained the position to Bevin: King Abdullah wanted to intervene in Palestine and occupy those areas allotted to the Arabs in the partition plan (but excluding Galilee and Gaza) so as to prevent either the Jews or the forces allied to the ex-Mufti from taking control. According to General Glubb, Bevin commented when this had been translated: "It seems to be the obvious thing to do." And then the Foreign Secretary

[1] See Chapter Two, p. 60.

added: "But do not go and invade the areas allotted to the
Jews." Bevin thanked the Transjordanian Premier for his
frankness, and they parted.

At that time neither Glubb nor Bevin, and certainly not
Abdullah, assumed that there would be a general Arab invasion of Palestine. But what did they assume? General
Glubb says that Abdullah and the British were intent on a
simple occupation of the central areas of Palestine which the
United Nations had allotted to the Palestinian Arab State,
and that no assault on the areas allotted to the Jews was
intended. Bevin made the same claim in Parliament. Are
these claims correct?

Before we can go on we have now to resolve one of the most
difficult problems of the unfolding Palestine situation: the
relationship between British and Arab policies during this
critical phase. The account which has been given by General
Glubb is unintentionally revealing. For it explodes the Arab
and Israeli belief that Glubb was an important link in the
chain of Anglo-Arab relations, or that King Abdullah treated
him as his close confidant. In fact, neither the British Government nor King Abdullah viewed Glubb as an instrument of
policy, or used him as such. Glubb was kept in ignorance of the
secret discussions of the Arab League Council (though, had he
been interested, he should have had no difficulty in finding out
what was going on); he was also left in the dark about what the
British Government wanted to happen in Palestine. His own
account is surprisingly ill-informed on both scores for one who
held so central a position. But the most noteworthy feature of
Glubb's version is that it explains his otherwise inexplicable
ineffectiveness, and also the incompetent ignorance of his
intelligence on what was going on across the border, on the
Jewish side of the fence.

Glubb and the Transjordanian Prime Minister returned from
London carrying the British Government's blessing for
Abdullah's policy of taking over by peaceful occupation the
Arab part of Palestine—but not the Gaza region, nor that part
of Galilee which had been allotted to the Arabs. Abdullah felt
that these might be offered as a sop to the Egyptians in the
south and to Syria or the Lebanon in the north. The feeling
grew in Amman that the Jews would not object to this
arrangement, and that there was thus a prospect of a peaceful

settlement in sight, with only the ex-Mufti left unsatisfied. Abdullah was now prepared to show his hand at the next meeting of the League.

This opened in Cairo on April 10th, 1948, and continued for twelve days. It started calmly and more soberly than had become customary. General Safwat began with a review of the military situation. The latest news from Palestine was not encouraging, he explained. The Liberation Army's drive on Haifa had been halted, and Kaukji had had to withdraw from his attack on the Jewish settlement of Mishmar Ha'emek, which had barred his advance. At the other end of the front, the Jews had stormed the dominating village of Qastel, killed the Arab commander on the Jerusalem front, Abd el-Kader el-Husseini (the ex-Mufti's cousin and agent), and opened the road to Jerusalem. Safwat argued from these developments that the despatch of regular armies to Palestine could no longer be postponed.

This was the cue for Abdullah's delegation. They announced that the Arab Legion would enter Palestine immediately the Mandate had come to an end. This announcement caused a mixture of consternation and confusion among the other delegations. After an involved discussion it was decided to make another appeal to all Arab states to provide equipment and men for the Arab Military Committee to save Palestine, to send a representative to the headquarters of the Liberation Army, and to order the Arab forces that were to rescue the Palestinian Arabs to be ready on the frontier on May 1st, 1948. Despite these decisions, the Lebanese delegate Riadh-es-Solh argued strongly against a formal invasion of Palestine, and the Egyptians again reiterated their emphatic opposition to the use of regular armies. But the debate could not be left in this state of indecision while Abdullah was formally preparing for an invasion of Arab Palestine by the Arab Legion. For the moment, the League discussion was not dominated by the question of the Jews but by the open declaration of Abdullah's ambitions.

Accordingly, two days later, on April 12th, King Farouk invited the leaders of the delegations to visit him. He addressed them jointly, and said to them: "The occupation of Palestine by any Arab army must be considered as a purely temporary expedient; under no circumstances can it be treated as a

conquest or partition of Palestine. After its liberation,
Palestine is to be returned to its inhabitants, who will choose
their own government."

The shaft was clearly directed against King Abdullah. He
understood it as such and ordered his delegation to reply in
kind. Transjordan agreed with King Farouk, the delegation
answered, that the Palestinians shall decide for themselves;
but, added Abdullah, "Palestine and Transjordan are one,
for Palestine is the coastline and Transjordan the hinterland
of the same country." Abdullah was satisfied. He had served
notice on his fellow rulers that the major part of Arab
Palestine would be linked to his kingdom, and they had
accepted it, even if they did not like it.

Back in Amman, King Abdullah agreed with the Iraqi
Government that two Iraqi regiments should take over a part
of the Palestine front allocated to the Arab Legion. By the
end of the month they were reported to be on their way. On
April 26th the Transjordanian Parliament formally approved
of the plan to send the Legion into Palestine, and on the same
day King Abdullah issued a statement to the Press in which he
said: "All our efforts to bring about a peaceful solution have
failed. The only way left to us is war. To me has fallen the
honour to save Palestine." Yet two days later, on April 28th,
the British Foreign Secretary told Parliament in London that
"it is our intention that the Arab Legion will leave Palestine
before the end of the Mandate. . . . There are no signs that King
Abdullah intends to take any warlike acts."

There was still a hopeful belief in London that war might be
averted and that Abdullah would simply become the heir to
Arab Palestine. That was the Government's opinion. But
meanwhile there was a second school of thought (especially
among Bevin's Foreign Office advisers, and in the upper
reaches of the Imperial General Staff) which held that
Abdullah need not confine himself too closely to the partition
frontiers. He ought to aim at Haifa and the Negev as the two
key positions to be occupied by the Arab Legion; but some-
where *en route* the planning and execution of this second
concept went astray. Glubb denies any knowledge of it, though
it was explained to a gathering of British Staff officers by a
senior British officer in Haifa a few days before the end of the
Mandate. Yet even so late in the day the British had no real

conception of the scale of the coming Arab invasion of Palestine.

On April 30th, two weeks before the end of the Mandate, the League met again—this time, symbolically, in Amman. In many ways this was to be the most fanciful of the whole chain of League meetings. The political Committee had come round to the view that all the Arab countries need do was to mobilise their armies on the borders of Palestine to demonstrate their intention to march on Tel Aviv. This demonstration of Arab power would cause the Great Powers to intervene and compel the Jews to accept the Arab peace conditions. With this happy prospect in view, the delegates agreed that the armed forces of the Arabs should jointly prepare for the invasion of Palestine on May 15th, 1948. But, even so, the Egyptians still hesitated. They did not commit themselves. Simultaneously there was a meeting of the commanders of the Arab armies. These decided that a war against the Jews in Palestine would require five fully equipped divisions and six squadrons of fighters and bombers to support them. This army would have to be under a unified command. The Political Committee rejected these figures as unreal and exaggerated. Abdullah laughed at the commanders. "The Zionist fortress will fall after the first attack, and the Jews will stretch out the hand of peace to the Arabs," he told a journalist. It was his way of preparing the public for a *de facto* partition between Jews and Arabs on the lines of the United Nations borders.

And then suddenly Abdullah's dream was shattered. The prospect of the automatic occupation of Arab Palestine without a major clash with the Jews vanished overnight. The more ambitious plan for a quick dash to Haifa of which his British friends had spoken seemed no longer feasible. He found himself faced not only by the Jews but also by hostile Egyptians and Syrians who wanted to anticipate his occupation of Arab Palestine, and, to fill his cup to overflowing, he found himself at odds with his own commander, General Glubb, over the main objective in the intervention in Palestine. All had seemingly gone so well right up to the end. And now that the hour of decision had come all appeared to be in jeopardy and confusion. For in a general conflict he might not emerge with the territorial gain of Jerusalem and most of Arab Palestine on which he had set his heart. He decided to make one more attempt to halt the threatening catastrophe. There was nothing he could do with the Egyptians, or with the ex-Mufti. The British were intent on leaving. Three days before the British departure he grasped at one more chance. The Jewish Agency representatives were coming to see him once more. Travelling disguised through the lines of the assembling forces of the Arab Legion came Golda Myerson and Ezra Danin. They met at the house of the King's personal driver. Abdullah looked grey and drawn. It was all over, he told them. The combined Arab armies would march in another three days. He needed time for a peaceful solution. Could not the Jewish leaders delay the proclamation of their independent State for another two years? In that case there would be no war. But even Abdullah was no longer convinced that this might be a solution. Golda Myerson and Ezra Danin returned and reported.

There were one or two among Ben-Gurion's advisers who wanted to accept Abdullah's offer, but there remained the great uncertainty in the background. Both Abdullah and Ben-Gurion were still preoccupied with the British. Would they really depart on May 14th and clear the decks for war? Neither Abdullah nor Ben-Gurion were convinced of it; nor were some of Bevin's most intimate advisers. Only the British commanders in Palestine had no doubts. They were carrying out the complicated process of evacuation; and it would be too difficult to stop this half-way, let alone to reverse it completely. But the consequences of these contradictory British postures were the general uncertainty, disquiet and suspicion which centred on British intentions during these last days of the Mandate. What then were these intentions?

There can have been few questions about British foreign policy which were more difficult to answer. Even later access to documents, or to the men engaged in the actual shaping of the policy, provides no conclusive answer. For the two dominant themes of British policy ran counter to every effort towards understanding its intentions. One was the refusal of the Foreign Secretary to give any precision to his policy. His principal assistant at the time has described it as based essentially on a series of "unstated assumptions" about what the British would like to see happen, and what in the Foreign Secretary's opinion was likely to happen. But that was not all.

If this emphasis on imprecision of policy was the first of the principal themes, then the second was the multiplicity of channels through which this policy was applied in the Middle East and at the United Nations.

On its different levels, British policy was given expression by many officials—by the Foreign Secretary during his rare pronouncements to Parliament or to visiting dignitaries; by his principal assistants on Middle East matters during less formal talks with diplomats or visiting officials; by two of the Chiefs of Staff, Field-Marshal Montgomery and Air-Marshal Tedder; by Sir Alexander Cadogan at the United Nations; by Brigadier I. N. Clayton (a shadowy figure at the Cairo Embassy, a kind of British unofficial ambassador to the Arab League, whose importance as a spokesman for British policy was greatly exaggerated by Arabs and Zionists alike); by General Glubb and Sir Alec Kirkbride in Amman; by General Cunningham, the High commissioner, and General Macmillan, the G.O.C., in Palestine; by General Gale in Egypt; and by a variety of more or less shadowy officials and organisations operating in the Middle East in the name or merely in the interests of the British Government—intelligence agents, political warfare media, radio stations, information offices and self-appointed unofficial ambassadors in the shape of newspaper correspondents, businessmen and oil companies. The sum total was like a modern symphony—both unharmonious and atonal. Unfortunately, it also lacked a competent conductor.

For six months, from the passing of the United Nations resolution at the end of November 1947 until the outbreak of formal war in Palestine in May 1948, the friends of Britain, and her more numerous antagonists over the issue of Palestine, were trying to comprehend the nature and purpose of British policy. What it lacked in authority and precision it made up in variety and contradiction—to which British spokesmen were inclined to add an element of obscurity. One consequence was that it was like the counter in a multiple store: friend and critic alike could pick and choose those aspects of British policy which they either liked or disliked and praise them or denounce them as they wished.

Thus the Jews in Palestine saw in British policy a Machiavellian plan to deprive them at the last moment of the fruits of the United Nations decision to partition Palestine and establish a Jewish State. The Arabs saw the contradiction between the assurances of British support which had been made to them at one level and their repudiation at another. The United Nations Palestine Commission, speaking also in this case for the United Nations Secretariat and the United States Administration, found in its report of April 13th, 1948, that the general policy of Britain had been to take no measure which might be construed as involving it in carrying out the Assembly resolution. About this negative objective of British policy there was no dispute. The British Government justified its attitude with the argument that the world could not expect British troops alone to carry the burden of enforcing the partition of Palestine against the will of its Arab majority. But in Palestine this argument was suspect in the eyes of the Jewish leaders, because they feared that British troops might still be employed to prevent the establishment of a Jewish State as laid down by the United Nations Assembly.

What justification, then, was there for the suspicion, or even the fear, that there would be a last-minute switch in British policy which would lead to the return of British troops to Palestine and to British military intervention against the policy adopted by the United Nations Assembly?

Because of the characteristics of British policy-making at the time, which we have already described, the record is contradictory, confused and inconclusive. And that, we may assume, was also the actual character of the policy pursued at the time. The "men on the spot" in Palestine, soldiers and civil servants, were carrying out their orders to withdraw from Palestine without any kind of secret second thoughts about staying on, or coming back. Admittedly, they did not like the short time allotted to them for carrying out the withdrawal, but they had no real military desire to hang on. They wanted to get out, and they did get out.

The British commander in Haifa, Major-General Stockwell, initiated the withdrawal from almost the entire area of Haifa on April 21st, and the Haganah took over.[1] Despite informal suggestions to the contrary from the commander of the Transjordanian Arab Legion, General Glubb, General Macmillan, the G.O.C. Palestine, ordered the total withdrawal

[1] As described on p. 118.

from Jerusalem by May 14th. But even more conclusive was the action of General Macmillan in Jaffa. He had intervened to stop the fighting there between the Jews and the Arabs during the first week of May because it interfered with his smooth withdrawal from Sarafand, the principal army camp in Palestine. By then Jaffa was almost entirely under Jewish control. At this point, when it was all over, Macmillan received a signal from the War Office in London. It said: "Recapture Jaffa, and hand it back to the Arabs." He was informed that a cruiser and two destroyers had left for Jaffa with reinforcements. When they arrived Macmillan's troops were engaged in escorting the fleeing Arab population of Jaffa to Transjordan. It was not surprising that General Macmillan felt at the time that this intrusion from London was not only unhelpful, but "quite unrealistic."

What, then was going on in London to produce these "unrealistic" orders and decisions? Were the men on top, the politicians and soldiers, regretting their hasty withdrawal? Had they been waiting for some such opportunity to reassert British authority in Palestine? Or were they just confused and no longer aware of what had happened in Palestine, and no longer master of the events there? It would seem that there was more improvising in the Government than planning, and more speculation at the War Office than information as the basis for the Government's actions.

In the Cabinet discussions, Bevin asserted his belief that there would be war in Palestine, that the Arabs would get the upper hand, that the Jews would appeal to the British to intervene on their behalf, and that the result would be a partition of Palestine in which the Jews would control neither Haifa nor the Negev. Creech Jones, the Colonial Secretary, did not believe that there would be an open war; both he and his Ministry feared rather a general state of administrative chaos resulting from the Mandatory Civil Service being withdrawn.[1]

[1] One of Bevin's principal advisers put it like this: "No clear directives had been given to the Arabs or to the British forces in Palestine that the Arabs were to occupy only those areas allotted to the Palestinian Arab state by the U.N. It was understood by him—and presumably also by King Abdullah—that some Jewish areas were to be occupied. It was generally assumed but never specifically stated that there would be fighting in Palestine which would result in partition, but Israel's portion would be rather smaller than that proposed by the U.N."

In Jerusalem the G.O.C. British troops in Palestine, General Macmillan, concluded by April 1948 that, in terms of troops, equipment and geography, the combined Arab armies "would have no difficulty in taking over the whole country." In London the Chief of the Imperial General Staff, Field-Marshal Montgomery, shared this opinion. So did many officials and officers of lesser rank. Macmillan was ordered not to intervene in the course which events were anticipated to take. He was to adhere strictly to the directive drawn up by the War Minister, Emanuel Shinwell, and dated April 1947. This ordered Macmillan to confine himself to maintaining law and order only in the areas held by British troops during evacuation; he was not to become involved in the Arab-Jewish conflict, and his primary job was to ensure an orderly withdrawal.

But there were a few doubters in official London as to the outcome of the policy. Thus, after having almost completed the sale of the largest British army camp at Sarafand to the Jewish authorities for some £750,000, General Macmillan received orders from London to the effect that "Sarafand is Arab property and must be sold to them." Accordingly, the Arab forces in Palestine were given possession of Sarafand when the British left the camp. Twenty-four hours later the Haganah drove out the Arabs and took over. There was nothing to pay.[1]

The same procedure was followed up and down the country. Macmillan received orders that priority should be given to Arab requirements in the disposal of strategically placed police fortresses and other government property. These were later to become the scenes of some of the fiercest fighting of the Palestine War. Their names read like the battle-roll of the Palmach or the Haganah: Mount Canaan, Nebi Yusha, Beit Dajan and Iraq Suweidan—or, to put it another way, like memorials to the British official certainty that Palestinian Jewry faced certain defeat.

Out of the confusion and improvising a British military policy was almost unwittingly taking shape: a kind of semi-intervention policy which would enable the superior Arab forces to take over all of Palestine, except perhaps a small all-Jewish enclave. And as this developed, so did the political

[1] Some years later, the State of Israel settled the account and paid H.M.G. £600,000 for the camp.

concept that was to provide its legitimisation. After months of stalling, obstructing, impeding, qualifying, denouncing, manoeuvring and protesting at the United Nations, the British delegate, Arthur Creech Jones, told the Special Assembly what was in his Government's mind. It was the day after the Haganah had taken over Haifa and was in the process of consolidating the Jewish position in the north, in the Jerusalem corridor and in Jaffa. Creech Jones informed the Assembly on April 23rd that in his Government's opinion the United Nations was now obliged to aim at a "more modest objective" than partition, without seeking at this time to arrive at a final solution of the conflict between Jews and Arabs in Palestine. In these efforts the British delegation would co-operate to the best of their ability.

This, then, was the British position, frankly declared and openly stated. What had made Creech Jones do it? Was his Government so ill-informed about events in Palestine, so misguided about the future prospects, that they really believed on that April day that the time was ripe for a public pronouncement of this kind?

The reason for this sudden intervention has to be sought in a curious scene which had taken place at No. 10 Downing Street on the previous evening, April 22nd. Ernest Bevin had called on the Prime Minister in the late afternoon in a state of rare panic. Newspaper reports from the Arab capitals, Bevin told Attlee, had reported that the Jews had massacred 23,000 Arabs in Haifa while British troops, under Major-General Stockwell, had stood by and done nothing about it. Bevin said that the army had "let him down" and placed him in an impossible position in his relations with the Arabs. Attlee was impressed and summoned Field-Marshal Montgomery to No. 10. This was at 7.30 p.m. The Minister of Defence, A. V. Alexander, was also present at the meeting. There was a heated discussion; we have Montgomery's evidence that "Bevin was very worked up"[1] and that Attlee was inclined to support him. By early next morning, Montgomery reported, Bevin and he met again and Bevin "was even more agitated." It was against this background of panic, anger and rumour that the Colonial Secretary's otherwise surprising statement was made. For we now have it on Field-Marshal Montgomery's

[1] *Memoirs*, p. 473.

authority that the Foreign Office was actually so ill-informed on the morning of April 23rd as to have concluded that, in the light of the massacre of 23,000 Arabs in Haifa,[1] world opinion would support a British proposal which would leave the proposed Jewish State without the Negev, without Jerusalem and without Haifa—a kind of greater Tel-Aviv.

But at the United Nations no one was in a hurry. Neither the British nor the Americans, neither the Assembly nor the Arab delegations felt any sense of urgency. The discussions in the Assembly continued as the fateful May 15th came nearer. There was an endless progression of new ideas, all with only one end in view: the postponement, or even the abandonment, of the partition plan. The Special Assembly passed resolutions, empowered the United Nations Mediator to seek a peaceful adjustment in Palestine, and relieved the Palestine Commission of its further responsibilities. It went on talking until May 14th, but the November resolution was destined to stand.

[1] The actual number of Arab casualties in the fighting in Haifa on April 21st and 22nd was about 300 killed; exact figures are not available. I was in Haifa during these days and watched the fighting. The Foreign Office's representative in Haifa was Cyril Herbert Alfred Marriott who expressed some rather unusual opinions on the situation in Palestine at the time. Some of his more astonishing reports to the Foreign Office (or their copies) came into the hands of Haganah intelligence and made very odd reading.—J.K.

7

THE LAST WEEKS OF THE MANDATE; "PLAN DALET" AND THE DEFENCE OF JERUSALEM

As late as April 1948, many members of the Jewish High Command were still sceptical of the British intention to leave Palestine. But as, one by one, every army camp was evacuated and every police fortress given up by the Mandatory forces, it became increasingly clear that the British meant to keep their word. The Haganah order was, therefore, issued, that in all areas wholly evacuated by the British the local Haganah commanders were "to fill the vacuum left by the British," to capture strategic heights overlooking possible lines of advance by the expected invading Arab armies and to link Jewish-held territory into one continuous area.

Army camps, police fortresses and government buildings given up by the British were, naturally, of considerable tactical importance for both the Arabs and the Jews, and both sides planned to be first in after the British had left. The advantage was frequently with the Arabs. They often received advance notice of impending moves from sympathisers in the Palestine Police or in the British army. General Taha Hashemi, the Iraqi general in charge of training Arab volunteers in Damascus, tells in his *Diary of the War* how the Arab leaders had been advised of the exact time of evacuation of the important police fortresses of Safad and at Nebi Yusha in Galilee, both of which were immediately occupied by the forces of Adib Shishekli, commander on the northern front of the Arab Liberation Army. They were also told of the British departure from the main electricity works at Gesher Naharayim, and a force of 200 Arab Legionnaires took it over. According to Taha, the fortress at Samakh and the large army

117

camp nearby were taken by the Arabs in similar fashion; Taha also alleges that a British Deputy Police Commander in Jerusalem provided the Jerusalem Arabs with full details of the impending British evacuation of the city.

In some places the British officers invited the Arabs to take over strategically located positions before the British had actually left. Thus, Iraqi irregulars were seen inside the Allenby Barracks in southern Jerusalem a week before British troops had given up the camp. The dominating Abu Ghosh police fortress in the Jerusalem hills was handed to the local Arabs, but these called in the Jewish settlers of Kiryat Anavim, as they did not want Kaukji's irregulars to take over their area.

But the Jews, also, were not slow to move into evacuated strong-points. Their intelligence service was well-organised, and occasionally reinforced by a well-placed bribe. They had had years of experience of working against the British. Consequently, they also got their share of police fortresses and army camps abandoned by the British.

The first "mixed" town in Palestine where the British forces decided to withdraw from maintaining law and order was Haifa, and it was here, in filling the vacuum created by the British withdrawal, that one of the decisive actions of the war was fought. For weeks the two sides had been preparing for the battle that would have to be fought for the city once the British really departed. Reinforcements were sent in by both sides, and as the hour of the British departure drew near, tension seized the 150,000 Arab and Jewish inhabitants of the city. The Arabs were in the majority, but were poorly organised and lacked weapons. Rival defence organisations competed for control of the Arabs in the city, and the young commander who had been sent there by the Palestine Committee in Damascus was hard put to it to maintain his command. But Mohammed el-Hamd el-Haniti was a forceful commander, and he succeeded in bringing order to the quarrelling factions and in organising the defence of the Arab quarters, which were overlooked by the Haganah on Mount Carmel and were difficult to defend.

But the Arabs lost their able commander even before the battle of Haifa was fought. El-Haniti was killed in an ambush on the outskirts of Haifa when an Arab convoy bringing

fifteen tons of arms and explosives from Damascus was
intercepted by the Jews.[1] His place was taken by Amin Az
ad-Din, an ex-officer of the Transjordan Frontier Force. Az
ad-Din, however, had neither the courage nor the organisational skill of his predecessor, a shortcoming which was to tell
heavily in the impending battle. He also had the misfortune to
face, in Haifa, one of the ablest command combinations which
the Jews had anywhere in Palestine. The front commander
was Moshe Carmel, confidence-inspiring and solid, with an
unfailing eye for the main chance and a dogged determination
to see things through. He had a solid planner and staff
officer, Mordechai Makleff, as his local commander. But no
less important was the "Arab section"[2] of the Haganah which
was at his disposal. It gave Carmel and Makleff a decisive
advantage over their Arab opponent even before the battle
for Haifa was joined.

On Sunday, April 18th, the British commander in Haifa,
Major-General Stockwell, summoned the Jewish Agency's
liaison officer, Harry Beilin. He told him that the British
forces would be withdrawn from all parts of Haifa except the
port area and part of the French Carmel. His withdrawal
would be completed within forty-eight hours, by Tuesday,
April 20th. Stockwell walked over to a large wall map of
Haifa and asked Beilin whether the Haganah could take over
the town. According to British intelligence estimates, Stockwell added, the Haganah would need 4,000 men for the job.
Beilin did not tell Stockwell that all that the local Haganah
could muster was little more than a battalion.

Fortunately for the Jews, both the British and the Haganah
intelligence estimates of the number of Arab combatants in
Haifa were grossly exaggerated. They had put the total at

[1] The Haifa Haganah had ways of getting information, and one
highly placed agent in the body which controlled all Arab policy. They
were thus able to intercept no less than nine of the eleven convoys
bringing arms and reinforcements for the Arabs in Haifa, at a cost in
bribes of about £50 per convoy.

[2] Haganah intelligence was fed mainly by information supplied by its
Arab section and its English section. The former consisted of Arabic-
speaking Jews, who infiltrated into the Arab sectors of the country as
Arabs, and gleaned in this fashion valuable information; the latter
section consisted of Haganah members who spoke perfect English and
who usually worked either in offices of the British administration or in
British army camps.

between 1,500 and 2,000. The actual number of armed and
trained Arab combatants was not much larger than that of
the Jews—560, to be exact. But this crucial information was
still hidden from the Haganah command as they prepared for
battle which was to decide Haifa's fate.

Stockwell had also summoned the Arab commander to
inform him of his decision to withdraw. When Az ad-Din did

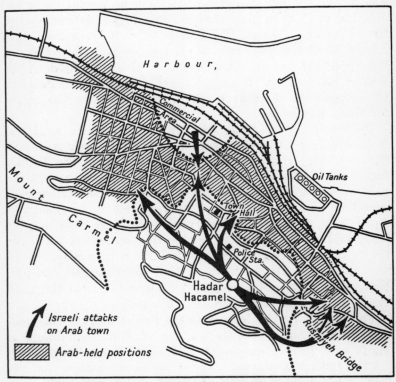

Map 4. The battle for Haifa. April 20th–22nd, 1948.

not come Stockwell drove down to the Haifa Sukh to look for
him. But he could not be found. Stockwell then had the Arab
notables informed of the British intention.

The Haganah took the initiative. A small force was detailed
to occupy buildings overlooking the strategic Rusmiyeh
bridge, over which all traffic to the east of Haifa had to pass.
After a room-to-room fight, the Haganah gained its objective,

only to be cut off immediately afterwards by the Arabs from
the nearby Halisa quarter. All day long the Haganah command attempted to relieve its badly mauled force on the
Rusmiyeh road, but without success. However, at sunset on
April 20th three columns of Haganah troops converged on the
Arab quarters of the city: two pushed downwards from Mount
Carmel, and the third advanced from the Commercial Centre
close by the port, aiming to link up with the other two units.
The battle continued all through the night. By mid-morning
on the 21st the link-up was almost complete; Arab resistance
had weakened considerably when the Arabs found that their
commander had left the city. He left them a message to say
that he had gone to bring back reinforcements.

The outcome of the battle was no longer in doubt, and
General Stockwell offered to mediate the surrender of the Arab
forces. Moshe Carmel agreed, and set out his conditions:
surrender of all weapons to the Haganah; immediate curfew
in the Arab quarters; the Haganah to have complete control of
the city; all inhabitants, Jews and Arabs alike, to have equal
rights and duties.

At seven in the morning of April 22, 1948, Haganah H.Q.
in Haifa received a message from Maj.-General Stockwell.
It said that he had been formally asked to transmit the
Haganah's terms for the Arab surrender. Fighting ceased two
hours later at 9 a.m. and by noon Stockwell was in possession
of the Haganah's "armistice" terms. He thought that they
were reasonable and moderate.

At four in the afternoon, the Jewish representatives met at
the Haifa Town Hall with the Arab representatives. Stockwell
was in the chair. The meeting was opened by the Jewish mayor
of Haifa, Shabetai Levy. He said that the Jews did not want
a single inhabitant of Haifa to leave. They had lived peacefully
together for forty years and could continue to do so. Then
the terms were explained to the Arabs. He stressed that he
wished them to remain as equal citizens in every way and to
be free to carry on their normal business and way of life.

The Arab delegation[1] then asked for a recess so as to be

[1] The Arab delegation of six was made up by two Moslems and four
Christians: Farid Saad and Sheikh Abdul Rahman Murad (Moslems)
and Elias Koussa, Victor Khayat, Anis Nasr, and George Muammar
(Christians).

able "to contact the Arab states for advice."[1] They had been in touch with Damascus since the early hours of the morning and they now withdrew to consider their next step. About the events during these critical three hours there has been much said and written and it has served to confuse rather than clarify the picture. But the basic story is now beyond dispute.[2]

At 7 p.m. the four Christian Arab members of the delegation returned to the Town Hall without their Moslem colleagues. Their bearing had changed. The former friendliness had been replaced by a sombre fatalism. They announced that they would not sign the "armistice" because it was degrading to sign such a document together with the Haganah. In fact, they would not sign anything.

Instead, they requested that the Jews should permit the Arab population to leave the city. They would not live for a single day under Jewish rule; "we do not recognise you and we shall return when you are no longer here," the Arab statement concluded.

Stockwell asked the four Arabs whether they had gone mad? Shabetai Levy, with tears running down his cheek, pleaded with the Arab leaders to stay with their people in Haifa. It was of no avail. Victor Khayat later claimed (through his brother) that he was against the evacuation, but he did not explain who or what made the Arab delegation decide on this step.

Nor does the explanation given by Mr. Koussa, who also was one of the Arab delegates, explain the pronouncement by the delegation after the recess. He asserts that there were no orders from the Arab Higher Committee in Damascus to advise the Haifa Arabs to abandon their homes, that in fact the whole exodus was an unpremeditated, elemental catastrophe, the result of the Haganah's calculated psychological

---

[1] Quoted in a report from the Arab delegation to the Arab Higher Committee in Damascus on April 30.

[2] The Arab exodus from Haifa is an important element in this story, both because it marked a new turn in Arab policy and Jewish outlook and because it became the prototype of the refugee problem in general. An attempt to establish the full facts of the exodus was first made by Walid Khalidi in the Beirut *Middle East Forum* in July 1959 and followed up in December 1959. Both these articles contain important new material and some significant omissions. For these see the *Jewish Observer and Middle East Review* for 11.9.59 and 18.9.59.

terror campaign reinforced by the real terror caused by the I.Z.L. massacre at Deir Yassin on April 12th when a whole Arab village of over 200 men, women and children was wantonly put to death.[1]

But all this does not explain the sudden rejection of the Haifa "armistice" by the Arab delegation at the Town Hall talks, nor does it explain the exodus of Haifa's 70,000 Arabs. For this had started already in December 1947, immediately after the partition vote at the U.N. and had affected especially the Christian Arabs—about half of Haifa's Arab population— who were being pressed by the Moslems to be more active in the fight against the Jews and to provide more financial support for it. The Haganah, on the other hand, was actually worried by the growing Arab emigration from Haifa. The Jewish leaders were convinced that they could keep the Haifa port going only if Arab labour continued to be available. Haganah policy, therefore, was to encourage the Arabs to stay.

Yet by the end of March 1948, before any serious fighting started—before Deir Yassin and while the tide of battle strongly favoured the Arabs—twenty-five thousand Arabs had already left Haifa. A further twenty thousand left in the first eighteen days of April, following Kaukji's offensive against Mishmar Haemek and persistent rumours spread among them that they should clear out to enable the Arab air force to bomb Haifa without harm to themselves. They were assured that the departure was temporary and would help the Arab fighting forces in the Haifa area.

The Arab leaders took an active part in aiding this process. The Christian leader, Archbishop Hakim, had arranged the removal of children in large groups to Damascus and Beirut

[1] Now a Haifa lawyer, E. N. Koussa, claims in a letter to the authors that "it is utterly untrue that Mr. Khayat had received an order to evacuate. I was a member of the Committee and personally delivered to the Syrian Consul at Haifa, Mr. Thabet Al-Arees, at about 12 a.m. on April 22nd, 1948, a telegram to the Syrian Government setting out the terms of the proposed truce, a description of the panicky flight of the Arab inhabitants of Haifa, and asked for instructions. Nothing was received in spite of repeated wireless reminders. It would be more consistent with reason and reality to assume that the Arab leaders were simply stunned by the gigantic magnitude of the flight which they did not foresee and which defied, unfortunately, their ability to tackle. But neither the Mufti, nor the Arab Higher Executive or any other Arab leader gave any order to the Palestine Arabs to leave their homes."

as early as February and March 1948. The parents followed the children.

The fighting, and the failure to sign the truce, increased the trend and on the day after the abortive Town Hall discussion another 20,000 Arabs abandoned their homes and left the city; but this was no new development. What was new in Haifa was the evidence that the Arab leadership had encouraged the exodus, if it had not actually ordered it. It had done this both by either direct or indirect instruction to the Arab negotiators[1] and by its scare-propaganda designed to frighten the Haifa Arabs into the belief that if they did not leave they would suffer the same fate as Deir Yassin.

The Arabs in Upper Galilee had all the advantages. They outnumbered the Jews by nearly thirty to one. Their villagers were adequately armed, and they operated near to the base of the Liberation Army over the Syrian and Lebanese borders. Their greatest advantage, however, was derived from their unmatched topographical position: the Jews of Upper Galilee sat trapped in the Valley, overlooked by the Arabs. And, as the British pulled out in the last weeks of April, the trap seemed about to be sprung. This, at any rate, was the expectation of the Haganah High Command.

The danger zone for the Jews lay to the east, where Galilee tapers northwards into a narrow tongue of land wedged between Syria to the east and the Lebanon to the west. There was also danger for the Jews in ancient Safed, with its 12,000 Arabs and about 3,000 Jews, nestling close into the folds of the Galilean hills.[2] In the valley to the east some twenty Jewish settlements, interspersed by many times their number of Arab villages, had been largely isolated. The only road leading to the south had been blocked by the Arabs, who occupied the heights along both sides of the road. The Arabs, furthermore, had succeeded in dominating the cross-country roads within the valley. Jewish settlers were thus prevented

[1] Haj Mohammed Nimr el-Khatib and Taha Hashemi, two Arab writers who were closely concerned with Arab policy-making at the time provide considerable evidence to justify the assumption that such orders were given.

[2] Since the outbreak of hostilities at the beginning of December, Safed, together with the other mixed towns, had had its full share of sniping and bomb outrages.

from moving to the assistance of threatened settlements, which had therefore to fend for themselves.

To the west rose the hills of Naphtali, with the Lebanese border on the skyline. Here three small settlements in the hills were the only defence line between the Jews in the valley and the feared Lebanese invasion. To the east was the Jordan river—little more than a stream. It marks the beginning of the foothills which rise to the high Syrian plateau; here also were a number of Jewish settlements which acted as guardians of the frontier. But the key to the whole area lay at the base of the Galilean "tongue." If the Arabs could drive forward in two columns from Syria and the Lebanon, and meet at Rosh Pina, they could effectively seal off the whole of Eastern Galilee. The trap would then be closed.

By now time was short. The Haganah had only two weeks left before May 15th, when the British Mandate was to terminate—the signal for the Arab invasion. Accordingly, the Haganah High Command decided not to wait. As the British moved out at the end of April, the Haganah was to move in. It was the kind of decision which is easier to make than to execute. Command of the operation (Operation Yiftah) was given to Yigal Alon, the twenty-eight-year-old commander of the Palmach.

Alon proposed to concentrate on three general objectives: to capture the key positions from the enemy, to free the roads for Jewish traffic, and to "prepare" Galilee for the impending Arab invasion. But when Alon arrived at the local headquarters at the settlement of Ayelet Hashahar he found conditions much worse than he had expected. Many of the settlements were desperate; the settlers clamoured for more weapons, more defenders.

Alon rejected their demands; in a stormy, almost violent meeting with representatives of the settlements, he told them that they would have to give up more of their meagre manpower and arms so that he could reinforce the offensive striking force of the one battalion of the Palmach which already operated in Galilee. This was no easy order for the settlers. Alon was asking them to denude their defences, and to gamble their homes and the lives of their families on what seemed to many of them a risky venture. But the urgency of Alon's plea convinced them. They realised that they had no choice; if they wanted to survive they had to fight Alon's way.

His advance began on April 28th, as the British withdrew from the large police fortress at Rosh Pina and the army camp nearby. Alon had waited for this moment; his Palmach battalion was deployed in the vicinity, ready to intercept any Arab forces attempting to take over either the fortress or the camp. Meanwhile, the British rearguard, seeing that the camp was about to fall into the hands of the Palmach, set fire to some of the buildings. The Palmach force, seeing this, began to advance on the camp in battle formation. As they reached its outer perimeter the British opened fire. A sharp skirmish developed. But as suddenly as the shooting had begun, it ended. The British rearguard had withdrawn. Rosh Pina camp and the police fortress were in Palmach hands.

Alon now proceeded with the planned offensive. His first objective was the city of Safed. The Jewish quarter was inhabited mainly by extreme orthodox, unworldly Jews who knew little of self-defence. They had been reinforced by a group of 35 Palmach members. They were no match for the large Arab population and the irregulars who had come to support them—a force of almost 3,000 besieged the Jewish quarter. Colonel Adib Shishekli had taken command of this force of the Arab Liberation Army. But above all, the Arab position had been greatly strengthened when the British handed over to them the three police-stations which dominated the city: a great Teggart fortress built on the summit of a hill approximately 150 feet higher than the rest of the city, and two other fortified posts, one to the east of Safed and the other in the central part of the city, where the Jewish and Arab quarters met. With these buildings in Arab hands, the Jewish positions were placed in a steel vice, and with every passing day the Jews felt its pressure tightening on them.

On the night of May 1st the Palmach force set out from its Mount Canaan base and attacked the two Arab villages of Ein Zeitim and Biriya on the outskirts of Safed, and so opened a way into the Jewish quarter of the city. But the Arabs were now on guard. When the Palmach soldiers moved forward in a series of waves up the steep hill towards the fortified Arab position, they were repulsed and suffered severe losses. First round in the battle for Safed had gone to the Arabs. Shishekli was now ready to take the initiative and assault the Jews in

Safed. A great anxiety gripped the city. In the Jewish quarter morale had sunk very low after the Palmach failure. But it was even worse in the Arab sector. Despite the Arab victory, the Arab population began to leave the town in large numbers. No one, however, spoke yet of "refugees".

Meanwhile, elsewhere in Galilee, by an odd coincidence, the Arabs also had chosen May 1st as the day on which to launch their offensive. Strong attacks were launched against most of the Jewish settlements in the vicinity of the Syrian border. Other Arab units ambushed Jewish transport rushing aid to the settlements. At the same time, the main Arab force was directed against the settlement of Ramot Naphtali, in the hills close to the Lebanese border. The Arab intention was clear: if they could take Ramot Naphtali they could sweep down into the valley below, cut off the Palmach forces in Safed from their base in Rosh Pina, and, together with a force from the east—which, presumably, would overwhelm the settlements being attacked there—would seal off the whole of Galilee.

The attack on Ramot Naphtali was, therefore, pressed all day long. Under covering artillery fire, armoured cars and infantry of the Lebanese Army, together with units of the Liberation Army, fought the settlement. After some hours the settlers began to retreat from the hill-top overlooking the village. Shortly afterwards the first Lebanese armoured cars reached the settlement's courtyard. It was a decisive moment. Ramot Naphtali was on the verge of abandonment by its defenders. The local commander advised Alon that he would have to evacuate if no reinforcements arrived soon.

This was the moment which Alon had dreaded. The only reinforcements he could send were from Safed; but this would almost certainly mean losing his initiative. Moreover, it would mean that he had lost the initiative in the fighting, and that his offensive would come to an end. On the other hand, if Ramot Naphtali were to fall the entire Jewish front in the north was in danger of being turned, and the whole of Galilee might be lost. Alon decided that instead of sending forces to the beleaguered settlement he would redouble his efforts in Safed, and thus force the Arabs to switch their forces from Ramot Naphtali to the focal point of his attack. Accordingly, he sent a signal to the commander of Ramot Naphtali which said: "At the bottom of the hill will be a Palmach machine-gun detachment: anyone attempting to leave the settlement will be shot." By sunset, Ramot Naphtali lay in ruins, but it was still in the hands of its defenders. With nightfall, the Arabs broke off the engagement, as was their wont. The respite was sufficient to evacuate the wounded, and to bring some reinforcements from the valley.

The Arab attack next day, on May 2nd, fared no better. By now a second Palmach battalion had reached Galilee, and quickly cleared the winding road leading upwards from the Sea of Galilee to Rosh Pina. (Tiberias had previously been evacuated by its Arab inhabitants after the British had pulled out of the town.) This timely reinforcement tipped the balance at Ramot Naphtali, and also for the other hard-pressed settlements along the Syrian border.

But in Safed the issue was still undecided. The Arab leaders had suddenly realised that Safed was particularly important to their invasion plans. These depended on Safed being securely in Arab hands by May 15th. On that day the Lebanese army was scheduled to advance down to Safed, and to take over the whole of Central Galilee.

Early on May 10th, with only five days to go before the Arab invasion, the Palmach battalion launched its second assault. It attacked all three Arab strong-points simultaneously. This battle for Safed turned into one of the most hard-fought encounters of the war. Eventually Shishekli and his two deputies, Sari Anfish and Amin Jamian, gave the order to withdraw. The shock to the Arab population had not been anticipated, the last of the 12,000 Arabs in Safed left their homes and fled with the retreating troops. Safed was left in Jewish hands.

The fall of Safed had a chain-reaction on the Arabs of Upper Galilee. In ever increasing numbers they left their villages and joined the stream of refugees to the Lebanon and Syria. Alon's forces, freed from the responsibility of Safed, were now able to reinforce the settlements and prepare them for the impending invasion. The Galilee offensive—Operation Yiftah—was almost complete. Among other things, it had proved the calibre of Alon as a commander. For his decision to maintain the initiative when the settlements were near collapse, proved to be the decisive act in the battle for the Galilee.

Alon wanted to exploit his success and continue his offensive sweep into Lower Galilee, with Nazareth as his next objective. This plan was turned down by the High Command because of the critical state of Jerusalem, and after Alon had consolidated the situation in the north, he was ordered south to take command at the Tel Aviv end of the Jerusalem corridor. Before accepting the appointment, Alon made one further bid for a more adventurous strategy which might produce a decisive victory. He proposed that with his available troops in the north, and one extra battalion, he should invade the Arab-held central part of Palestine, the so-called triangle which embraced the districts of Jenin, Nablus and Ramallah. He proposed to do this by means of a three-pronged attack: one arm would move down along the Jordan in the rear of the defenders, a second arm would attack in the north-west, and the third would assault along the western flank. Alon was convinced that his plan would demoralise the Arab defenders of the triangle and force the Arab armies to turn away from Jerusalem and face north. Yigal Yadin—the Haganah Director of Operations—was impressed, but he had no troops to spare, and the situation on the Jerusalem front was too serious to take any risk. He needed Alon's personal help on this front. So Alon had eventually to go south, and the assault on the triangle remained a paper project—one of the might-have-beens of the Palestine war.

In other parts of Palestine, also, the Jews had gone over to the offensive. In Western Galilee the forces which had captured Haifa advanced on Acre.

The Haganah's attempt to take the fortress fared better than that of Bonaparte: within a day of the British evacuation, the town was in Jewish hands. On May 14th the imposing Napoleon Hill, where Bonaparte had directed operations against the city, fell to Carmel's troops, and on the night of the 17th the city itself surrendered.

In the centre there remained Jaffa, the largest of the Arab cities. The pattern had by now become familiar, and though in Jaffa there were two discordant notes (through the action of the I.Z.L. and the intervention of the British), the end was the same. Most of the Arab inhabitants who were still in the city abandoned their homes, and the city surrendered on May 12th, 1948 after the Haganah had come to the rescue of the I.Z.L. and had conquered most of the surrounding villages.

In this manner, the "clearing of the decks" on the eve of the invasion continued. Wherever the British evacuated, battle was joined. No place of importance went by default. The Haganah objectives outlined in Plan Dalet were being implemented. The Haganah filled the vacuum left by the departing British, and they captured the strategic heights which overlooked the roads which the invading armies would be most likely to use.

The Jews had won this round. But the war had not yet begun, and the Arabs still held one superb advantage. This was Jerusalem. It would determine the outcome of the war. The Arabs had maintained their superiority in the Jerusalem area despite their setbacks elsewhere, and it is to this critical theatre of war that we must now turn before we can adequately assess the events which followed the termination of the Mandate on May 15th.

The position of Jerusalem was different from that of any other part of the country. It was the king-pin of the conflict. Both to King Abdullah and to Ben-Gurion, Jerusalem was the prize which would award either victory or defeat. For both, the capture of Jerusalem meant much more than prestige; strategy played no less a role in determining their policy towards the Holy City.

Abdullah had set his heart on the capture of Jerusalem, the third most holy city of Islam. To be king of Jerusalem would be at least a partial consolation for his father's loss of Mecca and Medina nearly thirty years earlier. But Abdullah also understood that if he let the Jews hold the whole of Jerusalem this would jeopardise his calculations for annexing the Arab parts of Palestine. His Chief of Staff, Major-General Glubb (as he was then), agreed. As Glubb puts it: "If the Jews captured the whole of Jerusalem, they could drive down the main road to Jericho, and the whole position in Palestine would be turned. If the Jews could seize Allenby Bridge, the Arab Legion in Palestine would be cut off from its base, and suffer a military disaster."[1] But, while agreeing in principle with Abdullah on this point, Glubb baulked at the conclusion which

[1] Sir John Glubb, *A Soldier with the Arabs* (Hodder and Stoughton, 1957), p. 107.

Abdullah had reached: that the principal objective of the
Arab Legion would therefore have to be the capture of
Jewish Jerusalem.

Glubb saw in Jerusalem a Jewish bastion which his small
army would never be able to overrun. Much better, therefore,
to gain a truce in Jerusalem, if possible demilitarise it, and
concentrate the Legion in the open, where its superior fire
power and mobility could be used to greater effect. "If we
move into Jerusalem," Glubb argued, "we shall use up half
our army. Then we cannot hold the rest of the country. If the
Jews hold the rest of the country, Jerusalem itself would be
outflanked and fall. So in the end Jerusalem also would
fall."

Glubb was not the only one to read the strategic picture of
Jerusalem in this manner. The same argument was also
advanced by the leading strategist in the Haganah General
Staff—its Director of Operations, Yigal Yadin. Yadin disagreed with Ben-Gurion over the necessity of giving the
Jerusalem front absolute priority. For Ben-Gurion was
convinced that the whole country could be defended by
holding Jerusalem and by concentrating the major forces of
the Israeli Army on its defence. Yadin, and the whole of the
General Staff, thought the answer was the other way round:
Jerusalem would be saved if the rest of the country was made
safe. Ben-Gurion argued that Jerusalem was the only foothold
the Jews had in the Judaean Hills; if that were lost there would
be nothing to prevent the Arabs from swooping down from the
hills into the coastal plain below, and repeating a familiar run
of conquest in the history of Palestine. Yadin, on the other
hand, believed that the greatest danger to the Jewish community in Palestine would be an Arab break-through to the
coast further north—in the Qalqiya-Natanya region, or in
the direction of Haifa—or a massive attack by the Egyptian
army in the south. He therefore believed it essential to keep all
available troops in these potential danger areas, while leaving
Jerusalem with the minimum amount of reinforcements
necessary for its defence.

Thus, both Yadin and Glubb reached similar conclusions
concerning the place of Jerusalem in the general pattern of
strategy. But whereas Yadin based his argument on his
assessment of the holding power of the Haganah in the event

of an invasion of the Arab armies, Glubb took his stand on a wholly false appraisal of the opposition he had to face in Jerusalem. It was a striking example of the inadequacy of the Arab Legion's intelligence service, and of the consequences caused by this shortcoming. For Glubb was convinced that Jerusalem had been turned into a Jewish fortress, and that his small Legion would have to face 100,000 armed Jews. "The Jews had for weeks been erecting concrete defences in their city. Streets had been closed by concrete walls and road-blocks, and concrete pill-boxes and machine-gun emplacements, trenches and barbed-wire covered every approach," he writes. Half the Legion would be lost in so large a city, he adds. Strangely, perhaps, Glubb fails to mention in his account of the situation in Jerusalem on the eve of the invasion that there were nearly as many Arab civilians as Jewish in the city at that time.

Glubb's evaluation of Jewish strength in Jerusalem was considerably at variance with the reality. His overestimate of the opposition was one of his biggest mistakes in the war. It is surprising that he should have failed in this way, for there had been Arab Legion units stationed within Jerusalem, as part of the British army, until May. They had every opportunity to appraise accurately the strength of the Jews in Jerusalem.

The Arabs held all the high ground overlooking the city: the Beit Jala ridge to the south, the Mount of Olives to the east, the "French" hill to the north, Nabi Samwil to the north-west, and the hills behind 'Ain Karem to the west. They dominated all the communications into the city, including the road to Tel Aviv, which had been blocked again by Arab irregulars soon after the Haganah's offensive phase had come to a halt.[1] Within the city, the Arabs were also favourably placed.

In a report to the Haganah High Command made on March 21st, 1948, the Jewish Area Commander, Colonel David Shaltiel, estimated the Arab forces in Jerusalem and the

[1] On April 20th forces of the Harel Brigade (a Palmach unit) temporarily occupied the heights overlooking the defile of Bab el-Wad, in order to enable additional convoys to reach Jerusalem. But they were ordered back into the city. The operation was called "Operation Harel."

surrounding districts at 5,300 combatants. These included
350 Iraqi irregulars and sixty Yugoslav Moslem volunteers. At
this date there were altogether under Shaltiel's command 1,200
field troops (the Etzioni Brigade), 1,200 second-line troops and
2,500 members of the Home Guard. There were not enough
weapons for all the Etzioni Brigade, and the Home Guard had
virtually no weapons at all. Shaltiel ended his report to the
High Command by warning that the initiative lay entirely in
the hands of the Arabs. "Our forces are hardly sufficient for
defensive warfare," he concluded.

Moreover, of the field troops at Shaltiel's disposal nearly
half were stationed in the defence of a dozen isolated settlements situated in the Judaean Hills and entirely cut off from
the rest of Jewish Palestine and from Jerusalem itself. These
included the settlements of Atarot and Nvei Yaakov in the
Ramallah area and the "Etzion Group" in the vicinity of
Bethlehem; but from Bet Ha-Arava and the Potash Works at
the northern tip of the Dead Sea troops and some supplies
were brought through the Arab lines into the city. Nearly all
of the remaining troops were thinly spread out among the
outlying Jewish quarters within the city itself, which, in April,
were still cut off from the main part of Jewish Jerusalem by
Arab-held districts. Thus, Ramat Rahel, Talpiot, Mekor
Hayim, Yemin Moshe and the Hebrew University on Mount
Scopus, not to speak of the Jewish Quarter of the Old City, were
all in fact isolated Jewish enclaves within the Arab city, each
having only the most tenuous connection with the main body
of Jewish forces in the centre of Jerusalem.

Colonel Shaltiel's task was further complicated by the fact
that a considerable proportion of the city's Jewish inhabitants
belonged to the ultra-orthodox sects and were either unfit or
unwilling to join the fighting forces. About 500 more adhered
to one of the dissident organisations, which often refused to
take orders from the city commander. Thus, far from being a
bastion of strength, Jewish Jerusalem represented a mixture
of weakness and of grim determination to resist. In these
circumstances, Shaltiel believed it was militarily essential to
evacuate some of the isolated settlements, and in particular
the Etzion Group. In this way he could concentrate his troops
within the city, he maintained, and use them offensively.
But Ben-Gurion was unbending. The policy of no retreat

must be maintained. There would be no voluntary evacuation of any settlement or village, no matter how serious its plight might be, or how tempting the strategists' arguments.

So, Glubb's picture of an opponent armed to the teeth, fortified and entrenched, was hardly applicable. In fact, the Arabs faced a scratch force which, as late as April, still had less than one rifle for every two soldiers. A large part of the defending Jewish force was cooped up in isolated villages and settlements miles away from the city, and much of the rest was splintered up into fragmentary units defending small Jewish quarters surrounded by the Arab-held sector of the city. Far from having prepared fortifications, machine-gun emplacements and the like, the Haganah were forced to "shanghai" many of the religious Jews from the alleys of Mea Shearim in order to make them dig last-minute trenches—this in the days preceding May 15th, when the Haganah command in Jerusalem felt that an attack by the Legion was imminent.

The Arab position in Jerusalem was better. Whilst the Jews could not hope for any reinforcements or arms before the road to Tel Aviv was recaptured, the Arabs had adequate reserves of both close at hand. The villagers of the Hebron Hills to the south and of the Ramallah region to the north were armed and were renowned for their fighting abilities. There was no real problem in bringing them into the city. Arab traffic, though sometimes harassed by the settlers of Nvei Yaakov in the north and Kfar Etzion in the south, was never seriously interrupted. The Arabs had no isolated quarters within the city to defend. They could concentrate their forces. But they failed to exploit their advantages. The death of Abd el-Kader el-Husseini at Qastel had been a great blow to the local Arabs, and their leadership in Jerusalem lost its former dynamic. They never considered either Abdullah or Glubb as alternative leaders.

The Jewish quarters of Jerusalem, and in particular Yemin Moshe and Mekor Hayim, were subjected to almost daily attacks. But though Jewish positions were kept under constant pressure, there were no really determined assaults on them.

It was in the hills beyond the city that the Arabs attacked with greater effect. By retaking the heights overlooking the Bab el-Wad defile after Operation Nahshon and again after

April 20th, they succeeded in isolating Jerusalem once more from the rest of Jewish Palestine and forcing its 100,000 Jewish inhabitants into a state of siege. Long before May 15th, when the Arab Legion was to begin its march on Jerusalem, the Jewish position there had become precarious. By attacking simultaneously both within the city and in the hills beyond, the Arabs had shrewdly forced the Haganah High Command on to the horns of a strategic dilemma. On the one hand, the Jerusalem–Tel Aviv road had to be kept open; on the other, the position within the city was so critical that all available troops were needed there to hold back the Arab attacks. But the troops which the Haganah commander could spare for the Jerusalem front were only adequate for operations either in the city or in the hills overlooking the road; there were not sufficient soldiers available for both places. Thus, barely a week after the Harel Brigade had begun its offensive[1] in the Judaean Hills to recapture the hills dominating the road, they were hastily ordered back into the city. In the five days of its hill offensive, the Harel Brigade had succeeded in cleaving a way for three large convoys, each consisting of over 200 requisitioned civilian trucks, to reach Jerusalem with food and arms. But their offensive remained abortive. The fourth convoy, which brought the brigade itself to Jerusalem on April 21st, fought its way through only with great difficulty and heavy losses

These reinforcements arrived only just in time. The Etzioni Brigade, nearly half of which was defending the Etzion Group and the other hill settlements, had been in continuous action since December and had suffered heavy casualties. The troops cut off in Mekor Hayim, Yemin Moshe, and the Jewish Quarter of the Old City were in action day and night. The strain was beginning to tell. There were no reserves within the city to relieve them or to ease their lot. When, for example, the Arabs ambushed a convoy taking doctors and medical supplies up to Hadassah hospital on Mount Scopus, Shaltiel had no reserves to rescue the convoy's defenders, despite the fact that they fought against the attackers for seven hours within sight of the city. When they were finally overcome the Arabs set fire to the vehicles and killed those who attempted to escape the flames. By nightfall, there were

[1] Operation Harel.

some eighty dead, including the head of the hospital and many doctors and nurses. This incident took place several hundred yards from a British army camp. The British soldiers who witnessed the massacre received orders not to intervene, because of the danger to which they could be exposed. The British commander considered his force on the spot to be inadequate for an effective intervention.

The days of the British presence in Jerusalem were now drawing to their unpeaceful close. Uneasy expectation settled on the city. Arabs and Jews were asking the inevitable question: what would happen after May 15th? On April 26th, five days after the arrival of the Jewish reinforcements in Jerusalem, the Transjordanian Parliament ratified the decision to send the Legion into Palestine on the termination of the Mandate. Abdullah told journalists: "All our efforts to find a peaceful solution to the Palestine problem have failed. The only way left for us is war. I will have the pleasure and the honour to save Palestine." On April 27th the 2nd Motorised Brigade of the Iraqi army left Baghdad for Transjordan, on its way to Palestine.

Meanwhile, on the Jerusalem front a special command was established under the overall command of Itzhak Sadeh with Shaltiel in charge of the Etzioni Brigade in Jerusalem and Itzhak Rabin in command of the Harel Brigade in the Jerusalem hills. This force was to carry out Operation Yevussi and take the four commanding positions on which possession of Jerusalem largely depended: Nabi Samwil, Sheikh Jarrah, Katamon and the Victoria Augusta compound. But the offensive did not go well. On the Jerusalem perimeter, the Palestinian Arab irregulars scored their greatest victory yet when they succeeded in ambushing a company of the Harel Brigade, which had attempted to take the Nabi Samwil crest, the highest of all the Judaean hill-tops. The Jewish unit had to retreat, after having over forty killed. But inside the city the Harel forces were taking full advantage of the last three weeks of the Mandate. The arrival of the reinforcements enabled the Haganah to link up the isolated quarters within the city. Sadeh and Rabin now attempted to establish direct contact with Mount Scopus—the only strategically placed hill-top in the Jerusalem region in Jewish hands. His purpose was to threaten the rear of the Arab positions in the Old

City. After a house-to-house battle lasting through the night of April 26th, the Harel units succeeded in gaining control of the northern suburb of Sheikh Jarrah. They had thus severed the Arab road link between the Old City and Ramallah, and had re-established their own link with Mount Scopus.

But it was a short-lived victory. The morning after, an ultimatum from Brigadier Jones, commander of the British force, was handed to Sadeh. Sheikh Jarrah lay astride the British evacuation route; the British could not tolerate that the road should be the scene of battles; and the Jews were ordered to evacuate the quarter forthwith. When the ultimatum expired the Haganah were still in position. A squadron of British armour, supported by infantry, then advanced on their positions; a battery of 25-pounder guns, firing at point-blank range, also went into action. Jones meant business. The Haganah complied with his wishes, and Sheikh Jarrah remained in British hands until May 15th. Jones also kept his promises. He had told the Haganah that he would return Sheikh Jarrah to the Jews when the British evacuated. And before he withdrew, he did so.

The hardest fighting, however, took place in the southern part of Jerusalem, where a sharp battle raged for the possession of the large and rich Arab quarter of Katamon, which separated Mekor Hayim from the centre of the city. The battle was fiercest round the old Greek Monastery, which had been turned into the base of the Arab forces in this part of the city. When finally forced to withdraw, the Arabs left some eighty dead in the once-peaceful Monastery gardens and in the shambles that had once been a church.[1] With the fall of Katamon, Arab resistance in the whole southern part of Jerusalem began to break. But the Haganah forces were unable to exploit their advantage, for the British commander once more—for the last time—imposed on both sides a truce, which came into effect in the first week of May.

As the nervous quiet descended on the city, fighting flared up once more in the hills beyond. The Palmach reinforcements left the city and resumed their attack on the Bab el-Wad sector, in one more effort to open the Tel Aviv road to Jewish

[1] The attacking force suffered ten killed and some sixty wounded.

traffic.[1] But now the battle scene moved to the south of the
city, into the Hebron Hills. The Arab Legion had begun its
first attack, eleven days before the end of the Mandate and
the "official" invasion of the Arab armies.

Its target was the Etzion Group of four Jewish collective
settlements, fourteen miles to the south of Jerusalem, close to
the main Jerusalem-Hebron highway. The settlements, reinforced by troops of the Etzioni Brigade, had been isolated
from the rest of Jewish Palestine since December 1947, in the
midst of a thickly populated Arab area. They had been the
target for heavy Arab attacks, all of which they succeeded in
beating off. And despite their precarious position, the Jews of
the Etzion Group became a major nuisance to the Arabs.
From their vantage-point in the abandoned Russian Monastery, which they had occupied, they would open fire on Arab
traffic moving between Hebron and Jerusalem. During the
battle for the Katamon suburb within the city at the end of
April, the Etzion Group succeeded for a short time in making
the road almost impassable to the Arabs.

But their successes were to cost the Etzion defenders
dearly. The road was vital to the Arab Legion. Its trucks were

[1] On the night of May 7th—8th the Harel Brigade commenced
"Operation Macabbee," another attempt to open the Jerusalem—Tel
Aviv road. In the course of a week of heavy and continuous fighting the
village of Bet Mahsir and the heights overlooking Bab el-Wad were
captured and held by the Brigade. On the night of May 15th the villages
of Latrun and Deir Ayoub were also captured. The following night a
convoy of forty vehicles passed through, the last to reach Jerusalem
via the Latrun road. On May 17th Latrun and Deir Ayoub were reoccupied by the Arabs.

There exists a considerable conflict of opinion about the events of these
forty-eight hours during which the Israelis abandoned what turned out
to be one of the key positions in the war; the question at issue being
whether the Israelis could have held on. Yadin says that he was faced
with the threat of the advancing Egyptians moving on Tel Aviv from
the south with virtually no Israeli troops (other than the settlements)
to bar their way. He had to take the Givati force from Latrun and
send them south even at the risk of losing Latrun and its strategic
approaches. Yadin received a telegram from Ben-Gurion urging the
occupation of Yalu as the key to free communications with Jerusalem.
In reply, Yadin explained his position. Ben-Gurion was persuaded by
Yadin's arguments and agreed to the abandonment of the Latrun
villages; but it was an aquiescence which Ben-Gurion subsequently
regretted—but was there an alternative solution?

engaged in a continuous shuttle-service, bringing supplies and ammunition from the British camps in the Canal Zone to Transjordan. For the British Government had promised to supply Abdullah with equipment for one division, and the Legion was making haste to bring in this equipment before the Mandate should end and the road to Egypt become impassable. Thus, the irritating sniping of the settlers produced the inevitable retribution, and provided the necessary excuse for the Legion area commander to start his attack before the termination of the Mandate.

On May 4th a heavy artillery barrage unexpectedly opened up on the Russian Monastery. The noise of such a barrage was a sound which had not yet been heard in this war; now it could be plainly heard in Jerusalem, and sent a chill of fear through many of the local Jews who understood its meaning. The barrage, at point-blank range, was effective. A company of Legionnaires succeeded in capturing the Monastery. But all attempts to capture the hill-top behind the Monastery, and a further hill several hundred yards further north, ended in failure; by evening the Legion withdrew, and the Haganah returned to the Monastery.

The attack had failed, but it seemed as if the Legion had achieved its object. The settlers ceased sniping at Arab traffic using the road, and the Legion convoys and other Arab vehicles were able to pass unhindered. Moreover, the defenders had suffered forty-two casualties in the attack; with no hope of reinforcement, this represented a severe blow, and made their position even more precarious. For eight days following the attack quiet reigned in the area. But on the night of May 11th the defenders in the forward positions at the Monastery reported suspicious sounds. They were right in their suspicions: the Legion was preparing for an assault.

On the hill of Beit Fajjar two companies of Legionnaires had assembled. They were to capture the series of defences guarding the inner road leading to the villages, and thus cleave the area into two separate halves. They would then deal with each village separately. Meanwhile, throughout the night, hundreds of local Arabs, from as far away as Hebron, 'Idna and Dahariya were converging on the settlements. They had heard that the Legion was about to attack, and wanted to be in at the kill.

By noon the attacking Legionnaires had gained their objective of splitting the Jewish defence into two halves. Spearheaded by their armoured cars, the Legionnaires had quickly overcome resistance in the defence posts guarding the inner road. But at the approaches of Kfar Etzion itself all their attacks were beaten back, and with nightfall the attack ceased. By now, however, the defenders had abandoned all hope; in the day's fighting they had suffered seventy casualties, out of a total of under five hundred men and women. They had not the strength to counter-attack again.

At dawn the Legion resumed its attack on the defence emplacement guarding Kfar Etzion. After six hours of fighting, and after all ammunition in the Haganah outpost had been spent, the Legion overran the forward positions and broke into the settlement. The fighting continued inside the houses of the village, a communal settlement founded by orthodox Jews. The Legionnaires were joined by hundreds of local Arabs who swarmed into the village in their wake; the battle was turned into a massacre.

An officer of the Legion called on the defenders to surrender, and some fifteen men came out and gave up their arms. As they stood in a row at the command of the officer, who wished to photograph them, a local Arab stepped forward with a sub-machine-gun and mowed down the line of men, despite the protests of the officer. Altogether, of the whole population of the village, only three men and a girl succeeded in getting out alive; the rest were all killed. It was the end of Kfar Etzion. Shortly afterwards the villagers of the other settlements surrendered and were taken into captivity. They were protected from the local Arabs and treated correctly as prisoners of war. The Arab Legion had scored its first victory.

Meanwhile, in near-by Jerusalem, the fall of Etzion was the cause of jubilation among the Arabs. Church bells in the old city rang out the victory tidings, and crowds gathered outside the Jaffa and Damascus Gates, regardless of possible sniping. On that day, May 14th, it seemed to the Arabs and the British in Jerusalem that the days of the Jewish city were numbered. The way lay wide open to the Arabs. Only a few miles separated the victorious Legion force at Etzion from the city itself.

Among the Jews of Jerusalem a spirit of the desperation of Massada[1] was beginning to be felt.

In the Haganah units, troops had been standing around the walkie-talkies, listening tensely to the last farewells from Kfar Etzion as the Arabs finally overran the settlement. That evening a Haganah officer toured the platoons at their emplacements, telling them that the last of the Etzion Group had surrendered, and that the way was open for the Arab Legion, with its armour and heavy guns, to advance on Ramat Rahel and Talpiot, both of which had virtually no anti-tank defences at all. He called on all troops to fight till their last bullet—till their last breath. In the two suburbs in the southernmost tip of the city, Jews who had been rounded up from the streets of the city, including many of the ultra-orthodox, had been brought to dig trenches and build last-minute fortifications. The Legion was expected at any hour. And that night Legion artillery began to shell the north-western suburbs of Jerusalem from the dominating height of Nabi Samwil.

In the tense and divided city, hardly anyone noticed the Union Jack being hauled down from Government House, the home of the last British High Commissioner. As it finished work on May 14th, the Special Assembly of the United Nations had neither rescinded nor amended the partition resolution of November 1947. Almost at that very moment, in Tel Aviv the Jewish National Council proclaimed the establishment of the State of Israel.

The curtain had descended on British rule in Jerusalem, but there were neither cheers nor jeers as the last convoy of British troops and officials drove slowly up the Street of the Prophets on its way out of Palestine and into history; just silence. Jews and Arabs were now left to themselves. The odds seemed to be heavily in favour of the Arabs. The official War of Palestine had begun.

---

[1] The last Jewish stronghold held by the Zealots against the Romans after the fall of the Temple of Jerusalem A.D. 70. The Romans besieged the fortress for three years before it finally succumbed; the remaining garrison and their families committed suicide.

PART THREE

The Official War

8

THE WAR BEGINS; FIRST PHASE: MAY 15th—JUNE 11th 1948

THE Mandate had come to an end, and all that was left of British authority in Palestine was a tiny enclave in Haifa Port, where the last of the British troops were being evacuated.[1] The termination of the Mandate had in no way been carried out in the manner visualised by the United Nations. There had been no gradual take-over by Jewish and Arab authorities under the benign supervision of the United Nations Special Committee. Instead, the reins of government had been, as it were, contemptuously tossed into the ring for Jews and Arabs to contest. As early as February essential Government services had ceased functioning when intensive sniping prevented Jewish and Arab officials coming to work in Jerusalem. First the Law Courts closed down, then the central Post Office ceased functioning, next it was the turn of the telephone exchanges to stop ringing, and finally the water works, electricity installations, and all other Government and semi-Government offices and services came to a halt. There had been no attempt to transfer Government and administrative matters to the Jews and the Arabs. The British officials burnt their files, destroyed their records and departed. The United Nations committee which was to have supervised the take-over was only allowed into the country late in March. They were virtually ignored by the British and the Arabs, and, in the course of the fighting, were only supplied with food and drink through their two secretaries.

But despite this almost demonstrative non-co-operation on the part of the British Administration in Palestine, the

[1] General MacMillan, the last British soldier to leave Palestine, departed on June 30th, 1948.

expected chaos did not materialise. On the Jewish side, Jewish Agency officials took over the task of administration where the British had left off.[1] A scratch postal service was installed, the electricity and water works in the Jewish areas were brought into operation again, and order was maintained by Jewish auxiliary police. On the Arab side the invading armies declared martial law in the areas they occupied, and cared for the local populace. Thus, the division into Jewish and Arab areas which the United Nations had called for came into being. The Jews were left in command in the area allotted to the Jewish State—with the exception of the Negev, whose Jewish settlements were to all intents and purposes already isolated. The Arabs were left in command of their area, with the exception of Western Galilee, where, as May 15th dawned, a hard battle for possession was still being fought.

The two protagonists were now left on their own. But neither the Haganah nor the Arab High Command were yet ready for war. Both suffered from a multiplicity of authorities with uncertain competences, which had to be sorted out before either could undertake effective action. Thus it came about that, on the eve of the outbreak of the Palestine War, both sides were undergoing a serious crisis of command which resulted in the emergence of one effective commander-in-chief for the Jews, but which left the Arab problem unresolved, and their command divided.

The Haganah High Command had remained virtually unchanged since the days of irregular combat in March and April, except that the then virtually unknown and untried Yigal Yadin had emerged increasingly as the central figure in planning the overall conduct of the war. In effect, as the fighting had spread and war had become imminent, it was Ben-Gurion who had become the *de facto* commander-in-chief, and Yadin his *de facto* chief of staff. This caused the formal command structure of the Haganah to become an anachronism—and also, increasingly, an obstacle to decisive action and planning.

Ben-Gurion had been pondering this situation for some

[1] For this purpose, the Zionist Executive appointed in April a committee of thirteen members with Ben-Gurion as chairman which was called the "Minhalat Ha'am"—the Directory of the People—but were more popularly known as the "Yud-Gimmel"—the thirteen. This Committee became the Provisional Government on May 14th, 1948.

time—certainly all through the vicissitudes of April. There were too many political representatives—nine altogether—in the High Command, and far too few professional soldiers—in fact, none. Yitzhak Sadeh and Yadin were brilliant amateurs, but Ben-Gurion doubted whether they could handle a full-scale war, with all its organisational and technical complications. About Israel Galili, who was the head of the Haganah High Command (RAMA) and also the Jewish Agency's representative in it, Ben-Gurion felt increasingly uneasy. He had become convinced that Galili and his Haganah colleagues still underestimated the size and character of the imminent Arab invasion, and therefore failed to understand the nature of the Jewish resistance which would be required.

Ben-Gurion himself had only lately become acquainted with the inner workings of the Haganah High Command. Until the end of 1946 he had no direct connection with it. Only after the World Zionist Congress, which was held in Basle in December 1946, was he appointed the Jewish Agency's Director of Security, and it was then that he began to play an active part in the military preparations of the Palestinian Jews. He had little to do with the political High Command, but appointed an operations executive of three, which was known as "Makhlekah Bet." It consisted of Israel Galili (in charge of operations), Izraeli (in charge of finance), and Yosef Jacobson (in charge of supplies). On the purely military side, Yaacov Dori was the Chief of Staff, Yitzhak Sadeh his deputy, and Yigal Yadin the Director of Operations. By the end of April 1948, Ben-Gurion had made up his mind. He had developed some doubts about the soundness of Galili's judgment in his choice of commanders. He was seriously disturbed by the slowness of his arms procurement programme and, above all, by the division of authority between Galili and himself. It was this that really mattered. Ben-Gurion decided to act in his characteristic manner. He would take the Haganah bull by the horns.

On May 2nd he sent a personal messenger with a letter to Galili. This informed him that the political High Command had become redundant with the establishment of the "Yud Gimmel"—the executive committee of thirteen with overall powers. And, as the High Command was no longer needed, there was no longer any need for a Head of the High

Command (RAMA) which had ceased to function. In line with the new arrangements which had been made, Galili's appointment was ended forthwith. As from noon that day, the message concluded, the Haganah would receive its orders from the Jewish Agency's Director of Security, David Ben-Gurion. A number of Haganah staff officers and brigade commanders were at headquarters when the letter arrived. Galili read it out to them. They were shocked by the contents and surprised by its arid tone. But Galili urged them loyally to accept the decision. It was then 9.30 a.m., only two and a half hours before the change-over was to take effect. Galili also informed his Party—Mapam—and asked them not to make a political issue of it.

The news was received with mixed feelings at the front. There was one group of senior officers, most of whom had served in the British Army during the Second World War, who viewed with relief the action by Ben-Gurion to remove the influence of pressure groups from the Haganah and to bring greater uniformity into the general command structure. But many others, the hard core of the Haganah, particularly Galili's Mapam comrades, who played a leading part in the Palmach, were hurt and shocked. They came that evening to Kibbutz Na'an, where Galili lived, to protest at Ben-Gurion's action. Galili gave them strict orders not to take any independent action.

Meanwhile, Ben-Gurion had heard of these reactions and he pondered over the damage it might do to the Haganah at a critical moment. He weighed this against the indubitable advantages of a reorganised High Command without political representation. He had also encountered considerable difficulty in finding a suitable deputy. He had first asked Zvi Ayalon to take over, but Ayalon had refused; next, Yadin had also declined to accept the new position. At the same time the heads of many sections of the Haganah had expressed their concern. Ben-Gurion understood.

Therefore, five days later, he sent his military secretary, Nehemia Argov, with a personal letter to Galili. In this Ben-Gurion said that he had no intention of being commander of the Haganah, and he asked Galili to resume his post. The next day, Ben-Gurion and Galili issued a joint statement to the heads of all Haganah sections, and on May 9th Galili

returned to his post in the Executive Committee of Three
which directed all Haganah operations. The crisis was postponed, but not solved. In fact, Galili's position became increasingly shadowy, and as May 15th approached the Haganah
section commanders began to understand that they had one
commander-in-chief alone, and that this was Ben-Gurion.
And now there was no one to question his authority. There
was an element of classic tragedy in this clash of two powerful
wills and characters. Both were concerned only with the good
of their nation, yet each distrusted the other's sense of judgment. They had worked together for years. In the early
nineteen-thirties, Ben-Gurion had hand-picked Galili as the
man to reshape the Haganah—and Galili had done this with a
single-minded devotion which he also inspired in his sub-
ordinates. He had shaped the Haganah, he had turned it into
the military instrument which gave Ben-Gurion the breathing-
space he needed, the commanders he sought and the spirit
which was Israel's salvation. But now something different was
required, and Ben-Gurion was convinced that Galili could not
meet these requirements. So the break came.

The Arab leaders were also beset with problems of command. They did not confide their respective plans to each
other. There was no co-ordination between their armies or
their commands. The Military Committee of the Arab League
existed only on paper and it exercised authority over none of
the Arab armies. The Egyptians told neither Abdullah nor the
Syrians how they proposed to act; the decisions of the Arab
commanders of Syria, Iraq, Lebanon and Transjordan, who
met at the Transjordanian army base of Zerka on May 12th
(while King Abdullah had his last secret meeting with the
envoys of the Jewish Agency, Mrs. Myerson and Ezra Danin),[1]
were not conveyed to General Glubb. Although Glubb was in
command of the one efficient Arab army, it had been decided,
with the approval of King Abdullah, not to inform him of
Arab plans and intentions. Glubb asserts that he was kept
uninformed of all the major League decisions in connection
with the invasion of Palestine. The Arab leaders did not trust
him; apparently even Abdullah had his reservations. For, on
his own evidence, Glubb was not drawn into the inner circle
of Arab commanders dealing with Palestine affairs.

[1] See Chapter Six, p. 110.

The blueprint of the Arab invasion plan was first prepared at the headquarters of General Taha Hashemi in Damascus some time before the beginning of May, and was brought before the Arab commanders when they assembled in Damascus during the first week of May. The plan received its final confirmation at the meeting of the Arab League Political Committee in Damascus on May 11th. On Iraqi instigation, the Committee also decided to appoint the Iraqi General Nur ad-Din Mahmoud as supreme commander of the Arab forces, with the title of "Commander of the Regular and Irregular Forces for the Saving of Palestine."

The plan for the invasion of Palestine was based on a wide pincer-movement whose meeting point would be at Afuleh and which was designed to cut off the Galilee and the eastern part of the Jezreel Valley from the rest of Jewish Palestine. With the fall of Afuleh, the Hashemite armies were to advance on Haifa, which was the main objective of the invasion. Thus, according to the plan,

* the Lebanese army would advance from Ras el Naqura down the coast towards Acre and Haifa;
* the Syrian army would advance from its base at Bennt Jbail in the southern Lebanon into central Galilee, take Safed and advance towards Nazareth and Afuleh;
* the Iraqi army would advance from Naharayim towards Afuleh; a second force of the Iraqi army would cross the Jordan further south together with the Arab Legion and these two forces would advance through Arab-inhabited Samaria—via Jenin—to Afuleh. Once the link-up with the Syrians was completed, the Iraqi and Jordanian armies would continue their advance from Afuleh through the Jezreel Valley and Shafa Amr to Haifa, while the Syrians would concentrate on mopping up operations against the Jewish positions in those areas of the Galilee and the Jezreel and Jordan valleys which were cut off from the rest of the Jewish area. The Lebanese army, advancing from the north, would participate in the final assault on Haifa;
* the Egyptian army would advance on Tel Aviv from the south and thus divert maximum Jewish forces from the main Arab thrust on Haifa.

On May 12th, the day after the plan was brought before
the Political Committee in Damascus, the Jordanian representative returned to Amman. He informed Abdullah of the
plan and of Mahmoud's appointment. The Arab historians
say that the King showed the plan to Glubb, who turned it
down and changed it. Glubb claims he never heard of or saw
this invasion plan. He certainly never changed it. Actually,
the King did not consult Glubb on this matter. He had
definite plans of his own. On May 13th he contacted the
League's Political Committee, which was still in session in
Damascus, and demanded that he be given the supreme command of the Arab armies. The Arab representatives agreed
to comply with Abdullah's demand, but they also stipu-
lated that Nur ad-Din Mahmoud continue as his deputy. The
King himself told Nur-ad-Din that he did not accept the plan,
that he had quite different plans. First priority was to be given
to Jerusalem; he had no intention of committing the Legion to
a battle in the north, even with Haifa as a prize, so long as the
fate of Jerusalem was in the balance. The Legion would
concentrate on Jerusalem and its surroundings and, together
with the Iraqi forces, would occupy those parts of central
Palestine which were scheduled to become the Palestinian
Arab State. He advised Nur-ad-Din to switch the Syrian
attack from the centre, where it would be open on both flanks,
to the southern end of the Sea of Galilee, and to cross into
Palestine at Samakh—to the north of the Iraqis, who would be
crossing the Jordan at Gesher (five miles further south), so
protecting the left flank of the Syrians. Nur-ad-Din accepted
these alternatives. But Abdullah's changes meant that the
pincer-movement on Afuleh could no longer be executed. The
Syrians, therefore, were ordered to switch their attacking
force from Bennt Jbail, where they were already concentrated,
to Samakh, to the south of the Sea of Galilee. The long convoy
of Syrian vehicles was plainly visible to the Israelis as it
wound its way through the hills. The Israelis then could not
understand the significance of this last-minute movement.
The Syrians did not place too great importance on the element
of surprise, otherwise they might have been more cautious in
their troop movements. At that time they still believed that
they would not encounter serious opposition from the
Jews; in fact, they were so confident that their original

invading force comprised less than half their entire army.

While the Syrians moved from Bennt Jbail, part of the Lebanese army which was concentrated at Ras el Naqura was switched to Malkieh to the east. The new orders given by Nur-ad-Din Mahmoud to the Lebanese were that they were to advance into the Arab-inhabited Central Galilee and use it as a base for further advances on the Jezreel Valley and Haifa. It was this force which Dan Laner was to meet in his unexpected and costly encounter.

The main thrust in Mahmoud's new plan was to be made by the Iraqis and the Syrians against the settlements of the Jordan Valley. From the strategical point of view, Mahmoud's new plan was much inferior to his previous one. Instead of a pincer movement with the two lines of advance through Arab-inhabited territory, Mahmoud was now planning a frontal attack on a relatively heavily populated and well-defended Jewish area, which was, moveover, isolated and relatively far from the heartland of Jewish Palestine where the decisive battles would have to be fought.

While the Syrians were to attack at Samakh, the Iraqis were to break through at Gesher, several miles further south along the Jordan. Nur-ad-Din Mahmoud, however, realised that the left flank of the Iraqi attack remained exposed, as the Legion would be concentrating their forces much further south in the Jerusalem area. Thus a dangerous gap existed in the Arab front which he feared the Jews might exploit by a thrust through the virtually undefended hills of Samaria towards Jenin. For this reason the first of the two Iraqi Brigade Groups which made up the Iraqi Expeditionary Force[1] did not take part in the initial attack on Gesher. It was held in reserve to counter any possible Jewish attack in central Palestine. Later, it succeeded in saving Jenin from falling

[1] As the Iraqi army of 1948 was built on a territorial basis, with each brigade responsible for the defence of a certain area, two special brigade groups were set up for the Expeditionary Force. These consisted of the first brigade group, and the second mobile brigade group. The Force had twelve Avro Ansons as air cover. At the end of May a third brigade group, which included a company of tanks (ten Italian tanks), as well as additional planes, were dispatched to Palestine. Additional units were sent in July and August, and by autumn 1948 the Iraqi Force consisted of twenty-six battalions and was the largest of the Arab armies in Palestine.

into Jewish hands by arriving on the scene when the town was about to capitulate.

In Damascus, King Abdullah's action created a state of near-panic. On the morning of May 15th President Kuwatly of Syria telephoned King Abdullah from his palace. He told the King that the Secretary-General of the Arab League was with him, and that they had come to the conclusion that it was essential to delay the planned advance of the Arab armies into Palestine. Instead, they should send increased financial aid and weapons to the Palestinian Arabs until these had created conditions more favourable for a general invasion. Abdullah rejected the proposal out of hand, and President Kuwatly then agreed to send the Syrians to Samakh; but, he explained, there would be some delay, in view of the Syrian state of unpreparedness for this switch.

While the Syrians dallied, Abdullah was receiving a stream of frightened appeals from Jerusalem. Despite the opposition from Glubb, who feared for the well-being of the Bedouin Legion in the built-up area of Jerusalem, Abdullah insisted on the capture of the city; but he was no less anxious to occupy as much of Palestine as time and his meagre forces permitted. Like Ben-Gurion, he was aware of the important political issues which would be decided by military occupation. He saw much further than the confined military horizon of Glubb Pasha and much more clearly. Abdullah wanted to get there before the Egyptians. He need not have worried quite so much.

For the Egyptians had their own command troubles. The Egyptian Army Command had accepted the political directive of the Nokrashy Government that it would be folly exemplified to invade Palestine with the regular armies of the Arab states. Instead, it assisted the Moslem Brotherhood irregulars in Palestine with occasional volunteers and arms. But it was wholly unprepared for the Egyptian Government's sudden decision at the beginning of May to move into Palestine on May 15th with two brigades. Only a few days before the Nokrashy Government changed its mind, the Minister of Defence, General Haidar, had thumped the table when Mohammed Haikal had asked him about Egypt's intentions. "We shall never even contemplate entering an official war," Haidar had replied. "We are not mad. We shall allow our men and officers to volunteer for service in Palestine, and we shall give them weapons, but no more."

The Egyptian Defence Minister knew what he was talking about. When, a few days after this conversation, he was informed of the change of plan, he summoned the officer commanding the Egyptian forces in the Sinai desert to Cairo for consultations. Major-General Ahmed Ali el-Muawi came. Haidar asked him about the condition of his troops—this was in early May 1948. Muawi replied that it could not be worse. Haidar then informed him of the possibility that Muawi might have to lead his men to war against the Jews. Muawi protested that his army was not trained for war. The Defence Minister then arranged that Muawi should address the General Staff and leading Cabinet Ministers. After listening to Muawi's distressing account of the state of the army in Sinai, the Prime Minister, Nokrashy, commented that Egypt's position among the Arab states made it necessary for her to change her policy and enter the war. However, he reassured Muawi. There was no need for undue alarm. There would be very little fighting, for the United Nations would intervene. Indeed, Nokrashy concluded, such clashes as there might be would be more in the nature of political demonstrations than military engagements.

Thus reassured, Muawi returned to el-Arish to prepare for this kind of war. He had no idea what was going on on other fronts. He called in his deputy, Colonel Mohammed Neguib, and told him of the decision. Neguib protested that there were only four battalions fit for battle, and they had neither the men nor the material for a successful campaign. "Why court disaster?" Neguib queried. "We have our orders. Our duty is to carry them out, not to question them," Muawi replied. And he proceeded to prepare for the invasion of southern Palestine. As far as he was concerned there was no other Arab army in the field. He had his own game to play.

And so we come to the point of no return—in Amman, in Cairo, and now in Tel Aviv, where the National Council of Palestinian Jewry assembled in the Museum in the afternoon of May 14th, 1948.

At four o'clock precisely Ben-Gurion, flanked by his twelve fellow Ministers of the New Jewish State, stood up. This was, without doubt, the greatest moment in Ben-Gurion's career. There and then he made himself responsible for the fate of the Jewish people. The small hall was packed with people, with emotion and with history. Ben-Gurion, in a blue lounge suit, began to read in a matter-of-fact voice. For five minutes he recalled centuries, tragedies and aspirations in short, tense paragraphs that moved like a Greek drama to their predestined climax.

> The land of Israel was the birthplace of the Jewish people. . . . Exiled from Palestine . . . Impelled by this historic association . . . . In the year 1897, the first Zionist Congress . . . Acknowledged by the Balfour Declaration of 1917 . . . The Nazi holocaust . . . The survivors . . . In the Second World War . . . On November 29th, 1947, the General Assembly of the United Nations . . .

Ben-Gurion paused for a moment. This was history. Now he was to make history. As if with an afterthought, he added: "It is, moreover, the self-evident right of the Jewish people to be a nation, as all other nations, in its own Sovereign State." And then, in ringing tones:

> Accordingly we, the members of the National Council, representing the Jewish people in Palestine and the Zionist movement of the world, meet together in solemn assembly today, the day of termination of the British Mandate for Palestine, by virtue of the natural and historic right of the Jewish people and of the Resolution of the General Assembly of the United Nations.
>
> Hereby proclaim the establishment of the Jewish State in Palestine, to be called ISRAEL.
>
> The State of Israel will be open to the immigration of Jews from all the countries of their dispersion; will promote the development of the country for the benefit of all its inhabitants; will be based on the precepts of liberty, justice and peace taught by the Hebrew prophets; will uphold the full social and political equality of all its citizens, without distinction of race, creed or sex; will guarantee full freedom of conscience, worship, education and culture; will safeguard the sanctity and inviolability of the shrines and holy places of all religions; and will dedicate itself to the principles of the Charter of the United Nations.

We appeal to the United Nations to assist the Jewish people in the building of its State and to admit Israel into the family of nations.

In the midst of wanton aggression, we yet call upon the Arab inhabitants of the State of Israel to return to the ways of peace and to play their part in the development of the State, with full and equal citizenship and due representation in all its bodies and institutions provisional or permanent.

We offer peace and amity to all the neighbouring states and their peoples, and invite them to co-operate with the independent Jewish nation for the common good of all. The State of Israel is ready to contribute its full share to the peaceful progress and reconstitution of the Middle East.

Our call goes out to the Jewish people all over the world to rally to our side in the task of immigration and development, and to stand by us in the great struggle for the fulfilment of the dream of generations—the redemption of Israel.

With trust in Almighty God, we set our hand to this Declaration, at this Session of the Provisional State Council, in the city of Tel-Aviv, on this Sabbath eve, the fifth day of Iyar, 5708, the fourteenth day of May, 1948.

The Proclamation had taken seventeen minutes. There had been much speculation and disputation about the name of the new state. Now it was known and accepted. Immediately after the reading and signature of the Declaration of Independence, Ben-Gurion announced the new state's first Government decrees.

Dawn broke early over the Eastern Mediterranean. Soon after four o'clock the first sun rose over the new State of Israel on the morning-of May 15th, 1948. Tel Aviv seemed to be in a deep slumber after the exhausting festivities of the preceding day which had followed on the proclamation of Israel's independence. It was also the new Israel's first Sabbath day. But all through the night the lights had burnt behind the blackout screens in the squat pinky building on the sea shore—the "Red House," where the Haganah High Command had deliberated all night with the first Prime Minister of Israel, David Ben-Gurion. Israel Galili, de facto deputy to Ben-Gurion was there, and so was the now rapidly emerging but still untried Chief of Operations, Yigal Yadin.

The fog of war hung heavily over the deliberations in the Red House. Ben-Gurion, Galili and Yadin were almost certain, but not quite, that by dawn the regular Arab armies would be marching against Israel. They had to the end a one per cent doubt about Arab intentions. However, they could do nothing but wait until they were sure. For it was essential to Israel's stand at the United Nations that the first act of open war should come from the Arab states and not from the Israelis. In any case, militarily, Ben-Gurion and his commanders had no choice: with the limited numbers and equipment at their disposal, and in their peculiar strategic situation, they had to wait for the first moves of the Arab armies before deploying the Israeli army.

While they waited, they recalled the staff discussions of the last two days. They knew the real state of affairs on their own side of the hill, but they had a somewhat exaggerated opinion of the strength and resources of their opponents. Yadin concluded that Israel had no great chance of winning unless fresh supplies of weapons and equipment arrived soon. If they did arrive, then Israel had an even chance of holding her own against the attack; and both Ben-Gurion and Yadin were convinced that the ships at sea and the transport Dakotas precariously hopping the airfields of Europe would get through, despite the proclaimed blockades of the Arab countries, of the British and of the United Nations.[1] But none of Israel's leaders in the Red House on that night believed that it was possible for Israel to win the war that lay ahead with the resources then at their disposal.

Yadin reported that little of this uncertainty could be found in the armed forces or in the civilian population. As a result of the chain of successes which they had enjoyed in the forty days from the beginning of April, public morale (outside Jerusalem) was exceptionally high and self-confident—almost

[1] On April 17th, 1948, the Security Council voted a resolution (against Soviet opposition) which in effect imposed a general arms embargo, and a ban on potential fighting personnel going into Palestine. This was extended, after May 15th, by the British Government to apply also to the Arab governments engaged in the invasion of Palestine. In the event, it made the acquisition of arms and equipment more difficult for both parties to the conflict, but it did not prevent it. Even the British authorities found convenient loopholes through which Egypt, Transjordan and Iraq were able to get extra equipment.

too much so. Soon after midnight came the exhilarating news from Washington that the United States had recognised the new State. This countered somewhat the earlier depressing news of the fall of Kfar Etzion and the surrounding settlements (fourteen miles south of Jerusalem on the Hebron road), after a three-day encounter with the Arab Legion. Yadin drew attention to the implications of this defeat: they would have to devise a more effective defence for the settlements against artillery attack. The discussions continued inconclusively. The first light of dawn had come, but not yet the Arab answer. Ben-Gurion prepared for a special broadcast to the United States. It was five o'clock in Tel Aviv.

Out of the now clear morning sky, coming in from the sea, and unnoticed by the almost non-existent air-raid defence system, came three Spitfires with the markings of the Royal Egyptian Air Force. They made for the unmistakable landmark of the Reading Power Station on the sea-shore, behind which lay the sandy Tel Aviv airfield. They aimed their not very powerful bombs from only about 1,000 feet, did some damage, and turned back towards the sea. One Spitfire, however, was hit by the solitary machine-gun which was mounted for anti-aircraft defence on the roof of the power station. The pilot came down not far from Tel Aviv and was taken prisoner.

This was the signal for which the men in the Red House had been waiting. And before the smoke had cleared from the airfield, other messages were also coming in. In the Negev the settlement of Kfar Darom had been attacked, and another settlement had been bombed from the air. On the Transjordanian and Syrian borders a number of settlements had been shelled. It was still too early to see a pattern in these attacks, or to make decisive dispositions. But the Haganah High Command had had its one per cent doubt removed. The attack had begun.

The Haganah defence was based on ten territorial brigades. In the north there were three brigades:

"Yiftah," a Palmach brigade,[1] together with all the

---

[1] The size of the brigades varied very considerably throughout the war. The complement of each brigade should have been 2,750 men at the beginning of May. In actual fact, however, most brigades had much less. Thus, on April 1st, the 1st Brigade had a complement of 1,454 men, the 2nd Brigade 1,667 men, the 3rd 1,880, the 4th 846, etc.

Map 5. Disposition of the Israeli forces on May 15th, 1948, and the general lines of the attacks by the Arab armies. The 7th Brigade was formed a week later.

settlements in the area, were under the overall command of Yigal Alon and later under Mullah Cohen.

"Golani," the 1st Haganah Brigade, commanded by Moshe Montag and his deputy, N. Golan, held Tiberias and the Jordan Valley.

"Carmeli," the 2nd Haganah Brigade, commanded by Moshe Carmel, (who later became Commander of the Northern Front, while Makleff took over the Carmeli Brigade).

In the centre there were two brigades:

"Alexandroni," the 3rd Haganah Brigade, commanded by Dan Even, held the Nathanya front.

"Kiryati," the 4th Haganah Brigade, under Michael Ben-Gal, held Tel Aviv and its surroundings.

In the south there were two brigades:

"Givati," the 5th Haganah Brigade, commanded by Shimon Avidan, held the Rehovot-Isdud front.

"Hanegev," the 12th Palmach Brigade, under Nahum Sarig, held the deep south.

In Jerusalem David Shaltiel commanded the 6th Haganah Brigade (the "Etzioni" Brigade).

In the Jerusalem corridor Yosef Tabenkin took over Palmach "Harel" Brigade from Itzhak Rabin.

The 7th Haganah Brigade was formed, just over a week later, for the attack on Latrun, and was commanded by Shlomo Shamir.

The total number of effectives which were under the Haganah High Command on May 14th, 1948, was 35,000.[1] This included everything: all mobilised infantry, the Home Guard, the air force, the naval services and the special service corps. But its most significant feature was that out of the total establishment of 35,000 there were 25,000 actual combatants—it was a striking tribute to Haganah training and organisation.

[1] The figure given by Israel Galili and the most accurate available was 28,760, but this figure did not include some of the auxiliary services.

The weapons over which the High Command disposed on that day were as follows:

22,000 rifles (including many obsolescent types)
11,100 sub-machine-guns (mainly locally manufactured Sten guns)
1,500 light machine-guns
A few medium machine-guns
105 3-inch mortars
682 2-inch mortars
16 Davidka mortars[1]
75 PIATS and anti-tank rifles
4 65-mm. guns

Ammunition was short. It worked out at 50 rounds per rifle and 700 per machine-gun.

Ben-Gurion and his colleagues therefore had to face a very different situation from that which their opponents imagined. The best informed of the Arab commanders, General Glubb, was under the impression that the Israelis had at their disposal over "some 65,000 armed men." He also accepted as a fact the fantasy that among the Israelis were something like 20,000 men who had served in the Russian and Polish armies. He therefore reached the conclusion that the Arab Legion faced an enemy of overwhelmingly superior strength. The other Arab commanders were inclined to improve on General Glubb's imaginative appreciation until they were convinced that they faced an Israeli army of almost 100,000 trained soldiers, fully equipped to match the Arab armoury.[2] In fact, the line-up of the fronts was rather different.

The invading regular Arab armies were roughly equal in number to the Haganah effectives of the Israelis, and this balance of forces also applied to most of the fronts. Most of the tales of the overwhelming superiority of one side and the heroic inferiority of the other, to which both Arabs and Israelis have lent currency, are not substantiated by the actual numbers which were engaged.

[1] A crude home-made mortar which tossed a lump of explosive for some 300 yards, accompanied by a noise out of all proportion to the weight of the explosive.

[2] Major E. O'Ballance, in his book, *The Arab-Israeli War*, 1948 (Faber, 1956), treats these figures as if they were accurate.

The total strength of the invading armies was approximately 24,000, divided up in this way:

Egypt	10,000
Arab Legion	4,500
Syria	3,000
Iraq	3,000
Lebanon	3,000 (including 2,000 men of the Arab Liberation Army)

Along the principal fronts the line-up reflected the same trend. This was the picture on the morning of May 15th:

	Israelis	Arabs
South	5,000	5,000 Egyptians
Deep south and Hebron	1,500	4,000 Egyptians
Jerusalem and corridor	4,500	4,000 Arab Legion
		1,000 Egyptians
Central front; Tel Aviv		
Natanya	3,000	3,000 Iraqis
North	5,000	3,000 Syrians
		1,000 Lebanese
		2,000 A.L.A.
Total	19,000	23,000

These figures vary a great deal and are only rough outlines divided into arbitrary fronts. But they underline the existing numerical balance in the field. They do not show the rather more powerful fire-power of the Arab armies, which,—despite their shortcomings, mercilessly outgunned the Israelis on every front. They also had fighter planes, and bombers of a sort. The Israelis had scarcely any artillery and no modern aircraft during the opening phase of the conflict and no armour whatsoever.

This, then, was the general position as the Arab armies moved into Palestine. It did not appear very reassuring to those Israeli leaders who knew the realities of the situation. It was fortunate for them that Glubb and the Arab commanders had such an exaggerated opinion of Israeli strength; it was even more fortunate for the Israelis that the political leaders of the Arabs had encouraged their soldiers in the opposite belief to that which their commanders held. The rank and file were convinced that they would have a walk-over, that easy victory and rich booty were now within their grasp. The shock of reality for them was great and profound; Glubb and his fellow commanders, judging from their memoirs, were spared the shock of realising how wrong they were. They have enshrined their faulty and often laughable appreciations in their published records of those days.

As the Israelis watched the armies of invasion approach, they had not much chance of executing their plans—"Dalet" or any other letter of the Hebrew alphabet. They had to meet somehow four simultaneous threats. It was not possible to allot priorities; all four fronts were critical. On none of them could the Israelis afford to give ground.

Yet the Haganah High Command was nervous about committing too many troops to the containing of the attack. For it too was very much in the dark about conditions inside the Arab command; its field intelligence also was not too good. The kibbutzim under attack, and many of the local commanders, were inclined to exaggerate and multiply Arab strength. But what worried the Israeli command most were two factors. The first was that *on paper* the Arab invasion made sense; it looked like a subtle co-ordinated move on the lines of which the Israelis had some advance information. According to this, the defenders were to be drawn south by the Egyptians and north by the Syrians, while the Arab Legion and the Iraqis would strike the decisive blow at the soft centre. The second factor was uncertainty about the part which British policy would play in this development. The Haganah command therefore hesitated to send reinforcements either north or south, for fear of the expected attack in the centre. But without reinforcements neither the north nor the south could be held. This was Israel's strategic dilemma; only the Arabs did not know it. Let us therefore see what actually happened and how the invasion progressed.

General Glubb has claimed that the state of confusion on the Arab side was such that the Israeli commander could have occupied Jerusalem, Latrun, and important positions on the Egyptian front without meeting very much, if any, opposition.

To this General Yadin has replied that however sound

Glubb's reasoning may be about the situation as he saw it from his side, it overlooks Yadin's problem and dilemma. He had to deal not only with the Arab Legion but also with the other attacks in the north, south and centre. In the brutal final analysis, Yadin claims, he had neither the troops nor the means to contain the four attacks and at the same time embark on independent offensives of his own. The truth of the matter was that Glubb was right in pointing to this tempting vacuum, but he was wrong (and this error permeated all his calculations about the Israelis throughout the war) in failing to appreciate how much the whole Israeli war effort at this stage was geared to a shoe-string.

The situation on the southern front on May 15th, when the Egyptian army began its move into Palestine, illustrates this inherent conflict in the Israeli command between opportunity and emergency.

An Egyptian Expeditionary Force had been assembled at El Arish, comprising the 2nd and 4th Brigades under the command of Major-General Ahmed Ali el-Muawi. His second-in-command was Colonel Mohammed Neguib, and Neguib's principal staff officer was Major Abdel Hakim Amer (who was to become Egypt's Commander-in-Chief after the revolution of 1952). These two brigades were ready to move into Palestine on April 29th, 1948, but they did not anticipate having to do so as a fighting unit. The sparse briefing which they received from Cairo indicated that at the most they would have to act as an occupation force to prevent King Abdullah from taking more than his allotted share of Palestine.

It was not until May 9th, barely a week before the date set for the invasion, that Muawi received orders to take over southern Palestine and to move in the general direction of Tel Aviv and Jerusalem. His brigades were neither equipped nor trained for this move, if it entailed overcoming serious opposition. Neguib protested, but was ordered to take charge of the force which was to move along the coastal road through Gaza towards Tel Aviv. The troops, however, were not upset. The men, and virtually all the officers, were convinced that there would be no serious fighting against the "Jewish civilian rabble" which had been formed into an *ad hoc* army. While Neguib's force was given the task of advancing along the coastal road towards Tel Aviv, a second, smaller Egyptian column, under the command of Lieutenant-General Abd el-Aziz, advanced north-eastwards in the direction of Beersheba and the Hebron Hills. Its objective was to safeguard the right wing of the main column, and to prevent Abdullah laying claim to the Negev and the Hebron Hills. Abd el-Aziz reached Bethlehem on May 21st, and the following day began his attack on the southern outskirts of Jerusalem.

The Egyptians were not quite so unprepared as it would seem from Neguib's published account, or from the propaganda which now hangs like a heavy fog over the history of the Egyptian war effort in 1948. As the Egyptians moved north through friendly and enthusiastic Palestinian Arab areas, they received considerable aid from the local guerilla leaders who operated along the Egyptian line of advance, Husni el Minnawi in Gaza and Tarik el al Afriki in Majdal. It was largely because of their help that Neguib was able to move fairly quickly. By May 17th the main force of this brigade had already passed through Gaza, invested the Jewish settlement of Yad Mordechai which lay astride the road, and moved on beyond Majdal towards Isdud.

From the hills overlooking the road, Israeli observation posts watched the advancing Egyptians. Most of the Israeli scouts were inexperienced in distinguishing detail. They counted some 1,500 vehicles, they identified some armour and a good many guns, and they concluded that a fully equipped Egyptian armoured division was approaching the cluster of Jewish settlements and towns which protect the southern perimeter of Tel Aviv. The report was passed back to Shimon Avidan, the commander of the Givati Brigade, who had been ordered south only four days earlier with instructions to halt the Egyptian advance.

Avidan took stock of his men and means and reported back to headquarters details of the plight of his front, which seemed to be menaced by a massive thrust at Tel Aviv. It was not a happy picture.

The Givati Brigade had been in continuous action since December 1947. Its casualties had already been almost a thousand, 250 killed and 700 wounded. Avidan had to fill the gaps with new and raw recruits from Tel Aviv and Rehovot, and they were not always of the same tough fibre as the earlier volunteers. His five battalions were spread out in seventeen defensive positions, and he had neither armour nor artillery. That night when the news reached the Givati troops that so powerful an Egyptian force was heading their way, there was, according to Avidan, near panic among the inexperienced troops and grave concern among the more hardened. For this was the first time that they would be in contact with a "real" army.

In this desperate mood, orders were given to the settlements in the south to give up every possible man and gun to the Givati Brigade, and some further reinforcements were sent from Tel Aviv. There it was assumed that the Egyptians were heading for a link-up with the Arab Legion in the Lydda-Ramle region before combining with them in an attack on Tel Aviv. The settlements astride of the Egyptian advance were told that they could expect no help, but that they had to fight to the last round and the last man to save Tel Aviv. Four of the precious Messerschmitt fighters which had only just arrived were diverted to head off Neguib's thrust at the heart of Israel.

Yet nothing was further from Neguib's mind. He was a worried man. The vehicles which the Israeli observers had counted were mainly trucks, not tanks, and they were rather fewer than the 1,500 imagined by the Israeli scouts. He had advanced northwards along a single road. The isolated settlements offered much more resistance than he had anticipated, and his informants among the local Arabs reported a great concentration of Israelis waiting for him further north. But unexpectedly and encouragingly his advance continued without major mishap. He reached Isdud and decided to consolidate his position before striking into the heart of the Jewish positions.

Thus it came about on this front—which, in Tel Aviv, was rated as possibly the most dangerous—that two commanders and two forces assembled, each believing that the other was determined to attack, each assessing the other's strength as being much greater than it was, and both acting accordingly with considerable caution in the face of the presumed superiority of the enemy.

But although faulty intelligence alone would not have halted Neguib for long, he was confirmed in his belief by the initial reaction of the Israelis in the Negev and at Isdud.

Avidan had overcome the initial nervousness among his troops (which was accompanied by a number of desertions from among the new conscripts). He was backed up in his measure by the conduct of the defenders of Kfar Darom, Nitzanim and Yad Mordechai. They fought hard and long before they were overcome. Yad Mordechai, in fact, fought for six days, diverting a considerable part of Neguib's troops and artillery, which might have been decisive had they also reached Isdud before the Israeli defence was consolidated.

By the time Neguib had assembled the 2nd Egyptian Brigade at Isdud, in preparation for his next move, he had with him 2,500 men, 10 tanks, 6 field guns and a few mounted 2-pounder guns. Another Egyptian brigade, the 4th, had meanwhile moved into position along the lateral road from Majdal to Hebron, and thus cut off the southern Negev altogether—at least, on the map. The Egyptians occupied a number of key positions which enabled them to invest Negba, the settlement which blocked their inland route to the north. The police-station at Iraq el-Suweidan and two important hills (113 and 105), as well as a number of villages, had been unoccupied since the British left them, and there was some criticism of Avidan for not having taken them while he had the opportunity. His answer, again, was that he had no troops to spare for holding positions of this kind. He was satisfied that the settlers had the situation in hand. The Israelis were to regret later that they took this somewhat complacent view, for hard battles had to be fought before the Egyptians were again driven from these positions, which turned out to be of great importance in the contest for southern Palestine.

Against these two Egyptian brigades, with their 5,000 men, the Givati commander had been able to muster three first-line battalions and two reserve battalions. Altogether he had 4,800 men. Of these, as Avidan put it, 3,000 were "eaters," and only 1,800 were "bayonets." In addition he had a mobile unit of eight lorries and three horses. It seemed therefore that, taking an overall picture, the Israelis and the Egyptians were fairly evenly balanced in numbers, while the Egyptians had the advantage of concentration and of superior fire-power, for what it was worth. In fact, it was worth a good deal against an army and against settlements neither of which had any experience of artillery bombardment.

But overall estimates can be misleading. Neguib had 2,000 men at Isdud as the spear-head of this thrust, but Avidan had nothing like it to match him there. He had placed his main defensive positions further back along all the possible lines of Egyptian advance towards Rishon le Zion and Rehovot, and covering the more immediately threatened forward settlements around Negba. Only a comparatively small force was actually in position at Isdud to engage Neguib when he arrived there. The Givati troops were tired out. Only one company was fit for action. It engaged the Egyptians, although many of the soldiers were suffering acutely from food-poisoning. They made no great impact militarily on the Egyptians, but Neguib concluded that he faced a formidable force of "4,000 Zionists" and did not press on when the attack was called off. The Givati forces maintained their pressure and confirmed Neguib in his belief, but the Israelis made no appreciable impact on his front. They captured Yibna and forced the local Arab bands to abandon positions north of Isdud. But misfortune or bad leadership dogged some of their attempts to force Neguib to withdraw.

On June 3rd the Israelis captured Hill 69, which dominated Neguib's supply line, but lost it again five days later when the local commander lost his nerve during an Egyptian counter-attack. In another attack on June 3rd, the Egyptians had been forewarned, and the attacking company had thirty of its men killed—a third of its strength. There was no unified command between the Givati Brigade on the northern sector and the Hanegev mobile Palmach brigade in the south, and when the first United Nations truce came, on June 11th, the Egyptians were still in position twenty miles south of Tel Aviv. But the defence had managed to contain them; this, the first big threat to Israel had been met by a mixture of improvisation, courage, able fieldmanship and luck.

The Egyptian move which had set out to capture Tel Aviv in forty-eight hours had not succeeded, but the Egyptian commanders had ably switched their target. They now concentrated on isolating the Negev and forcing the Jews completely out of southern Palestine, thus holding the south not only against the Israelis but also against Abdullah. It was a danger which the Israelis fully appreciated, and Abdullah also took the point. For it was driven home for him on the

Jerusalem front, where his forces merged with the Egyptians. The Egyptian commander disposed of a force which was nearly as large as the whole Arab Legion. He refused to recognise the authority of Abdullah as the Arab Supreme Commander and refused Abdullah permission to visit the Egyptian front. In fact, when the first period of fighting ended on June 11th, the Egyptians felt that they had at least improved their position even if they had not gained their objectives. They were poised on the perimeter of Tel Aviv and on the outskirts of Jerusalem, and they controlled all the main roads in the Negev. They looked hopefully to the future, which might enable them to settle accounts with both the Jews and with King Abdullah. This was the key to the appreciation of the situation in the south. And the Egyptians were thus quite content with their achievement during this opening phase. Their troops needed more training and some rest and fresh supplies. In Cairo therefore the Nokrashy government and King Farouk proclaimed massive victories in Palestine and denounced the United Nations for having prevented the Egyptian forces from finishing the job on which they had embarked through the imposition of the cease-fire on June 11th.

The Givati Brigade had prevented a break-through during the critical first days. It had paid a heavy price, with 200 men killed and 1,000 wounded. It needed new men and fresh supplies of arms and equipment. For the brigade, the truce was more than welcome—it was a necessity. It was the same with the unconquered settlements in the Negev which had been under air attack, artillery attack and assault by local Arabs. They too were in need of fresh arms, supplies and food, if they were not to be sitting ducks for the Egyptians when the fighting was resumed. And this was even more true of the exhausted mobile Negev "rats", the Palmach's Hanegev Brigade, which had harassed the Egyptians and sustained the settlements through the trying period when all seemed lost. Many of the Hanagev Brigade had been without leave for seven months and yet it had kept its fighting spirit throughout, it had also encouraged the harassed Negev settlers, and, on the last day before the truce, it had captured Bir Asluj together with a number of Egyptian prisoners. This was a much needed stimulant which the Negev troops needed and deserved.

But now both the Egyptian and Israeli commands looked

to the truce imposed by the United Nations as providing an opportunity to make up for their failing strength during this initial phase of the war in the south.

We can now turn to the other fronts.

The Haganah High Command was much less worried by the northern threat. It felt reasonably confident that it had some of the best Palmach and Haganah units operating there, and two of the outstanding commanders, Alon and Carmel, were in charge of the operations. But there was another reason for its confidence. Compared with either the situation in Jerusalem or the potential threat to Tel Aviv represented by the Egyptian advance, the northern situation appeared to be less urgent. Furthermore, both Alon and Carmel had just completed a series of offensive actions in Western and Eastern Galilee which had greatly raised the Israeli morale and improved their military position. Local Arab opposition in the whole of Western Galilee had collapsed with the fall of Acre on May 17th. In Eastern Galilee, Operation Yiftah commanded by Alon was drawing to a successful conclusion.

But this feeling at headquarters that the north could be left to look after itself was quickly shattered by alarming news from the Syrian front. The Syrian command had carried out the switch of front which was made necessary by Abdullah's refusal to accept the combined operations plan (see p. 151.) with much greater speed than the Israelis had anticipated. Alon was still preoccupied with the possibility of an attack from Malkieh across the neck of Northern Galilee when a Syrian column with some 200 vehicles, a few French tanks and artillery, came swiftly down from Kuneitra towards the southern tip of Lake Tiberias. When it reached the Yarmouk river, four miles from the Lake, it broke up into five separate columns and turned on the cluster of rich Jewish settlements which were here situated on both sides of the Jordan.

First the Syrians captured Samakh, which had been held by the Jews. But this key position on the road to the settlements was dominated by the police-station which the Haganah had occupied. This held up the Syrians for almost three days. They took the station only after its forty-two defenders had all been killed. A Palmach attempt to relieve them had failed with heavy losses. The Israelis were shocked into realising

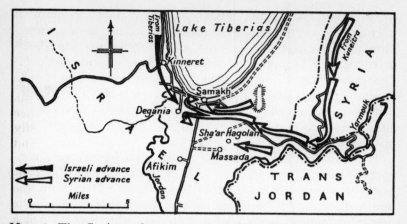

Map 6. The Syrian advance on Samakh and the Jordan valley
settlements.

that the Syrians were not quite so negligible a factor as they
had assumed. With the fall of the police-station, there was
now nothing defensible between the oncoming Syrians and
some of Israel's most famed settlements, Degania and Afikim
among them. There was alarm in the Jordan valley, and two
of the most exposed settlements, Massada and Sha'ar Hagolan,
were evacuated. It looked as if others might follow.

Urgent appeals for reinforcements now reached the Haganah
headquarters. It was clear to Ben-Gurion that he had to do
something to prevent a collapse in the north-east which might
affect the whole country. There were no troops to spare. Every
unit everywhere was engaged, and most of them were hard
pressed. The exception was a Carmeli force which had attacked
and taken Acre in the west and was moving northwards to the
Lebanese frontier, occupying Western Galilee without meeting
any opposition. But this was an opportunity which Ben-
Gurion did not want to forego. He ordered Carmel to continue
his operation, and to Degania he sent a Haganah officer who
was to make a name as a lone wolf and as a commando leader
of exceptional calibre—Moshe Dayan. His orders were to
hold the Jordan valley settlements.

Dayan explained later that there was no military justification for such an order, but that it was "a Zionist decision,"
an act of faith. With Dayan came two pieces of artillery—not

very impressive 65-mm. guns—very few shells to go with them, and a prototype sample of a locally made flame-thrower. The Syrians had already broken into the show-settlement of Degania when Dayan, the guns and the flame-thrower went into action. The guns scored two hits on the Syrian armour, and the Syrians faltered while the defence stiffened. But precisely what happened next has never really been established, for the Syrians suddenly disengaged and withdrew.

It seems that they (like the other Arab forces) were con-vinced that they would be able to move across Palestine without meeting serious opposition, or, like Neguib in the south, they may have imagined that they were up against a powerful Zionist army. May 20th was the turning-point. Perhaps it was the evacuation of the two settlements of Massada and Sha'ar Hagolan by the Israelis which first encouraged the Syrians to think that the same would happen at Degania, and the shock of resistance was accordingly greater. For they withdrew four days later from the two settlements which they had occupied, and also abandoned Samakh after a series of confused engagements which sug-gested that the Syrians had no clear idea of what they wanted, once their initial plan of linking up with the Arabs in Nazareth and Central Galilee had not materialised.

But the Syrians did not simply retire to lick their wounds. The lessons of the failure at Degania were quickly considered in the privacy of the Syrian General Staff. The failure was held to be due to a lack of careful preparation, and above all to the absence of surprise. A second operation was now prepared with great care which was to come as a complete surprise to the Israelis. It did. On June 10—almost the last day of the fighting before the truce—the Syrians came down the hill towards the Bridge of the Daughters of Jacob, about four miles south of Lake Huleh (as it was then).[1] They seized the bridge and launched an immediate attack on the settle-ment of Mishmar Hayarden. They took it, and held it until the truce was proclaimed. It was the only Arab bridge head on Israeli territory. But there appears to be no justification for the assumption that this Syrian force had the task of cutting

[1] The lake and surrounding swamps have since been drained as part of the Israel development programme.

across the valley and moving into Safed and beyond.[1] Instead, the Syrians managed to consolidate their bridgehead. They held the river crossing and territory about two miles to the south and two miles to the west, and turned the settlement into a formidable defensive position which tied down Israeli forces which were badly needed elsewhere.

Across the valley to the north-west, Israeli plans had also gone not quite as intended. Yigal Alon was convinced that it was necessary to clear the Lebanese from Malkieh, in order to remove the constant threat to Nebu Yusha and Ramot Naphtali. He sent his best officer, Dan Laner, with the 1st Palmach Battalion, against Malkieh and the 3rd Palmach Battalion to attack bridges, supply points and roads on the frontier. But for once Alon's intelligence was faulty. As Laner moved on Malkieh, he found himself face to face with 3,000 Lebanese. He was not prepared for defence. He was far from the nearest Kibbutz base. He had no choice but to fight it out in the open against an enemy who outnumbered him by six to one. He fought one of the best battles of the war; he and his very able company commanders (among them Assaf Simhoni) fought a withdrawing action for forty-eight hours without break. He retreated with all his casualties—over a hundred—without losing his head and able to come back on May 19th, six days later, to capture Malkieh and Kadesh. But they were lost again when the Yiftah Brigade was pulled out in June to move south.

There were thus no catastrophic developments in the north during this first period of fighting, and things had gone reasonably well for the Israelis. They had fought as hard as ever, but one notices signs of over-confidence, faulty intelligence and errors in assessing the situation among some of the local commanders in the north.

Alon seemed to sense this. They were operating on too narrow a front to be really effective. He therefore proposed to Carmel that they should make a combined drive from west and east across Central Galilee and take the whole area from

---

[1] Both Harry Sacher in *Israel: The Establishment of a State* (Weidenfeld and Nicolson, 1952), and Major O'Ballance (a keen follower in Sacher's footsteps) in his book, claim that this was the Syrian intention. There is no evidence to sustain this view. In any case, the Syrian force was far too small for this purpose.

Nazareth to the Lebanese border. But before he could get very far with his plan he had to begin his move south, where a more urgent task awaited him at Latrun (see Chapter Nine).

But there are still two more sectors of the northern front which call for some consideration. Though situated further south and facing yet another Arab front, both came under the command of Carmel, and both, from the Arab point of view, were intended to be part of the general Arab offensive against northern Israel.

The Iraqi contribution to the invading armies was one brigade of about 3,000 men, with one armoured car regiment. It was originally intended to use this force for the break-through at Gesher, and that the Arab Legion should attack some ten miles further south at the Sheikh Hussein crossing of the river. When Abdullah insisted on his priority for Jerusalem the Iraqis were still intended to break through at Gesher and take the Israeli defences at Beisan from the rear,

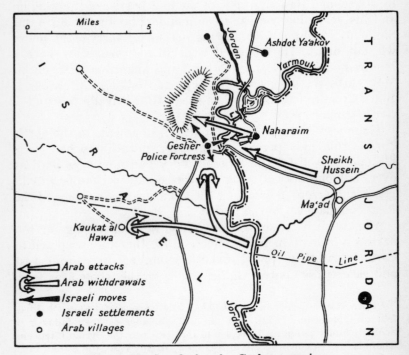

Map 7. The battle for the Gesher crossing.

before moving on Afuleh and the Plain of Esdrealon, but
without flanking assistance from the Legion. The Iraqi
attack began on May 20th with a three-pronged move. One
assault was launched from Naharayim to the north of Gesher;
a second, frontal assault, was aimed at Gesher itself, and was
backed by considerable artillery support; and a third—the
most dangerous—force crossed the river Jordan to the south
of Gesher to attack the heights of Kaukab el Hawa.

This last-mentioned attack was to be the preliminary move
to the taking of Gesher, and if it had succeeded the main
Israeli positions around Gesher would have become untenable.
It was fortunate for the Israelis that their local commander
had appreciated the importance of Kaukab el Hawa and had
occupied it on May 16th. The Iraqis arrived on the following
day and evidently expected to find no one there. There was a
sharp engagement; the Iraqis withdrew for the moment, but
maintained a small bridgehead on the Israeli side of the river.
Meanwhile, the main assault on Gesher had started, and a
part of the bridgehead force was ordered to make a flanking
attack on the settlement. They approached the defence from
the north, but here again the able local Israeli commander
blocked their approach by firmly holding the police-station
against the Iraqi attack. On the fourth day the Iraqi commander decided that he was not getting anywhere; so did
Glubb. Glubb was getting increasingly worried about the lack
of troops in the northern part of Palestine, especially between
Nablus and Jenin. He had an Arab Legion brigade locked up
there and he urgently wanted to move it south towards Latrun,
which was the crucial outpost in the defence of Jerusalem.
Glubb therefore proposed that the Iraqis should break off
their Gesher engagement, especially as the Syrians were
withdrawing further north.

The Iraqis disengaged forthwith, moved south to Allenby
Bridge, and crossed the Jordan to take over from the Arab
Legion brigade which had already been moved south as the
threatening battle of Latrun developed on the road to
Jerusalem. The Iraqis arrived at the crucial moment to avert
a total disaster on this front; this time fortune was on their
side.

As soon as Carmel found that the Iraqi pressure on Gesher
had been relaxed he began to consider the position of that part

of his front which faced southwards towards the Arab triangle opposite Jenin. The forward Arab positions were barely a mile from the main road between Beisan and Afuleh, and very close to four large Jewish settlements. He decided therefore to push back the Arabs and feel his way in the general direction of Jenin. But the errors of his intelligence began to tell.

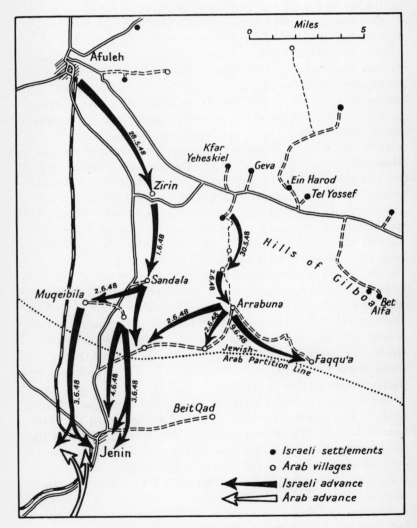

Map 8. The first battle for Jenin.

Carmel had been given to understand that it was the Legion that had attacked at Gesher, and that the Arab brigade south of Jenin was that of the Iraqis. This led him into a chain of fatal miscalculations.

The operation began according to plan on May 28th and proceeded smoothly and surprisingly uneventfully. The forward positions and those in the Gilboa hills were held by local Arabs, and they put up no great resistance. The pattern of advance was slightly confused, as its initial phase was more of a mopping-up operation than a forthright attack. One column cleared the Gilboa mountain villages; the other, secured thus on its flank, moved down on both sides of the main road to Jenin. Headquarters was delighted. There appeared to be no serious opposition, and by June 3rd three battalions of the Carmeli Brigade had reached the hills overlooking Jenin from both sides and from the rear. Scouts reported that the town was empty, that the population had fled, and that there was no sign of troops. Jenin was ready for the kill. Makleff hesitated. He had been described by one of his superiors as a safe commander: "no advance without security." He suspected that this was too easy. It might be a trap. He paused, and he lost.

For meanwhile, in his alarm at the news from Jenin, Glubb had urged the Iraqi commander to detach one battalion from his force and hasten it northwards. The Iraqis did not rush. They had just had one brush with the Carmeli forces at Gesher and they now held them in marked respect. But their good fortune held. Once again Makleff's intelligence failed him. He was informed that a powerful Iraqi force was approaching Jenin. He decided, however, to stand and fight. About the succeeding events there is a good deal of confusion and contradiction. Something had gone wrong with the advanced three Israeli battalions. Makleff sent orders by messenger to stand and fight at Jenin and that somehow this got confused into an order to withdraw. At the same time when the relieving Iraqi battalion arrived on the scene the Israelis were sure that they faced a much larger force. Next, an Iraqi shell hit the forward Israeli headquarters and killed all the officers present, thus throwing the forward commanders into a state of uncertainty and confusion. Lastly, the Jenin operation was planned as part of a much larger act. It was to coincide with a drive from the Sharon plain towards Tulqarm, carried out by Dan Even and the Alexandroni Brigade. But the Alexandroni attack did not materialise. Thus the cumulative pile up of accidents and errors conspired against the Israeli Commander and against the success of his operation.

The fact remained that the Israelis lost a great opportunity at Jenin. They misjudged the situation, they had some bad luck and fairly heavy casualties. The very variety of the explanations of the defeat suggests an initial state of confusion in the planning of the operation. But it had not been all in vain.

The advance on Jenin still left a valuable strip of territory in Israeli hands, but it did not bring the striking strategic gain which it easily might have done. Meanwhile, at his Ramat Gan villa, which had become Ben-Gurion's headquarters, the Prime Minister carefully weighed the reports from the Jenin front. They confirmed him in the conviction that drastic changes were necessary in the Israeli army before it could become a really powerful instrument.

Thus this phase of the war in the north drew to its close, in much the same way as it did in the south. The Israeli front had held, but only just. The Arab invasion had been halted, but the strain had been greater than either the Israeli public or the world at large had realised.[1] Yet neither the north nor the south had become the focal point on which both the principal protagonists had concentrated. For Ben-Gurion, as for Abdullah, the issue was to be decided by the fate of Jerusalem.

[1] Carmel reported later that every battalion under his command had at least a hundred dead and had been reduced in effective size from 450 to 200 men.

9

JERUSALEM TRAPPED; THE BATTLE OF LATRUN

I<small>T</small> was to Jerusalem that Abdullah sent the best of his Arab Legion troops. He had set his mind on capturing the city, and he had overruled the arguments of the commander of the Arab Legion, General Glubb. Glubb had hoped that the city would be neutralised, and that the efforts of the Consular Truce Commission to continue the truce which the British had imposed would be successful.[1]

But Glubb hoped in vain. As the British moved out of Jerusalem, the fighting in the vacuum which they had left behind continued with mounting violence, and the efforts of the Truce Commission were of no avail. In the Old City Arab irregulars launched repeated attacks against the Jewish garrison there, while in the New City Haganah troops occupied the key buildings evacuated by the British. At that time the Haganah might have agreed to some sort of truce in the city, for its position was far from happy. A representative of the Jewish forces, Vivian Herzog, who was acting at that time as head of the Security division of the Jewish Agency, was in contact with the Truce Commission at the French Consulate, and gave repeated assurances that the Haganah was prepared to cease fire, on condition that the Arabs did likewise. But there was no Arab commander in Jerusalem with sufficient authority to comply with the Commission's demands.

[1] On April 23rd the United Nations had appointed the French, Belgian and American Consuls in Jerusalem as a Truce Commission. They attempted to prolong the truce imposed by the British at the beginning of May into a permanent cease-fire in the Jerusalem area, but were not successful. Their last meeting was held on May 15th in the house of the French Consul, Neuville. During the meeting the house came under fire, and the American representative was wounded.

Abdullah did not want the truce, and Glubb did not have the authority or ability to override Abdullah and impose one. The fighting continued.

In fact, it provided Abdullah with the excuse he wanted. He was now going to save Jerusalem from the Jews and capture the entire city. For him Jerusalem was a far more

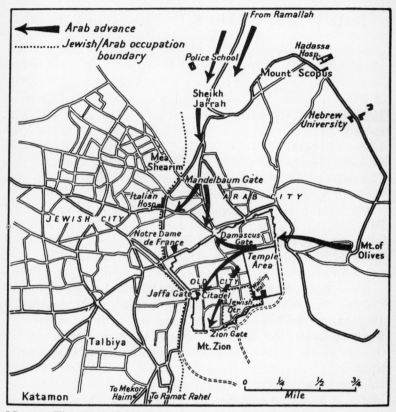

Map 9. The Arab Legion moves into Jerusalem after May 15th, 1948.

glittering prize than either Samaria or Haifa. From the outset he had set his heart on taking the city and becoming King of Jerusalem.

The first units of the Arab Legion entered the Old City of Jerusalem on May 18th, and that night a second force reached the northern outskirts of the city. This consisted of one company of infantry and one squadron of armoured cars, four

6-pounder anti-tank guns, four 3-inch mortars, with four 25-pounders as artillery support.[1] Later, reinforcements arrived, and, all told, some 700 Legionaires were engaged in the fighting in the northern and eastern suburbs of Jerusalem. Opposing them were two battalions of Haganah infantry, each consisting of about 500 men; 200 men of the Irgun and the Stern group, with arms for only about a hundred; and several formations of the Home Guard—men over forty-five, very inadequately equipped and armed. The Jews enjoyed numerical superiority. The Arabs had the advantage of superior fire-power. They had artillery, supporting armour and fully armed and equipped units. The Jewish units were poorly armed. They were short of ammunition. And they had only relatively few home-made "Davidka" mortars as supporting weapons.[2]

This was the position in Jerusalem when, on the morning of May 19th, the Arab Legion launched its attack on the Jewish held parts of the city.

The first assault was directed against the important quarter of Sheikh Jarrah, on the road from Ramallah to the Old City. This quarter had first been captured by the Jews in April, but they had been forced out again by the British.[3] When the British left Jerusalem Haganah troops moved in again, but responsibility for its defence was given over to the company of the Irgun which was attached to the Haganah force. Instead of preparing the defences, the Irgun troops delayed until they had possession of the former Palestine Police School, which was within their area. Consequently, when the Legion attacked they found virtually no opposition against them, and they easily captured the entire quarter and all the Irgun positions. It was an important tactical victory for the Legion. By capturing Sheikh Jarrah they succeeded in linking up with the Arabs in the Old City. They had also cut off the Jewish positions on Mount Scopus, and these have remained separated from the rest of Jewish Jerusalem ever since.

Having gained their first objective so easily, the Legionnaires proceeded to attack the Jewish quarters of northern Jeru-

[1] According to the figures given by Glubb in *A Soldier with the Arabs*.
[2] On May 15th the Jews had only sixteen of these Davidkas in the whole of Palestine.
[3] See Chapter Seven, pp. 137.

salem; Bet Yisrael, Shechunat Pagi, Shmuel Hanavi and the "Hungarian Quarter." Their main force, supported by armoured cars and 25-pounders, attacked the now famous Mandelbaum Houses, trying to force their way up the Street of the Prophets towards Mea Shearim, the Italian Hospital and the centre of the city. Other attacks were launched at various points along the Shmuel Hanavi road on the two Jewish quarters of Bet Yisrael and Shechunat Pagi.[1]

Throughout that day, and the week following it, the fate of Jewish Jerusalem hung in the balance. In a sense, this was the most critical period of the war. The Haganah troops were strung out over a large area; they were weary after months of fighting, whereas the Legionnaires were still fresh. Above all, the Haganah had virtually no weapons against the Legion's armour, except home-manufactured "Molotov cocktails" and a few PIATS, nor were the defences built to stand up to the point-blank fire of 6- and 25-pounders. On at least three occasions, it seemed that the Legion was about to break through, but each time the Israelis counter-attacked and regained the houses they had lost.

After several days of heavy fighting in the northern suburbs, in which casualties were heavy on both sides, the Legion suddenly switched its attack. Its new objective was the strongly built Convent of Notre Dame de France. This imposing building overlooked a large part of the Old City. It was also not more than half a mile from the centre of Jewish Jerusalem. The Convent was therefore a desirable property for both sides. Once more the Legion speared its attack with armoured cars, and throughout May 23rd its infantry fought hard to gain entrance to the massive building. By the morning of May 24th the Legion headquarters received news that Legionnaires had forced an entrance.

All that day the fighting continued within the building and in the gardens of the Convent. But by five o'clock in the afternoon Notre Dame was still in Jewish hands. Of the 200 Arab infantrymen who had taken part in the attack on the

[1] Glubb, in *A Soldier with the Arabs*, does not mention these attacks at all, despite the fact that they involved some of the heaviest fighting in the city. They refute his claim that the aim of the Legion was only to link up with the Old City and form a defensive line within Jerusalem, without trying to capture the Jewish quarter.

building, nearly half were either dead or stretcher cases. One of Glubb's companies had lost all its officers and N.C.O's. except one. The attack was called off. One of the Jewish commanders of the defence was a well-known professor of the Hebrew University.[1]

The attack on Notre Dame proved to be a turning-point in the battle for northern Jerusalem. The Legion could not afford such casualties. It had no reserves. From then on, the fighting in the north of the city slackened considerably. The focal point of the attack switched to the southern outskirts.

Units of the Egyptian army had reached Bethlehem after an uninterrupted march from the frontier at El Auja. They consisted in the main of Moslem Brotherhood volunteers commanded by Lieutenant-Colonel Ahmed Abd el-Aziz. They now linked up with the Arab Legion units which had earlier captured Kfar Etzion. Ever since the April days when Kfar Etzion had fallen, the people of southern Jerusalem had been hourly expecting these Legion forces. It seemed to them that nothing now could stop the Arabs. There were no anti-tank weapons in any of the southern suburbs, nor was there any defence against the artillery which the Legion had used so effectively against Kfar Etzion.

The expected attack materialised on May 21st. Its objective was Ramat Rahel, a Jewish collective settlement at the southern tip of the city. It was strategically situated on a hill commanding easy access to virtually the whole of south Jerusalem. Talpiot, Mekor Hayim and Katamon would become untenable if the settlement fell into Arab hands.[2]

The attack was opened with an artillery barrage fired at point-blank range. It stunned the settlers and caused them heavy casualties. After several hours of preparatory fire, the Egyptians stormed the settlement. But they had hardly entrenched themselves when forces of the Etzioni Brigade counter-attacked and reoccupied the hill-top, with its burning shell of the settlement. But the Jewish infantry were needed in the north of the city, and they were immediately replaced

[1] The late Professor Bodenheimer, elderly head of the Enlymology faculty.
[2] In the days of Solomon the hill-top played a similar part. A large Jewish garrison was permanently stationed on it, guarding the southern approaches to Jerusalem.

by second-line troops. These were no match for the Arabs. In a second assault on the following day Ramat Rahel was once more captured by the Egyptians, supported by the Legion.

The threat to Jewish Jerusalem was now acute. The Legion renewed its attack in the north. The southern suburbs were under heavy fire from the Legion guns at Ramat Rahel and Mar Elias. But, in some of the heaviest fighting of the war, Harel reinforcements and Etzioni troops battered their way up the hill to retake Ramat Rahel once again. The settlement was to change hands three times more before the Haganah was finally left in possession, and the danger, for the time being, had passed.

While the Jews were kept mainly on the defensive, they made a number of sorties to improve their general position, and in particular to establish a link with the Jewish garrison in the Old City. The first of these attacks began immediately the British had completed their withdrawal from the city on May 14th. Both the Arab irregulars within the city and the Haganah forces were waiting to pounce on the evacuated buildings and army camps, and hardly had the British left when heavy fighting broke out for possession of these prizes.

In this race the Jews came off the better; not only did they succeed in occupying the massive block of government buildings in the centre of the city, but they also ousted the Arabs from such points as they had already occupied before the British had left, in particular the large El Alamein and Allenby barracks. Thus, by the time the Arab Legion arrived, the Haganah had succeeded in linking up its isolated quarters and in capturing a large part of new Jerusalem. The only quarter which remained completely cut off and isolated was the Jewish Quarter of the Old City.

The 1,700 Jews living there were in a difficult position. They had been separated from the rest of the Jewish city for the past six months, receiving meagre food supplies, by way of British-escorted convoys, once every fortnight. In the last weeks of the Mandate a truce had been imposed in Jerusalem, but with the British evacuation of the Old City the Arabs resumed their assault on the trapped Jewish quarter. Slowly they forced the Jews into a small perimeter, until by May 17th their position had become critical. They held no more than a hundred yards square of territory, with the inhabitants huddled in three large courtyards. Many of the small Haganah force living with the Old City Jews were wounded. The supply of ammunition was nearly exhausted. On May 17th, after a particularly heavy attack had been beaten off, the officer commanding the Old City defence signalled a series of anguished messages to the Jerusalem Command: "Most of us are wounded," "Our ammunition is nearly finished," "We cannot hold out much longer." Then, finally: "Our ammunition can last for only another quarter of an hour."

At this point help arrived. Troops of the Palmach captured Mount Zion on the night of May 18th[1] and broke through the Zion Gate into the Old City. Minutes later they had linked up with the Jewish Quarter. For the besieged and half-starved Jews there it was a day of jubilation and thanksgiving.

But their joy was short-lived. Once more the Israelis failed to consolidate their successes. Bad liaison between the Palmach and the Jerusalem command, and precipitate action by the commander of the Palmach troops who had broken into the Old City, nullified the advantage they had gained. Reinforcements, which were to hold the Zion Gate and maintain the link with the Jewish Quarter, had not arrived as planned. The Palmach commander could not wait for them and, by nightfall, had withdrawn his forces from the Old City, leaving behind eighty-seven untrained second-line soldiers as reinforcements for the Old City Jews. The Zion Gate was recaptured by the Arabs, and the siege of the Old City Jews was renewed. What might have become a serious threat to the entire Arab position in the Old City was thus thrown away by inadequate liaison.

That day, May 18th, the first units of the Arab Legion entered the Old City, and the attacks on the Jewish Quarter became more determined. In an attempt to relieve the Quarter, at dawn on May 19th the Haganah simultaneously attacked the massive Citadel of David, the Jaffa Gate, and Mount Zion. The attack on the Jaffa Gate failed, as did further efforts to retake the Zion Gate.

For ten more days the beleaguered Quarter withstood the Arab Legion, but on May 28th, two aged Rabbis, carrying white flags, approached the Legion lines. The Jews of the Old

[1] In this attack, two Britons and sixty Arab soldiers were taken prisoner.

City had surrendered. As the Legionnaires entered the Quarter and saw the small force against which they had been fighting, the few soldiers who had not been wounded, and the kind of weapons they carried, one of the Legion officers remarked: "If we had known you were so few we would have fought you with sticks instead of machine-guns and mortars." The incident demonstrated once more the shortcomings of the Legion's field intelligence.

For the Jews, the loss of the Holy Places, in particular the Wailing Wall and the Temple Area was a great blow. Militarily, however, the fall of the Old City garrison had surprisingly little effect on the war situation.

Meanwhile, the plight of the Jewish population of the rest of Jerusalem was getting worse. The Arab Legion, with its control of the dominating heights, had ringed the city with its batteries of 25- and 100-pounder guns. Jerusalem was shelled continuously and indiscriminately. The Egyptians too had brought up several 100-pounder guns, and used them with anti-personnel shrapnel-filled shells. The Jerusalem Jews were driven off the streets, shops remained shut, and the men who continued to distribute the meagre water ration risked their lives as much as any front-line soldier. In the three weeks' fighting before the first truce more than 8,000 shells were fired into Jerusalem. They killed 400 civilians, and over a thousand were wounded.

But this was only a part of the hardships which the Jerusalem Jews had to bear. By the end of May, food stocks had been almost used up. The population was receiving a daily ration of 140 grams of bread per person (about two normal slices). In over ninety per cent of the houses there was no food left whatsoever, and the people would rummage in back gardens for choice weeds and grasses to eat. The taps were dry. Water was distributed by truck—one small pail of water per family daily. There was no electricity and no petrol, and there were no newspapers and no cigarettes. Above all, there was very little ammunition left. Machine-gunners received orders to fire single rounds only, so as not to waste ammunition. Mortar crews were "rationed" to five bombs per day.

This was the background to the Legion attacks in Jerusalem. Trapped and besieged, with little food and less ammunition, attacked from north and south, the Jews of Jerusalem felt that only a miracle could save them. But a spirit of defiance permeated the city. Old and young worked feverishly building defences, digging trenches, and erecting road-blocks, while the shells fell. Members of the youth movements were sent to the front line, and in the overflowing hospitals were not a few boys of fifteen and sixteen who had been wounded while repulsing the attacks of the Legion at Shechunat Pagi or Bet Yisrael. The Jews felt that they were facing an enemy many times stronger than them—not only in fire-power, but also in numbers. Like Glubb—and like most commanders in battle—they overestimated the enemy strength. But at least they were only too well aware of the overwhelming superiority in fire-power which the Arabs enjoyed. Had the Legion armour broken through at the Mandelbaum Houses, or at Shechunat Pagi, the whole of Jerusalem might possibly have fallen to the Arabs.

For there were at this stage a number of serious weaknesses in the Jewish command in Jerusalem. Except for a short period, there was no unified command of the Haganah forces in the city itself and the Palmach forces in the hills. Yitzhak Rabin, first commander of the Palmach forces in the Judaean Hills, and later Yosef Tabenkin, commander of the Harel Brigade, were in constant conflict with David Shaltiel, commander of the Jerusalem forces, who would often bring these disputes before Ben-Gurion. One of the results of this lack of co-ordination was the failure to relieve the Old City Jews. Another was the loss of a number of opportunities for offensive action. Moreover, the fact that Ben-Gurion repeatedly intervened in tactical questions concerning the Jerusalem front seriously hampered the initiative of the local commanders. The Palmach, in particular, was not given the free hand it would have liked to have had on this front, though when it took independent action on occasion it was not always appreciated by Shaltiel. Its focus and outlook were proud and bold but not always easy to handle.

Within the city itself, brigade staff work was very poor. Shaltiel, the commander of the Etzioni Brigade, was too remote from his men. He was a stern disciplinarian as a commander, but appeared to be unable to gain the affection or trust of the troops fighting under him. Some of his orders and methods were high-handed and ill-suited to the difficult conditions prevailing in the city at the time. Matters reached a head when some of the company commanders of the "Moria" infantry battalion refused to obey his orders, and he threatened to have them arrested. Eventually the Moria Battalion had to leave the city and join the Palmach.[1]

In a different context, Shaltiel also had to contend with the private armies of the Irgun and the Stern Group. They had their separate command, independent equipment, and a strong inclination to act on their own. They only accepted such orders as they approved of. But most serious was the fact that they did not merely keep Shaltiel in the dark about their own strength, numbers and equipment—they led him to believe that they were far more numerous and much better armed than was the case. In the event, the Irgun and the Stern Group could each muster only a hundred active combatants, and they had barely enough rifles and equipment for half of them.

These weaknesses naturally told on the Jewish defence. But the Legion failed to take advantage of them, because, once again, it was uninformed about conditions on the Jewish side. The bogey which Glubb had created served Shaltiel well in covering up the shortcomings of his command. Thus, after the Legion's failure to capture the Notre Dame Convent and to hold Ramat Rahel, its attack lost its impetus, and, for the remaining two weeks of fighting before the first truce, it contented itself with local skirmishes and limited attacks. For the Legion was completely unaware of how near to success it had been. But there was also the imponderable factor of the Jewish civilian population in Jerusalem. The majority gave a remarkable display of courage and civic duty. The short-comings of the military command did not affect it. This civilian spirit made the work of the soldiers much easier. It was not so on the other side of the fence.

In the Arab sector of Jerusalem, the population, swollen in number with refugees from Katamon, Baka'a and other Arab suburbs captured by the Jews, were near to panic. Like the Jews, they felt that only a miracle could save them from losing the entire city, and this mood gradually affected the Legion officers also.

---

[1] It became the 10th Battalion of the Palmach, attached to the Harel Brigade. Later, before the second phase of the fighting, the Moria Battalion was returned to Jerusalem.

Thus, the fighting inside the city reached a stalemate. But the position of the Jews, cut off as they were from the rest of the country, remained desperate. To maintain their position they would have to loosen the vice in which the Arabs held Jerusalem. It was, then, in the hills to the west of the city that the deciding battles for Jerusalem would have to be fought. We must therefore now turn our attention to this front and the important developments unfolding there. For the battle of Latrun, the most controversial battle of the Palestine War, had already begun.

There exists no appreciation drawn up by the Israeli army's General Staff which argues the case for the attack on Latrun. There was none. There is no record of a careful weighing of the pros and cons before launching a frontal assault on this central cog of the Arab investment of Jerusalem. There was none. There were consultations between the Prime Minister and the Director of Operations; there was some discussion, but not much. There was just a small chit of paper, four inches by two inches. On it was Ben-Gurion's order to Yadin; Jerusalem had to be relieved. There was no time for finesse. The road had to be opened at the bottleneck where the Arabs had stoppered it —at Latrun. If there were no troops for the operation, then a new formation had to be raised. If there were no arms, then ships were about to land them. But there was to be no delay. There was no time for planning, only for improvisation; otherwise Jerusalem might be lost for ever. Above all, the action would have to be completed before the truce was imposed.

This was an order. Ben-Gurion did not want to hear of the difficulties. He knew them. It was Yadin's job to overcome them. It was an impossible proposition. Yadin did not believe in it, but he understood Ben-Gurion's reasoning; and as things stood he could offer no acceptable alternative that might relieve the impending threat to Jerusalem. So the decision was taken on Saturday, May 22nd: the 7th Brigade would be formed at Na'an, and it was to be ready for the assault on Latrun by Monday night, forty-eight hours later. Yadin shuddered at the implications of Ben-Gurion's decision. But he set out to have it implemented in a manner which is probably unique in the history of warfare. Its execution therefore deserves rather closer attention than it has yet received.

Yadin summoned Shlomo Shamir, a former major in the

Jewish Brigade during the Second World War, and told him that he would be in command. On Saturday morning, Yadin ordered Vivian Herzog, head of the security branch of the Jewish Agency in Jerusalem, to fly to Tel Aviv. On arrival he was told that he was to be the Operations Officer of the 7th Brigade. Shamir informed him that they would have to attack the following night, without even seeing their troops. Both Shamir and Herzog were agreed that this was not possible. Ben-Gurion was persuaded, but not easily, to delay the attack by twenty-four hours. The new command then moved to Na'an, where the brigade was forming. No. 5 "buses" and others from Tel Aviv were bringing the troops from Tel Aviv: the 32nd Battalion under Zvi German, a company of the Palmach with some half-tracks, and a new battalion of immigrants under Zvi Hurewitz. These immigrants had arrived only the day before. They were given cursory rifle training. They had had no experience of war, and they spoke a babel of languages, but hardly any Hebrew.

At the same time a large convoy of trucks loaded with supplies for Jerusalem was forming near-by at Bilu.

At 10 o'clock on Tuesday evening (May 25th) the first orders group was held. The instructions were to take Latrun and prepare for the advance on Ramallah as far as possible. The principal object was to let the food and ammunition convoy to Jerusalem pass through the blockade at Latrun.

The troops were assembled in lorries and Tel Aviv buses. It was hot (there was a blistering khamseen), and they had no water-bottles. By midnight the support weapons had not arrived. Herzog proposed to postpone the attack, and Shamir contacted Yadin who had moved to Kibbutz Na'an. Yadin agreed and advised Shamir to send a cable to General Headquarters. Yadin himself immediately returned to Tel Aviv to persuade Ben-Gurion to agree to the postponement. But Ben-Gurion was firm. The attack was to proceed according to plan. With heavy heart, Yadin cabled his reply to Shamir: "Attack, at all cost." At two in the morning the force moved noisily out of Hulda on the road to Latrun. As they moved, the support weapons—half-tracks, machine-guns and mortars— were arriving at Hulda straight from the port of Tel Aviv, where they had been landed that evening. There had not even been time for a reconnaissance of the ground. The information about the enemy had come from headquarters. It said that Latrun was only lightly held by some of Kaukji's irregulars.

But already a week earlier Glubb had sent the 4th Arab Legion Regiment to Latrun to prevent reinforcements from Tel Aviv reaching Jerusalem. They could not help being alarmed by the noise, the headlights, and the movement from the direction of Hulda, 6 miles away. There was no question of surprise or finesse. The buses and lorries rumbled on towards

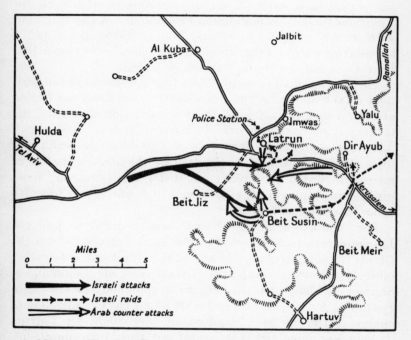

Map 10. The first Israeli attack on Latrun, May 25th, 1948.

their fate at Latrun as the first light rose over the Judaean Hills. They were received by gun and mortar fire from Latrun and Yalu, where the Legion guns were stationed. It was not a very devastating fire, but it shattered the nerves of inexperienced new troops who were already in bad shape because of the heat and thirst. They retreated, many of them into the arms of local Arab bands in the foothills south of Beit Jiz. It was the last straw for them. They broke and fled. Many collapsed from exhaustion. Haim Laskov, who was there with some armoured half-tracks, saved the majority when he kept his nerve, took charge and covered their retreat.

Next day Ben-Gurion visited the front to see for himself. It was not a pretty picture. The troops were demoralised, and the command also was not in the best shape. They had been through a gruelling experience. Ben-Gurion ordered that some trained reinforcements be sent to stiffen the Latrun front, and the American Colonel "Mickey" Marcus, who had already taken part in a series of striking commando actions on the Egyptian front, was nominated Commander of the front but without his own headquarters. His presence alone had a stimulating effect on the troops, and a second more ambitious plan was made for another attack on Latrun.

The essence of the new plan was that Laskov would make a feint attack on the Latrun police-station and draw the Legion attention and fire. Meanwhile, Prulov, in command of the trained reinforcements, was to move about six and a half miles across difficult country from Beit Susin to Yalu, and force the Legion out of its position by threatening its line of retreat. It was a good plan; but it depended on every commander in it playing his part, and now one more difficulty came to a head at Latrun.

The reinforcements which had been ordered to join the Latrun attack had consisted of the 52nd Battalion, from the Givati Brigade, in charge of one of the ablest of the brigade's officers. However, both the Givati Brigade commander, Shimon Avidan, and the officer in command of the 52nd Battalion, Prulov, had their doubts about the commanders in charge of the operation, and about their plans for Latrun. Avidan has explained that he did not trust their judgment. He had therefore instructed Prulov that he was not to engage in any action which might result in the unnecessary loss of his men. For Avidan felt strongly that, as commander, he was responsible for the welfare of his men. In the subsequent action Prulov heeded Avidan's injunction.

On the first night, the attack had to be postponed because Prulov had started out too late. But the following night everything started according to plan: the feint attack on Latrun was successfully made, and Prulov reached Deir Ayub. But after engaging the Legion there and suffering only two casualties,

Prulov decided that he could not succeed without heavy casualties, and he withdrew.

This left Laskov in the thick of it. He had broken into the police-station. He was suffering heavy casualties, and the immigrant infantry which was to back him up failed to advance into the fire. For the second time Laskov had to withdraw after reaching his objective. That night Marcus cabled Yadin: "I was there and saw the battle. Plan good. Artillery good. Armour excellent. Infantry disgraceful."

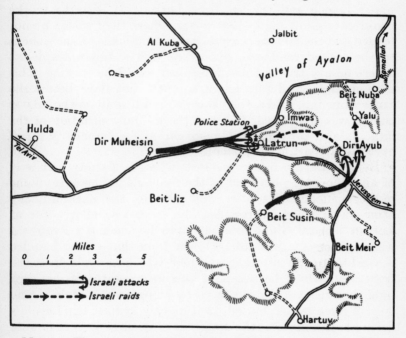

Map 11. The second Israeli attack on Latrun, May 30th, 1948.

The attempt had failed. Between May 25th and 31st the 7th Brigade had lost 137 men killed. But its work was not yet finished. For meanwhile the realisation had come to Ben-Gurion and Yadin that this was going to be the kind of war in which possession was more important than anything. Somehow therefore they had to get to Jerusalem. If the old road through Latrun was impassable, then they had to find or build a new one. For some time the Palmach had been using a path to the south of Latrun and Bab el-Wad to send troops on foot through the hills to Jerusalem. The path had first been used during Operation Maccabee on May 17th, when a solitary truck, loaded with supplies, had been manhandled through the hills, as the blockades on the main roads had not yet been cleared. This feat was now remembered, and work was immediately begun to make the path into a usable road. Five hundred workers were brought from Jerusalem and Tel Aviv to complete the road before the impending truce would make further work impossible. Work continued twenty-four hours a day, often under Legion artillery fire from Latrun. At first the trucks could only go as far as Beit Susin. There they would be unloaded and the labourers would carry their loads on their backs to the second roadhead, about one and a half miles away, where empty trucks from Jerusalem would be waiting. This distance was gradually lessened, until, two days before the truce came into effect, the "Burma" road, as it was popularly called, was completed. It saved the military situation in the city. It also provided the justification for Israel's political claim to its part of Jerusalem.

But the Latrun battle was instructive as a study, not only of an impossible plan, and of the frequent importance of the indirect effects of battles, but also of the extraordinary atmosphere which surrounded the Arab war effort. For at Latrun General Glubb and the Arab Legion's 4th Regiment were fighting quite a different war from that of the Israelis. According to the information which Glubb received from the front, and which he accepted and incorporated in his own published account, he was faced by an overwhelmingly strong Jewish force, which hurled itself nightly against the Legion's defences. Glubb notes the hundreds of dead Israelis that were found on the battlefield, and he writes that in the first four engagements the Israelis lost 1,400 dead,[1] rather more than the initial establishment of the entire 7th Brigade.

It was without doubt due to his strikingly unreliable information about the enemy forces that Glubb first opposed Abdullah's proposals to attack Jerusalem in strength, and was later to withdraw from Lydda and Ramle before the Israeli attack (see Chapter Eleven). For Glubb made no attempt at any time to check the claims of his Arab officers at the front. This unmilitary credulity cost him and the Arabs dearly.

[1] Glubb: *A Soldier with the Arabs*, p. 132.

For, on the basis of such information, Glubb designed his strategy to meet a powerful, fully equipped Israeli army that did not exist at that time. He spoke about the lost opportunity of the Israelis, but it might have been more appropriate to contemplate his own. For it was he who lost the war when he lost Jerusalem; there was going to be neither a second round nor a second chance for either Abdullah or Glubb.

On the other side, Ben-Gurion pondered over the lesson of Latrun. He felt that the gamble had paid off. It had needed just this much at that moment to turn the tables in Jerusalem. Yadin's and Alon's more ambitious plans might have been more successful, but they probably would have succeeded too late. Latrun, however, had also emphasised the shortcomings of Israel's new army. The lack of discipline, the absence of trust between the "pure" Haganah veterans and those who had served in the British army, and the inadequacies of the command structure—especially the danger of inaction and indecision produced by endless and undisciplined argument—had all impressed themselves on Ben-Gurion.

The impact of Latrun went far beyond the battlefield. It gave the impetus to the crisis of the High Command which was to rock the structure of government in Israel during the coming truce. It probably contributed more to the reshaping of Israel's armed forces than any other encounter in the war. It also confirmed Glubb in his complacent belief that the Legion had won a shattering victory. But deeper than all this was Ben-Gurion's conviction, as the struggle for Latrun came to an inconclusive end, that the issue of the war would be decided between the Arab Legion and the Israelis—unless the Egyptians made a major effort, which Ben-Gurion did not expect. "Either the Legion will break into our triangle, or we shall have to break into theirs," he argued. "If we succeed we shall almost have won the war," he added, "the main front therefore is the territory held by the Arab Legion—Jerusalem and the Judean hills, not the Negev or the Galilee. I have the greatest respect for the Legion," he concluded. One more attempt was made to crash through Latrun on June 9th. It failed, Colonel M. Marcus was killed accidentally by one of his own sentries.

10

THE FIRST TRUCE

During the early weeks of the war both Arabs and Israelis watched somewhat uncomprehendingly the events taking place at the United Nations at Lake Success. Neither the Arabs nor the Israelis were certain where the British now stood. Ben-Gurion admitted that this was still his main pre-occupation. The British might still increase their support for the Arabs, but if they did not do so, then he believed that Israel had a chance of winning the war. And the only indicator of British intentions was to be found at the United Nations. Therefore we must now follow the manoeuvres among the United Nations that led to the first Palestine truce.

The Security Council met on Saturday, May 15th, 1948—the day when the Arab armies invaded Palestine. The Egyptian delegate informed the Council that Egypt was concerned only in the preservation of law and order. None of the Big Three (Britain, the United States and the Soviet Union) intervened. On Monday, May 17th, the Security Council met again. The United States delegate now proposed that, as a breach of the peace had taken place within the meaning of Article 39 of the Charter, the Council should order an immediate "cease-fire" and stand fast.

The British representative, Sir Alexander Cadogan, did not speak until the following day; he expressed grave doubts about the American proposal. He doubted whether there had been a breach of the peace or if there had been a clear case of aggression. The news that day was still of Arab advances. Sir Alexander wanted no sanctions, even if the Security Council's appeal for peace was rejected by the Arab states.

Four days passed, while the world's press still reported Arab victories. The American delegate returned again with the charge that a breach of the peace had taken place, and once more invoked the sanctions of Article 39 to compel a "cease-fire." Again Sir Alexander opposed him, and the Council adjourned for another two days. On May 24th the Council received a message from the Provisional Government of Israel[1] accepting the "cease-fire" proposed in the American resolution. The Syrian member of the Security Council asked for an extension of the time-limit within which the resolution should be obeyed. Sir Alexander supported this request. Two days passed and then another two days, and still nothing was done.

On May 29th Sir Alexander again opposed hasty action. He also opposed a simple proposal by the Soviet Union, which was supported by the United States and France, to order a "cease-fire within thirty-six hours under threat of United Nations Sanctions." Instead, Sir Alexander Cadogan proposed another resolution of his own which, he said, might halt the fighting without the pressure of the sanctions chapter of the Charter. The heat was off.

The Arabs fought on. On the next day the Jewish Quarter of the Old City of Jerusalem capitulated. Sir Alexander's resolution was now voted upon and accepted as the lesser evil. Its principal provisions were (a) an appeal to all parties for a four week's cease-fire, and (b) that if this was rejected or subsequently repudiated or violated, "the situation in Palestine would be considered with a view of action under Chapter VII of the Charter." It was known, of course, to all members of the Security Council that the British Government was opposed to any form of sanction against the Arab states, and that it would take its position to the point of exercising its right of veto.

It was not until thirteen days later, when the Arab armies were near the point of exhaustion, that they accepted the "cease-fire." During this long interval Sir Alexander maintained a revealing silence on the Security Council. Not once did he express any need for more forceful action by the Security Council to bring the fighting to an end.

On only one occasion during all these Security Council discussions, in fact, had Sir Alexander Cadogan taken the initiative. On May 19th, when he had intervened to extract the

[1] The Government remained Provisional till January 25th, 1949, when elections were held for the first Knesset, the Israel Parliament.

"teeth" of any possible sanctions against the Arab states from the United States proposal, he had also, for the first time, proposed that a United Nations Mediator for Palestine be appointed. It was not an altogether unpremediated step. Count Folke Bernadotte had already been consulted about accepting the post six days earlier, before the formal war in Palestine had started. Now it was made clear that this was as far as the British Government was prepared to go: a Mediator without the power of sanctions, and one who enjoyed the confidence of Whitehall. With the conclusion that half a loaf was better than blank British non-cooperation, the Big Five[1] members of the Security Council agreed to the nomination of Count Bernadotte as Mediator, with powers strictly restricted by the British-sponsored resolution.

From the first the British Government took a somewhat proprietary interest in the Mediator, which was not altogether welcome to Count Bernadotte. He has recalled in his diary that the first "outsider" to call on him when he arrived in Paris on May 25th to begin his work as Mediator was Mr. Ashley Clarke, the British Charge d'Affaires in Paris, who told him "that the British Government was not prepared for the time being to take any steps against the Arabs." In fact, the Count was informed that the British Government was continuing to supply arms to the Arabs, and that British officers, who had joined the Arab forces as instructors, were also taking an active part in the war. Nor were British official circles anxious, Mr. Clarke confided to the Count, to accept the American proposal that the Arab action should be regarded as "provocation and a flagrant breach of the United Nations Charter."[2]

Meanwhile, the British Government's representatives were not slow in discreetly indicating to the Count the lines on which his meditation might prove fruitful and enjoy British diplomatic support, at least in the Arab capitals. The British Government wanted a revision of the partition plan: the southern part of the Negev (below the 31st parallel) was to go to Abdullah, and not to the Jews; the Jews were to get Western

[1] Nationalist China, France, the Soviet Union, the United Kingdom, and the United States.
[2] Bernadotte: *To Jerusalem*, pp. 6–7.

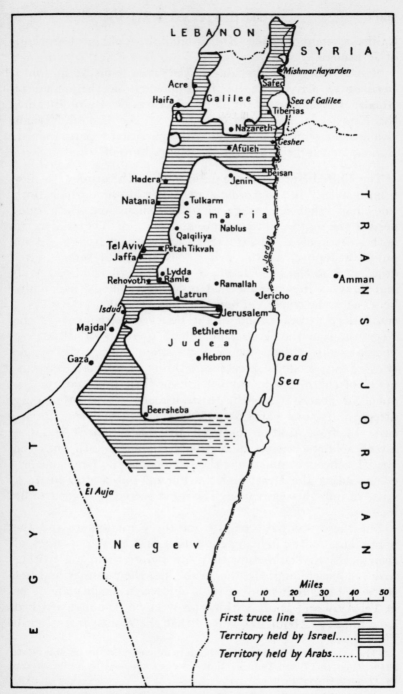

LEBANON

SYRIA

Mishmar Hayarden

Acre

Safed

Haifa

Galilee

Sea of Galilee

Tiberias

Nazareth

Gesher

Afuleh

Beisan

Hadera

Jenin

Natania

Tulkarm

S a m a r i a

Nablus

Qalqiliya

Tel Aviv

Petah Tikvah

Jaffa

Rehovoth

Lydda

Ramle

Latrun

Ramallah

Jericho

Amman

Isdud

Jerusalem

T R A N S J O R D A N

Majdal

Bethlehem

J u d e a

Gaza

Hebron

Dead

Sea

Beersheba

E G Y P T

El Auja

N e g e v

Miles

| 0 | 10 | 20 | 30 | 40 | 50 |

First truce line

Territory held by Israel......

Territory held by Arabs........

Map 12. The situation after the first truce, June 11th, 1948.

Galilee as compensation. King Abdullah would get the whole of Jerusalem.[1]

Shortly before the first day of the truce, June 11th, Count Bernadotte arrived at his headquarters on the island of Rhodes. His chief assistant and adviser was Dr. Ralph Bunche, the Negro who had been Secretary to the United Nations Commission which had prepared the partition report. Indeed, Bunche had largely written the report himself.

The United Nations truce descended on the armies "as dew from heaven," in the words of Brigadier Moshe Carmel. Both sides had reached a stage of utter exhaustion. Both sides needed the respite to reorganise and regroup. The soldiers on both sides knew it, but the truth was witheld from the Arab public at home. As the firing ceased, and a serene quiet descended on the Holy Land, it seemed to the soldiers, Arab and Jew, as if a miracle had occurred. Nobody had really believed in the truce. Yet now the guns were silent, the soldiers could sleep in peace, and in the besieged settlements of the Negev and in the Arab and Jewish quarters of Jerusalem people could venture out of doors again. Slowly the people trickled out; soon the streets were thronged with large crowds, many of the men and women taking their first walk in the open for nearly a month. In Jerusalem, where often only fifteen or twenty yards separated the two opposing forces, cases of fraternisation between the Legionnaires and the Israeli soldiers became increasingly common, until both the British officers commanding the Legion and the Israeli officers commanding the Israel Defence Forces[2] put a stop to it. A sense of unreality prevailed. The quiet seemed too good to be true.

But there was little respite for the commanders and the politicians. As the fighting came to a halt they took stock of their position. The picture they saw before them was neither rosy nor heartening. On the Arab side, their armies had not succeeded in gaining any of their objectives. Their plans to be in Tel Aviv and Haifa within two weeks of the invasion had been illusory. Abdullah's belief "that the Zionist fortress will

[1] ib., p. 10.

[2] The existence of the Haganah came to an end officially on May 31st, 1948, when the Israel Defence Force was established by order of the Provisional Government.

fall after the first attack" had not been fulfilled. Instead, the Legion had been held up at Jerusalem and had suffered casualties which could not easily be replaced. The Egyptian army had been contained at Isdud. The Iraqis, after their first success at Jenin, had not ventured beyond. The Lebanese had withdrawn over their frontier. Only the Syrians had succeeded in establishing a bridge-head on Israeli territory.

The united command of the Arab armies had disintegrated. Each Arab army had acted on its own. The Syrians had attacked at Semakh, and the Arab Legion six miles to the south at Gesher, without either side attempting to co-ordinate with or help each other. To crown the picture of gloom which confronted the Arab commanders at the beginning of the truce, all the Arab armies, excepting the Egyptian, reported a grave shortage of ammunition.

On the Israeli side the picture was even more depressing. The invading armies had been held, but more than a third of the territory allotted to Israel by the United Nations—the Negev—was in Arab hands. In the north, the Syrians had entrenched themselves on the western bank of the Jordan and threatened to cleave Eastern Galilee into two. In the centre, the Iraqis were only ten miles from the Mediterranean. In Jerusalem, the defence was near collapse; the soldiers had virtually no ammunition left, and the population was starving. Attempts to clear the road from Tel Aviv had failed.

But at least the Israelis had by now a reasonably united High Command. Even though there were some differences within it, the authority in military matters of Ben-Gurion, Galili and Yadin, was fully accepted. It met at G.H.Q. in Tel Aviv immediately after the truce came into effect on June 11th. But the full realisation of how close Israel had been to disaster in that first month of existence dawned only as each brigade commander in turn presented his report.

Brigadier Carmel, commander of the 2nd Haganah Brigade, opened the discussion with a report on the situation in the north of the country. The fighting units, he declared, were worn out. There were at least a hundred dead in every battalion, each of which had now shrunk to miniature proportions. Now the brigade was approaching a crisis from the tactical point of view. The fire-power of the Arabs had increased, and Carmel feared that his brigades would be forced

to confine itself to night and guerilla fighting unless reinforcements arrived. "On the Jenin front," Carmel added, "we are
under continuous artillery fire and under attacks from the air.
If the enemy intention is to use this fire-power as cover for an
infantry attack, we will not be able to withstand them."

A similar report was presented by Brigadier Dan Even,
commander of the 3rd Haganah Brigade.[1] "The units have
reached a stage of crisis. The main reason is fatigue, and
perennial shortage of everything. There were cases of men
going to battle in pyjamas. There were those who returned
from battle in their underwear and who received clothes only
three weeks later." There was still a great shortage of weapons,
he added.

Reporting on the situation in the Negev, Colonel Nahum
Sarig warned that settlements there were on the verge of
collapse. "They are subjected to artillery barrages by night and
artillery plus air attacks by day." In the Negev there had been
continuous action for all troops, with no possibility of training.
There were units which had had no leave for seven months.
Shimon Avidan reported on the state of the Givati Brigade in
the northern Negev; three-quarters of his troops were still
tied down on the Egyptian front.

And so the grim reports continued. Shaltiel spoke of the
weakness of his Jerusalem troops due to lack of food, and of
the fact that much of his infantry strength had been lost at
Kfar Etzion and Nvei Yaakov. "In the two infantry battalions
now defending Jerusalem there have been more than 600
wounded and many killed." He added: "Our first contact with
the enemy after the truce was proclaimed was with British
officers (of the Arab Legion). They hope to bring about the
surrender of Jerusalem through prolonged siege." More than
fifty artillery pieces had been firing on the city, including
100-pounders, he concluded.[2]

But the grimmest figures of all were given by the Palmach
commanders. It was the Palmach that had borne the brunt of
the fighting. Now their units were weak and weary. The Harel
Brigade reported that in its two battalions in the Jerusalem

[1] Known as the Alexandroni Brigade; it fought on the central front,
and was based on the Natanya district.
[2] General Glubb claims that the actual number of guns firing on
Jerusalem was much smaller.

hills 220 had been killed and 617 wounded. The remaining 200 were weak and exhausted. Mullah Cohen, of the Yiftah Brigade, gave the following figures: 250 killed; 300 wounded and still in hospital.

Such was the picture which faced the High Command at the beginning of the truce.[1] The harsh truth was that the fledgeling army was on the point of collapse. It needed arms and equipment. Troops had to be trained. Additional manpower had to be mobilised. Food and ammunition stocks in isolated settlements, and above all in Jerusalem, had to be replenished. The Israelis had a month's respite; a month during which, according to the truce regulations, neither side should do anything to gain any military advantage whatsoever. Neither side was to bring into Palestine either more men or more warlike material. Jerusalem was to receive sufficient food and water for four weeks' subsistence, but no more. These were the conditions which the United Nations Mediator, Count Folke Bernadotte, had laid down. But the Israeli High Command was hardly in a position to abide by them. Full adherence would have been tantamount to suicide. Unless the army could complete its reorganisation, increase its numbers and secure more arms and equipment, it could not hope to hold out much longer once the fighting was resumed. Moreover, the acquisition of arms was already in full swing. Three ships had already reached the Israeli coast, loaded with guns and light weapons, first fruits of the work of the "Rechesh" emissaries abroad. The Israeli High Command did not intend to halt this process now that the truce had been proclaimed. Too much was at stake. Thus it was without compunction that orders were given for increased mobilisation and for encouraging the immigration of young Jews of military age; and more emissaries were sent abroad to get more arms.

At the meeting at G.H.Q. partial answers had already been

[1] According to Yigal Yadin—Director of Operations at the Israeli G.H.Q.—the reports of the brigade commanders gave an unduly depressing picture of the situation. The commanders were psychologically tired and were pleading for more troops for their particular fronts. They therefore overpainted the picture. According to Yadin, the meeting of the High Command revealed a reaction to the first shock of battle, from which some commanders were still suffering. This might be true to a certain extent. But even if there was an exaggeration, the facts emerging from the reports, such as the high casualty figures, spoke for themselves.

given to the commander's pleas. "Within the next few days, 3,000 boys of seventeen will enter training camps," declared Moshe Zadok, chief of Manpower Wing of G.H.Q. Yigal Yadin told the conference that there were already sufficient rifles for forty battalions, for the second-line troops and for the settlements.

These arms had been procured in devious ways. Without them Israel would not have been able to stand up to the invasion. We have already described (in Chapter Four, pp. 75/6) how Ehud Avriel and Uriel Doron made the first contacts in Czechoslovakia for the purchase of rifles and machine-guns. We must now look more closely at this particular aspect of the war—the acquisitions of arms for the Israelis—because it forms an essential and integral part of the events of that period.

After Avriel had succeeded in his first mission in Czechoslovakia—buying 10,000 rifles and 450 machine-guns—he returned to Tel Aviv for further instructions. The Mandate had not yet come to an end, and arms still had to be brought into the country clandestinely. But Ben-Gurion's orders were clear and precise: "Go back to Europe and buy tanks, guns and planes. That is what we shall need most." Thus, when the Mandate came to an end, the Haganah were already prepared to bring in heavier weapons. Hardly had the new State been proclaimed when the first arms ship arrived in Tel Aviv. In addition to rifles and machine-guns, it brought the first six guns for the new Artillery Corps, 65-mm. light field guns.[1] Within a fortnight two more ships had arrived, carrying more artillery, including some 75-mm. guns—the first Israeli guns to be any match for the British 25-pounders used by the Legion, the Iraqis and the Egyptians.

Just as important was the need for fighter planes, to meet the Arab air superiority. The only aircraft in Israeli possession were of the Tiger Moth type. The Czechoslovak Government was prepared to sell aircraft to Israel. It was prepared also to help in other ways. On May 20th a military airfield in Czechoslovakia was turned over to the Haganah, and for the following three months it became the Haganah's main base in Europe for the shuttle-service of arms and planes to Israel. Operation "Black" had begun: dismantled Messerschmit fighters, Beza

---

[1] The Israelis had already some twenty light Hispano-Suiza anti-aircraft guns, used, not very effectively, as anti-tank weapons.

medium machine-guns and many other weapons were flown
in Dakota and Commando transports from Czechoslovakia to
Aqir airfield in Israel. Not all the weapons had been purchased from the Czechs; much of the equipment and the arms
had been obtained in the United States, where Haim Slavin
had established an extraordinarily efficient purchasing and
delivery organisation. The planes, piloted mainly by Jewish
veterans of the R.A.F., the U.S.A.A.F. and the South African
Air Force, were flown to Corsica, where they refuelled before
continuing their journey to Israel. When, later, the United
States successfully persuaded the French to rescind the
permission to land there, the Israelis received transit flight
permission from the Yugoslavs.

The Czechs had no qualms about selling arms to the Israelis,
despite the strict embargo which had been imposed by the
United Nations on the sale of arms to the Middle East. They
remained quite neutral. For they were equally prepared to sell
arms to the Arabs. A Syrian delegation, headed by Major Fuad
Mardam, nephew of the former Syrian Premier, had arrived in
Czechoslovakia a short time before the Israelis, and had
contracted an arms deal worth 11 million dollars. They were
to buy 8,000 rifles, ten million bullets and a quantity of hand
grenades and high explosives. Round this arms deal revolved
one of the most dramatic episodes of the Palestine War. For
the Haganah emissaries had heard of the sale, and they
received orders from Tel Aviv to prevent the arrival of these
arms in Syria at all costs.

Early in 1948 the arms were loaded on a Danube boat, and,
in the first stage of their journey to the Adriatic, reached the
Danube port of Bratislava. The Haganah was waiting for them.
and the port officials had been bribed to delay the boat as long
as possible. It was the first obstacle, but Fuad Mardam
succeeded in overcoming it, and the consignment, much
delayed, eventually reached the small Adriatic port near
Rijeka (Fiume). From here they were to be shipped to Beirut.
Again, the port had been "prepared." The shipment was once
more delayed. Then, while the arms were being transferred to
an Italian ship, the *Lino*, a group of Jewish partisans in Tito's
organisation secretly switched some of the rifles in the cases for
old, unusable ones.

Finally Mardam got his boat out to sea, and it seemed that

he had won through. But his luck was out. A storm blew up, and the ship was forced to seek shelter in Bari. A Haganah plane, which had been shadowing the ship, immediately informed Marder, Arazi and Ada Sereni—the three Haganah emissaries who were in charge of the operation. Soon after the boat had anchored at Bari a loud explosion shook the port, and the 450-ton *Lino* slowly heeled over and sank. A Palmach frogman had holed the ship with a limpet mine. But the water in Bari port was shallow, and the arms were packed in hermetically sealed cases. It was not difficult to salvage them. Now Mardam had to find a new boat to take the arms. He found this to be more difficult than he had imagined. The Italian shipowners did not relish the risk involved; some who hesitated were discreetly warned by Arazi that the fate of the *Lino* might befall any other ship which carried the arms. Weeks passed. The invasion of Palestine had by now got under way, and frantic telegrams were reaching Mardam, urging the immediate dispatch of the arms, which were badly needed by the Syrian army. Finally, when Mardam had almost given up hope, the captain of the Italian ship *Algiro* offered his services. Mardam was overjoyed. He could not know that two members of the *Algiro's* crew were veterans of the "illegal immigration" days and were in Arazi's pay. The arms were quickly loaded, and early in August the *Algiro* sailed for Beirut. But it never reached its destination. With the help of the Haganah men on board, who in the meantime had brought two more to the ship, the *Algiro* was intercepted by an Israeli vessel off the Dodecanese Islands. The arms and crew were transferred, and the *Algiro* was sunk. The arms provided a valuable addition to the build-up of the Israeli forces for the campaign against Egypt which was being prepared for the autumn of 1948 (see Chapter Twelve).[1]

There were many other strange and hardly orthodox methods employed by the Haganah in their acquisition of arms. The transfer of Beaufighters from Britain, the acquisition of three Flying Fortresses from the United States, or the flying

---

[1] After the war, Major Fuad Mardam was tried by a Syrian court martial and found guilty of having been a traitor to the Arab cause. He was accused of having sold the arms of the Zionists. He was sentenced to death. Before his sentence could be carried out, however, the Government was overthrown by Colonel Husny Zaim, and Mardam was freed.

out of Spitfires from a certain European country proved to be undertakings no less hazardous than "Operation Robber."[1] Such episodes, however, belong to another book.

Despite the truce, and the fairly tight international blockade of the Middle East, many of these arms reached Israel during the four weeks of quiet. But the acquisition of arms was only one of the tasks which occupied the Israeli High Command. Much of its time was taken up with internal differences, which now made themselves felt. For after having successfully held the invading armies at bay, Israel was suddenly in the grip of a secret crisis, of which all but a few remained wholly unaware. The country at large knew nothing of the head-on clash of personalities which brought the leadership of State and army to the brink of disintegration.

The earlier differences in the Haganah High Command had, as we have noted, been patched up. Galili had been reinstated in his position as deputy to the Minister of Defence, but without operational authority. On the surface, the work of the High Command continued smoothly. But actually the general situation at headquarters was becoming chaotic. Galili's status had become increasingly shadowy. Dori had become a figurehead. The real commander-in-chief was Ben-Gurion. It was he who made the decisions. It was he whose confirmation had to be obtained for every move, both of great and small tactical importance: even the transfer of a company of troops, or of mortars, from one front to another had to receive the personal confirmation of Ben-Gurion before it could be carried out. Members of G.H.Q. became increasingly restive— especially the Director of Operations, Yigal Yadin, who often differed with Ben-Gurion on major policy issues. The question of Jerusalem was a case in point: Ben-Gurion

[1] The Fortresses were flown out through South America, and after many hardships and much excitement reached the Haganah base in Czechoslovakia. On their last lap, to Israel, the planes bombed Cairo. The operation was commanded by an American Jewish air ace named Kurtz, who was later killed in the fighting in Israel. The Spitfires had to be flown on a journey of 1,400 miles. The maximum flying distance of the Spitfire without refuelling was, however, only 600 to 700 miles. Haganah engineers had to use all their ingenuity to adapt the Spitfires to take sufficient petrol for the long journey. Of the five Spitfires flown out in this way only three reached their destination; the other two were forced to land in Rhodes because of lack of petrol.

208 THE OFFICIAL WAR

still believed that the whole country would best be defended by concentrating everything on the defence of Jerusalem. The General Staff still thought that the answer was the other way round—Jerusalem would be saved if the rest of the country was first made safe.

These differences now came to a head. The army was being reorganised. Instead of the previous ten Brigade Commands, the army—and the country—would henceforth be divided into three "fronts." New appointments of "front commanders" had to be made. Ben-Gurion seized this opportunity of returning to his cherished plan of transferring the army command into the hands of regular ex-British army officers, instead of the partisan-trained Haganah commanders who were leading most of the brigades. He informed the General Staff that he intended to appoint two former British army officers, Mordechai Makleff and Shlomo Shamir, to take charge of the central and southern fronts respectively.

The announcement produced violent dissent from several members of the General Staff—from Yadin in particular. Yadin proposed the appointment of Yigal Alon—who had proved himself as one of the ablest of the Israeli commanders—in the south, and of Avidan in the centre. Yadin also disagreed with Ben-Gurion's schedule of priorities for the several fronts. But Ben-Gurion rejected Yadin's arguments. He insisted that the High Command accept his decisions. Yadin answered that he would resign. Ben-Gurion warned Yadin that he would have him court-martialled. Whereupon Yadin, together with all the other leading members of the General Staff, rose, tendered their resignations and left the meeting.

This was far more serious than the earlier troubles in the High Command over Galili. The resignations were not accepted. Instead, a ministerial committee of enquiry, headed by the Minister of the Interior, Yitzhak Gruenbaum, was set up to investigate the differences which had led to this state of affairs.[1] The subjects discussed ranged over a wide field, including the failure at Latrun, the Tubianski affair,[2] the

[1] Other members of the committee were: Moshe Shertock, Pinhas Rosenbluet (Rosen), Aharon Zisling and Moshe Shapiro. For Israel Galili's version of these events, see Appendix, page 278.

[2] Tubianski was a Haganah officer in charge of the Schneller army camp in Jerusalem. He was falsely accused of passing information to the enemy, sentenced to death and executed.

separatist tendencies of the Palmach,[1], and, above all, the situation in G.H.Q. and Ben-Gurion's place in it. Some of those called upon to answer questions became convinced that the committee was "out to get Ben-Gurion"—that it wanted him removed from supreme power.

Meanwhile, precious days of the truce were being squandered. It was an odd situation. The General Staff continued to work and plan without break despite the fact that every member of it had tendered his resignation, yet no high level decision concerning the planned offensives could be taken in this twilight of authority. But in all other fields Ben-Gurion continued to assert his authority as Defence Minister. He was now determined to push through his plans of reorganising the army on the lines of a conventional regular army on the British pattern, instead of the ill-defined partisan force which had provided the hard core of Israel's defence in the fighting until then.

Despite the opposition of Galili and other Haganah veterans, and in particular of the Palmach, Ben-Gurion issued new orders: the army was to have standard uniforms, officers were in future to wear distinguishing insignia, there was to be a difference in pay between the ranks, officers' mess-rooms were to be established. Military police, based on the British pattern, were to enforce these orders. It was a far cry from the days of egalitarian partisan warfare; it required much painful, and often resentful, adjustment on the part of the veteran Haganah troops before the regulations finally took effect. In many of the infantry battalions the officers' messes were boycotted till the end of the war. The Palmach was allowed to continue its separate headquarters and its separate existence a little while longer. But Palmach officers were compelled to wear their officers' insignia. At the same time, troops were given intensive training, courses were arranged in which instruction on how to handle new weapons was given, many soldiers were sent to officers' and N.C.O.'s schools, and new conscripts, many of them immigrants or volunteers from

[1] The committee investigated in particular an order instructing Palmach units to obey only orders emanating from Palmach headquarters. Ben-Gurion claimed that this was a proper Palmach order issued by Rabin and approved by Galili. Galili, on the other hand, claimed that the order was given by a junior Palmach commander.

abroad, were brought to the depleted fighting units. Thus, during the short period of the truce that remained, the army was transformed into a steamlined, coherent fighting force—at least, so it appeared to be when compared to the state of affairs on May 14th. Ben-Gurion had not been idle.

While all this activity was taking place, the Gruenbaum Committee continued its investigations and deliberations. The end of the truce was drawing dangerously near. Ben-Gurion's impatience with the proceedings was becoming increasingly apparent. On the morning of July 6th, he sent the following letter to Yitzhak Gruenbaum, the chairman of the committee:

> "Dear Gruenbaum,
> I do not wish to interfere in the activities of the committee, and even less do I wish to curb its freedom of action. But it is my duty to apprise you and your colleagues of the fact that these discussions of a governmental committee which have continued for five days do not help to speed up the essential arrangements which have to be made in preparation for the end of the truce—if indeed the truce will come to an end in another few days. . . . The organisation of two vital fronts is being delayed—it is difficult for me to put off the necessary arrangements indefinitely, but in the present circumstances I do not wish to make final decisions. On the other hand it is neither proper nor possible for me to lay aside the responsibility, and I therefore call upon you and your colleagues in the committee to bring your recommendations to the government at the earliest possible opportunity."

By this time the committee had already reached its decision. It remained only to formulate its proposals and to hand them in for final confirmation to the other members of the Government. These proposals included, among other things, that

* the Government appoint a War Cabinet which will decide on the general planning of the war and on the strategy to be employed;
* the Government appoint two Directors-General who will help the Minister of Defence carry out his duties—one to be responsible for the army, the other for defence finance;
* the Minister of Defence would give his instructions through the Directors-General. In case of urgent need, the Minister

of Defence would be able to give his instructions directly to the Chief of Staff, but in such cases the instructions should be in writing, and should be notified to the Directors-General;
* the appointment of battalion commanders would be made by the Minister of Defence in accordance with recommendations by the Chief of Staff. The Minister would appoint brigade and front commanders after conferring with the Chief of Staff. In case of difference of opinion on such appointments, the matter would be resolved by the War Cabinet.

The shafts of the Committee's findings were directed unmistakably against Ben-Gurion. Although no names were mentioned in the final recommendation it was clear that the committee intended Israel Galili to be the Director-General of matters dealing with the army. This had been openly stated by Sharett when the committee was discussing the duties of the Directors-Generals. Sharett had said: "The subject which we are dealing with is named Israel Galili. Israel Galili will bring benefit to every matter that he attends. There exists a tradition, a custom that he, as Head of the High Command, dealt with these matters and brought benefit to them. It is a natural wish to preserve for him this field of action and to retain all the resulting benefits." Sharett, however, had objected to the proposed functions of the Director-General. "The logical organisational basis must be separation of the Ministry from the General Staff." And he added, somewhat cryptically, "If Galili had been suitable to be Chief-of-Staff, it would be different, but there cannot be two Chiefs of General Staff. If he is suitable to be Minister, let him be Minister, and be in charge of everything."

The Prime Minister, however, was not the sort of man to submit lightly to his critics. He reacted swiftly and typically. On the evening of July 6th, he sent the following letter to the committee:

"The damage liable to be caused to the war effort and to our young army compels me to pass over in silence the reasons for the resignations of certain members of the Ministry of Defence, and all that followed these resignations.

"The discussions held by the Committee of Five and the proposals made by certain of its members have made it impossible for me to continue serving in the Ministry of Defence and in the Provisional Government. But the grave situation in which we find ourselves compels me, as it does every other Jew, to aid the Provisional Government to the best of my ability in the fulfilment of its major task—the maintenance of security. I will therefore support the Government in every way I can as if I were still a member of it—and above all in the war effort. The direction of the military effort and the preparedness for this war effort cannot be let up for even a single day.

"If the Chief-of-Staff cannot return to his duties and you find difficulties in appointing someone in his place, I suggest you charge Yigal Yadin, Yohanan Rattner and Shalom Eshet (Fritz Eisenstatter) with the task of planning the war, with Yigal Yadin remaining as he was previously Director of Operations.

"These three, together with the Heads of Supplies and Manpower will compose the body that, with the guidance and advice of the Government, will decide from day to day the planning and the operation of the war.

"I suggest that the Chief-of-Staff, or three members of the Government in conjunction with the Chief-of-Staff, immediately appoint a temporary Chief-of-Staff who will co-ordinate the different branches of the General Staff.

"I am prepared to work together with the three members of the Government as adviser, without right of vote, for as long as you wish, and to participate in the meetings with members of the General Staff.

"These arrangements and discussions cannot be postponed. Commanders of the northern front and of the brigades operating there should be immediately appointed; in addition, commanders of the brigades operating between Tel Aviv and Jerusalem should be immediately named, in view of the fact that the appointments I made were not implemented by those whose duty it was to carry them out. The operational plans for the Galilee, the Haifa district, Lydda-Ramle, Latrun, Jerusalem and the south have to be immediately clarified and confirmed. Special attention should be given to the coastal defence of Tel Aviv and even more so of Haifa. Haifa is liable to become one of the major objectives of the Arab attack. All the unexploited manpower in that town should be immediately mobilised. The armaments and anti-aircraft defence of the few warships at our disposal should be immediately strengthened.

"My help will be given to any other institution, if you see any need for arrangements other than those I propose. I am

willing to help you in any manner desirable to you—on the
condition that no official responsibility falls on me, and without
my advice being in any manner whatsoever binding on anyone.

"In order to save the valuable time of the Government,
I ask you to lay aside the proposals for the organisation of the
Ministry of Defence—if the intention is to have a Ministry of
Defence of which I shall be the head.

Ben-Gurion."

The letter caused confusion and consternation in the
committee. Ben-Gurion's refusal to accept further responsibility was his way of saying "try and manage without me."
Sharett, who was sent to reason with Ben-Gurion, did not
even make contact. He told the committee:

"I did not succeed in talking to him, as he was in a state
of collapse. When I reached him I found a doctor next to him.
I tried talking to him, but could not succeed in discussing
the subject which interests us. He began saying that it was
necessary to meet immediately with the General Staff in order to
complete the planning. I laughed and said: 'Who will meet
them?' I asked him: 'are you Prime Minister or not?' He said:
'no'."

The effect of Ben-Gurion's threat of resignation on the
members of the committee is well illustrated by the following
extracts from the protocol of the Gruenbaum Committee:

Y. Gruenbaum: "I have one thought of complete withdrawal,
as if the committee had not yet begun its sittings, had not yet
completed them, and that everything was continuing as it
was previously. If the truce continues, then we will continue;
if the truce will not continue—we will leave off entirely. As
our colleague Zisling said, the danger from the other side is
not less than that from this side."

M. Shapira: "I doubt if Mr. Ben-Gurion will accept even this."

A. Zisling: ". . . . The advice you give, Gruenbaum, would
mean the destruction of the army. The army is not made up
of dolls—there was no rebellion in the army—it is made up
of human beings, who hold responsibility for the non-imple-
mentation of things which cannot be implemented. There
are those who say: we must compel Ben-Gurion, we will not
accept his resignation, and we therefore have to accept the
arrangement he suggests and accept all his advice, but on no
account can he resign from the government."

Y. Gruenbaum: ". . . . who would be the fool to accept responsibility with the advice of Ben-Gurion. Would you do that?
If Shertok would say to me: I am willing to sacrifice myself
and am willing to take on the job together with Ben-Gurion,
with Ben-Gurion as adviser, I would agree immediately. But
Shertok is not prepared to say such a thing."

M. Shertok: "And what do you say?"

Y. Gruenbaum: "Supposing one of us were to say it, I suggest
we call Israel Galili, Yohanan Rattner and Yigal Yadin and
explain to them the situation."

P. Rosenbluet: "I suggest we tell him that we accept all his
proposals except his resignation, and at the same time tell
him that if he resigns all the government will resign. You
have to make him understand the gravity of the situation,
as a result of which the government will not be able to accept
responsibility."

Y. Gruenbaum: ". . . . who will give commands, and in the
name of whom?"

A. Zisling: "Either Ben-Gurion returns, or Shertok accepts
the job."

The disheartened discussion was interrupted when a note
was brought in to Gruenbaum. It was from Ben-Gurion. It
informed the committee that Ben-Gurion was prepared to
retract from his intention to resign. He was willing to agree
to have a "committee" composed of Kaplan and Gruenbaum,
working beside him. He did not state what the authority or
the functions of this committee would be. The proposals of
the Gruenbaum committee would have to be shelved.

Ben-Gurion's offer, however, did not in itself solve the
crisis. The deadlock which had existed between Ben-Gurion
and the army leaders still existed. Thus before the committee
could accept Ben-Gurion's compromise Gruenbaum met with
the leading members of the General Staff—Yadin, Rattner
and Ayalon. They informed him that they were willing to
obey any order of the Government, and not resign, even if
the order did not suit their book. Gruenbaum also met with
Galili, and received a similar declaration of loyalty to the
orders of the Government. Gruenbaum warned Galili that he
would probably be the "sacrifice" and that Ben-Gurion would
incorporate in his own duties the functions previously per-
formed by Galili. Galili told the committee that he was willing

to step down, if this would be necessary. Thus reassured that the army leaders would accept any decision taken by the Government, the Gruenbaum committee accepted Ben-Gurion's terms, and asked him to take over command again. The crisis was over, and Ben-Gurion returned from his "illness." The rapprochement was made easier as Ben-Gurion had in the meantime reached a settlement with Yadin over the question of the appointment of a commander of the central front. He agreed that there should be no front commander but that Yigal Alon be put in command of the Lydda offensive. This satisfied Yadin, and he retracted his demand that Alon become commander of the central front. According to Yadin's planning at that time the Lydda offensive was to continue without pause to take in Latrun and Ramallah. Thus Ben-Gurion's agreement that Alon be commander of this offensive was, in his eyes, tantamount to his appointment as commander of the central front, and he was, therefore, satisfied with this compromise. Ben-Gurion, on his part, declared later that he had only agreed to this compromise because Makleff, Ben-Gurion's candidate, had himself turned down the appointment on the grounds that he was not yet ready to take on such a responsibility.

Throughout the truce the Israeli public had had no knowledge that there had been a headquarters crisis, for none of the resignations were made public. Public attention was focussed instead on the process of unifying the Israeli armed forces, on the breaking up of the dissident organisations (the Irgun and the Lehy), and on the transforming of all Israel's armed forces into a "conventional" army. There was much heart-burning, and many explosive words were said over the disbanding of the dissident organisations, but Ben-Gurion acted with a singlemindedness of purpose. When the Irgun tried to bring in an arms ship of its own during the truce,[1] and refused to hand over the ship and its contents to the Provisional Government, Ben-Gurion ordered the troops to open fire on the ship. He was determined to have no private armies fighting in Israel. He wished to exploit the *Altalena* incident to rescind the previous agreement he had made with the Irgun, according

[1] The *Altalena*, which had steamed from a French port loaded with, mainly, light arms. On board were many Irgun sympathisers from European countries, including a contingent from the United Kingdom.

to which the dissidents would join the Israel Defence Army as complete units, fighting under their own commanders. But he encountered too much opposition in the government to his drastic proposals. He had to wait until his opportunity came in September when, after the assassination of the U.N. Mediator, Count Bernadotte, he gave orders that the Irgun formations were to be broken up within twenty-four hours and dispersed among the other existing regular units of the armed forces.

Later, Ben-Gurion took action to bring the Palmach into a centralised command. He had hinted at what he had in mind when he told the brigade commanders at the High Command conference on June 11th that he was "full of apprehension concerning the lack of discipline. Because of lack of discipline we lost at least two positions. We could have liberated all of Jerusalem, the road to Jerusalem, and perhaps captured Ramle and Lydda[1] as well—if we had been an army instead of armies, and if we had fought according to an overall strategic plan. This he felt very strongly. But he never sought to equate the Palmach with the terrorist organisations, the record, and the social and political outlook of the Palmach, were totally different.

Thus, despite the tension, the hard words and the strained tempers, Ben-Gurion had his way. Only on the question of new appointments to front commands did he give way. The central front (where the main offensive was to be launched) was put under the command of Yigal Alon, instead of one of the ex-British army officers whom Ben-Gurion had favoured. But in the course of the fighting which was now to break out with renewed violence, Ben-Gurion was to have no cause to regret this change.

In the meantime, no less important political and organisational upheavals were taking place on the Arab side of the hill. Immediately after the cease-fire came into effect, the Iraqi Chief of Staff, General Salih Saib al-Jabouri, made a protracted tour of the Palestine front. On his return to Baghdad he recorded his findings in a long report presented to the Iraqi Minister of Defence. His conclusions were most revealing, for, like the reports of the Israeli brigade commanders quoted

[1] See Chapter Eleven.

earlier in this chapter, they represent the findings of a military man who was at the scene of the fighting immediately after the cease-fire. It was a secret report—no apologia, no propaganda, but a simple reporting of facts. The general opened his report in the following manner:

> The Arab forces participating in the actions in Palestine could have gained much more noteworthy results, despite their smallness of number, had they fulfilled the following conditions:
>
> (a) full recognition of the authority of the unified command, and proper execution of its commands by all the Arab armies;
>
> (b) full implementation of the duties imposed on each army in accordance with the pre-invasion plans;
>
> (c) full implementation of these plans, instead of changing them at the very last minute, for reasons not clear to us;
>
> (d) maintenance of the irregular forces (Kaukji's forces and others) in those areas in which they had been active for many months, instead of withdrawing them to Syria at the time when there was most need of them, when the Arab armies went into action.

The general adds: "The above-mentioned reasons were the cause for our not obtaining better results during the past month." He continues his report with a warning to the Defence Minister that the Jews would probably make every effort to prepare themselves for the renewal of the fighting. The Arabs must do likewise, he urged. They must

> bring in large and varied forces in order to solve the problem once and for all by overcoming the enemy; prepare equipment, arms and ammunition in sufficient quantities for a prolonged war . . . attain full co-operation of the various Arab armies in the battlefield; prepare units of "irregular" fighters, made up of Palestinians and Arabs of other nations; and organise the dispatch of volunteers from other Muslim countries which were sympathetic to the Arab cause.

The report was written on June 15th, 1948. The month of truce still lay before the Arabs. Similar reports and suggestions were being put forward by the commanders of the other Arab armies. Glubb, for example, says that "as soon as the truce seemed established, I went to see the Prime Minister. I explained the precarious nature of our position, the heavy casualties and the absence of reserves. I asked if he would sanction further enlistments, so that we should be better placed if there were any more fighting."[1]

But, as al-Jabouri had stressed so much, what was needed most was a unified command and a co-ordinated, overall plan of action. In an effort to obtain this an Iraqi delegation (including al-Jabouri) and King Abdullah visited Cairo shortly after the truce came into effect.

The Iraqi delegation was unsuccessful. In their effort to renew the united command, they offered the post of commander-in-chief of the Arab armies to the Egyptian commander. But it was of no avail. Instead of giving clear answers, Nokrashy wavered, procrastinated and blustered. At the beginning of the truce he told the Transjordanian Premier, Tewfic Abul Huda, that he would oppose the renewal of the fighting.[2] A week later he spoke in generalities and platitudes to the Iraqis and to Abdullah, and, by the end of the truce, he had become the most extreme of all the Arab leaders in his demands for an immediate renewal of hostilities.

Thus, from the very outset the Arabs' effort to utilise the month's respite to reorganise and to reach agreement on an overall plan became bogged down in a mire of political horse-talk. Worst hit by this state of affairs was Abdullah and the Arab Legion. The Legion had suffered heavy casualties; it was also short of ammunition. For this the Egyptians were very much to blame. At the beginning of May, the British had agreed to allot a considerable quantity of ammunition to the Legion. This ammunition was taken from the British military stores in the Canal Zone, loaded on to a ship at Suez and should have reached Aqaba. But as the ship steamed out of Suez harbour it was overtaken by an Egyptian Government launch and ordered to return to port. There Egyptian soldiers unloaded the cases of ammunition, piled them on Egyptian army trucks and drove off. Soon afterwards Glubb was informed by the British army headquarters of what had happened, but, despite energetic and repeated protests, the Transjordanians never got their ammunition.

[1] Glubb, *op. cit.*, p. 145.
[2] Glubb, *op. cit.*, p. 145.

The incident illustrates the extent to which the principal objective of Egypt's entry into the war was to hinder Abdullah as much as possible and prevent him from annexing too large a slice of Palestine. Later, the British agreed to send another ship loaded with arms and ammunition to the Arab Legion, but, before it could leave harbour, the truce was proclaimed, and United Nations truce observers prevented it from sailing.

Abdullah himself, during his Cairo visit, attempted to arrange for the return of the confiscated ammunition, but he failed in this, as in his other objectives:

> When I asked the late Nokrashy Pasha what Egypt's intentions were, he assured me that Egypt was loyal to the cause, and that it would persevere in the struggle until complete success was won. I also expressed to the Palace my desire to visit the headquarters of the Egyptian supreme command in Palestine in my capacity as Commander-in-Chief, but it was indicated that this would not be fitting since His Majesty had not yet visited the front himself. Thereupon I suggested the necessity of His Majesty's visiting Jerusalem, but was told that flying would be dangerous. When I replied that it would be possible to do so via the Suez-'Aqaba-Amman route, other excuses were brought forth. If this visit had taken place it would have been a successful move which would have resulted in our taking all of Jerusalem through an attack by the three royal armies in the presence of the Regent of Iraq ('Abd al-Illah), His Majesty King Farouk, and myself. Thus I succeeded neither in securing the return of the confiscated ammunition nor in seizing the greatest opportunity of the war by employing the full strength of the united command. I was unsuccessful also in getting His Majesty to carry out the objective of the command, since the forces of the four states for all practical purposes were not under the command of the Deputy Commander-in-Chief, Brigadier Nur ad-Din (Mahmud) Pasha, who was commander of the Iraqi forces and responsible for all troops.[1]

Abdullah had succeeded neither in obtaining help for the Jerusalem front, nor in getting the ammunition his troops needed so badly. He realised only too clearly that his failure

[1] Abdullah, *Memoirs of King Abdullah of Transjordan*, edited by P. Craven and translated by G. Khuir (Cape, 1950), p. 240.

put the Legion in a difficult position. Much better, then, to delay the renewal of the fighting until more arms and ammunition could be procured, and until some sort of an agreement could be reached on an overall plan of strategy. For Abdullah, more than any other of the Arab leaders, realised that otherwise the Arab efforts might be doomed. The King, moreover, valued his troops even more than his territorial ambitions. He knew that his great prestige and authority in the Arab world rested to a very large extent on the prowess and efficiency of his fighting forces. He was not, therefore, willing to risk having those forces destroyed. Accordingly, he gave orders to his Premier, Tewfic Abul Huda, who had arrived in Cairo to attend a meeting of the Arab League, that in no circumstances was the fighting to be renewed "until the army had obtained the light and heavy material it needed."[1] At the same time, Abdullah left for a tour of the Arab capitals, in an effort to swing the Arab leaders round to his views.

Abdullah again failed in his mission. When the vote was taken at the League session in Cairo, Tewfic Abul Huda found himself alone in his view that the fighting should be postponed, and he hastened to fall in with the others so as not to be branded traitor to the cause. The other Arab leaders were not interested in more delay. For they, as opposed to the Legion, had made good use of the truce. The Iraqis had more than doubled their numbers of troops on the Palestine front, where they now had an army of approximately 10,000 men. In the guise of despatches of food and clothes, they had brought eleven large convoys of arms, ammunition and military equipment to Transjordan and Palestine.[2] Some of this ammunition was later given to the Arab Legion, which then succeeded in replenishing its ammunition stores. Moreover, the Iraqis took over part of the central front which had previously been held by the Legion.

The Syrians too had carried out an intensive recruiting campaign, while the Lebanese received under their command the reorganised formations of the Liberation Army, which, after all the losses in casualties and desertions it had sustained,

[1] Abdullah, op. cit., p. 25.
[2] This fact was revealed during the investigation by an Iraqi Parliamentary Committee into the defeat of the Arabs during the war.

now numbered only some 2,000 men.[1] Egypt had also made good use of the truce. Its army had not been ready for war. Many weak spots, both in organisation and in training, had been brought to light in the first few weeks of fighting. Now its commanders made haste to overcome these flaws. Intensive training courses were initiated, and additional manpower was mobilised—in particular, volunteers from the Sudan who later proved to be among the Egyptian army's best fighters. New equipment was acquired, both for the army and the air force.

The result of all these preparations was to instil new feelings of confidence in the Arab leaders. They ignored Abdullah's warnings and forebodings. They would not suffer the truce to continue. This decision was taken more for political than for military reasons. The Arab public had been led to believe that their armies had been victorious in the field. For weeks newspaper headlines had proclaimed great battles won. Only the truce had at the last moment snatched final victory from the Arabs. Now the people were impatiently waiting for hostilities to be renewed. Any further delay would cause dissatisfaction with the leaders, internal unrest, and the possible overthrow of governments. Thus, when the Arab League met in Cairo at the beginning of July to decide on their answer to the United Nations Mediator's plea to prolong the truce, the Arab leaders, led by Nokrashy Pasha, decided unanimously to renew the fighting.

Shortly before the Arab League meeting, the Mediator, Count Bernadotte, had published his tentative proposals for a permanent settlement. They had caused anger both in Israel and among the Arab states—except in Transjordan. For what the Count had proposed was to give Jerusalem to Transjordan. Jerusalem, which it had failed to take in a month of bitter onslaught, and the Negev, which was under the firm occupation of the Egyptians.[2] In return for giving up Jerusalem, the Jews were to be allowed to have Western Galilee,

---

[1] Many of the Iraqi members of the Liberation Army had left its ranks to rejoin the Iraqi army. This was an additional factor which caused its size to shrink.

[2] In his final proposals, published in September, the Count added the towns of Lydda and Ramle to the areas Transjordan was to receive back.

which they had already occupied, and in return for handing the Negev over to Transjordan, the Egyptians were to get nothing. Transjordan and Israel were to form a Union which would handle all the economic affairs, foreign policy and defence of the two countries. Haifa was to be a free port and Lydda a free airport. It was hardly surprising that the plan was rejected out of hand by both Jews and Arabs. Both the Israelis and the Egyptians became convinced that Count Bernadotte was a tool of British imperialism, and that his proposals were in reality British proposals in United Nations guise whose aim was to ensure that the Negev and Jerusalem were given to Abdullah. United Nations stock and prestige was lower than ever before in Israel and the Arab countries.

The Mediator had failed. His proposals for a prolongation of the truce had been rejected by the Arabs. The end of the month's respite was drawing near. Once more the answer to the "Palestine problem" was to be sought on the battlefield. On July 8th, twenty-eight hours before the truce was due to expire, the Egyptians decided to wait no longer, and their forces reopened the attack. The war had been renewed.

11

THE TEN DAYS' WAR: JULY 8th—JULY 18th

THE Egyptians had broken the United Nations spell. It could not have lasted much longer in any case. For there were too many unsettled issues left after the first period of the war to permit any kind of negotiated settlement. But more important was the conviction which became an act of faith in the Arab capitals: the Arab public—and, surprisingly, many Arab leaders also—were convinced that they had been robbed of victory by the first truce. The Egyptian decision to finish with the truce and finish the unfinished job against the Palestinian Jews reflected Arab public opinion. Abdullah's opposition and fears did not.

The truce had transformed the military situation. None of the parties concerned had taken more note than was formally necessary of the United Nations injunction not to increase the military potential. When the fighting ended in June there were about 50,000 active combatants—Arabs and Jews—in Palestine. When it was resumed in July there were almost 100,000, but the emphasis had now changed. The Israeli armies had risen from just over 20,000 to 60,000 men. The Arab armies had also increased, but not at the same rate; they now had about 40,000 men in Palestine.[1]

Even more striking was the change in equipment. The Egyptians had managed to replenish their stocks of ammunition from the Canal Zone dumps. They had more and bigger guns—all British. The British Government had scrupulously carried out its part in maintaining the arms embargo, but it was impossible to keep a close watch on the huge stores in the Canal Zone camps of Suez and Ismailia.

[1] The figures of the Israeli Army include rear-echelon troops—at G.H.Q., training and supply camps, while the Arab totals refer to field forces only.

It was the Israeli equipment, however that had changed out
of all resemblance to their equipment of a month before. They
now had some tanks, some artillery, many mortars and sufficient small arms. They were mobile, and, compared with its
state during the previous fighting, the Israeli army now
packed a punch.

The long-drawn-out discussion at the Israeli headquarters
had been resolved. Ben-Gurion had dropped his proposal that
Shlomo Shamir should take over command in the south as
well as agreeing with Yadin's proposal that Alon should take
over in the centre, see p. 215. Ben-Gurion had also agreed that
Lydda was to be the first target of an Israeli offensive. Yadin
prepared plans for the assault, but some changes were made
by Alon when he took over, three days before the resumption
of the fighting.

This discussion was conducted on a strictly military level.
Alon was anxious to take Lydda and Ramle without the
risks of a frontal attack, which Yadin had thought practicable in this case. Altogether, the regrouping of the armies had
brought a brilliant constellation of commanders into the
centre, and they prepared an operation worthy of their repute.
There were Ben-Gurion, Yadin, Alon, Rabin, Mullah Cohen
and Dan Laner—no shortage of military ability.

As they made their plans there came faint echoes of discussions at the United Nations and of the Mediator's plans to
avert another outbreak of war.[1] These reports were treated
at the Israeli army headquarters, and especially at Alon's,
as largely irrelevant. The fighting, not the United Nations,
would decide the war. The Israeli commanders made their
plans carefully. They did not want to be rushed. They had
learnt from their earlier mistakes. And they paid no notice to

[1] Most of the activities were based on Count Bernadotte's efforts to
get the two parties to come to Rhodes for talks, but as he based his offer
on his proposals of June 27th, it was wholly unacceptable to the Israelis
and to six of the seven Arab states, for it very clearly favoured Abdullah's
claim to the whole city of Jerusalem. In his diary, Bernadotte had noted
that "much depended, of course, on what attitude Great Britain adopted
in the prevailing situation. It could be taken for granted that the
British, with their intimate connections with the Arabs, already knew all
about my proposals. It was also safe to assume that the Arab countries,
in particular Transjordan, would be greatly influenced by what the
British said." (*To Jerusalem*, p. 139.)

the talking marathon at Lake Success, as it appeared to them. Yadin explained two weeks later that their plan of operation was "based on the assumption that fighting would last for much longer than nine days." He had ambitious targets.

In the north, the Israelis were to throw the Syrians back across the Jordan, before turning on Nazareth and its surrounding villages as a secondary objective. In the centre, Lydda and Ramle were to be captured, and the success was to be exploited in the general direction of Ramallah; also the Jerusalem corridor was to be broadened, and the fighting strength of the Arab Legion was to be reduced as much as possible, if not altogether broken.

In order to give Alon adequate time to develop his offensive in the centre, it was decided that the initial pressure should be against the Syrians holding the bridgehead at Mishmar Hayarden in the north. It was to a large extent a prestige operation—to get the Syrians off Israeli soil—but it was dressed up as a preventive offensive, to block the Syrian attempt to break out from the bridgehead. It was understandable that Alon should want more time. For it was no scratch operation that he had undertaken. He had under him the largest force yet assembled under one Israeli commander— some 6,000 men. His front for "Operation Danny" stretched from Tel Aviv to Jerusalem.

Carmel was in overall command of the forces which were to attack the Syrian bridgehead. He mounted an elaborate attack with every textbook ingredient that was required: surprise, assault from the rear, unexpected approach, and a trap for the enemy who were dug in at Mishmar Hayarden. Only it did not turn out that way. The preparations had been too casual, the troops were over-confident and the planning was inadequate. The result was that there was no surprise, and the Syrians were waiting for the attacking Israelis. Carmel pressed his attack, even though the master plan had to be abandoned. Casualties mounted. The Syrians used aircraft in close-in fighting with marked effect.

Carmel wanted to make a determined effort to get the Syrians out. He assembled all available transport, guns and men on his front. He also took all he could from the 7th Brigade, which was now stationed in Western Galilee, with headquarters at Nahariya. But now he switched his offensive.

The attack on Mishmar Hayarden was converted into a holding action. Troops and transport were quickly switched to the west. There the 7th Brigade was to spring a real surprise.

While all the attention of the Arabs in Nazareth and Central Galilee was focussed on the Shajara front where Kaukji was mounting his main attack (7 miles north-east of Nazareth), the 7th Brigade, under the command of Haim Laskov and the Canadian Brigadier Dunkelman, broke in from the west. It took Shafa Amr and Nazareth without great difficulty. There was much harder fighting for the large villages outside Nazareth, especially Suffuriya, the ancient home of rebels and guerillas. Within forty-eight hours—and only just before a second truce was imposed by the United Nations— lower central Galilee had been occupied by the Israelis. It had not been a planned decision but like the dash for Latrun in May it had been improvised when the Israelis realised that a truce was imminent.[1] But this time the 7th Brigade, which had been cut to pieces only a month earlier at Latrun, was able to show its mettle.

The ten days which had nearly brought disaster in the north had transformed the military situation in the centre. Alon began his movement on July 9th. An armoured force under Yitzhak Sadeh moved southwards from Yehudiya behind Lydda to Ben Shemen, an Israeli settlement in the midst of Arab territory. The southern force—the Yiftah Brigade— came from the Latrun area crossed the main Tel Aviv-Jerusalem road and met with Sadeh's force at Ben Shemen. Sadeh was to capture the airfield while the Yiftah force with the 82nd Armoured Battalion in support would go for the

[1] Here we came up against an apparent contradiction of evidence which we could not resolve. This account of the war in the north is largely based on the contemporary eye-witness evidence of one of the authors. But it is not borne out by the reports and documents in the Israel Army Archives. According to these, the combined operation, first against the Syrian bridgehead and then against Nazareth, was so planned from the outset and that there is no justification for the suggestion that the attack on Nazareth was improvised and decided on at the last minute.

But after consulting with some of the officers in charge of the Nazareth offensive, we have concluded that there remains an irreconcilable difference of emphasis between the participating eye-witness and the General Staff documentation.

town of Lydda. A further object of this operation was to isolate the Arab Legion garrison at Latrun.

But once again the Israelis had intelligence trouble. They were still under the impression that Lydda was defended by the Arab Legion, whereas Glubb had withdrawn his token force from both Lydda and Ramle, which he and the King had already decided they would not be able to defend. But as Alon's plan unfolded Glubb recognised its further intention to isolate the Legion garrison at Latrun. With sound appreciation of the territory he sent forward the 1st Regiment of the Legion with its armour to the road junction of Beit Nabala about three miles north-east of Lydda. To meet this threat to its flank and rear Sadeh's 82nd Armoured Battalion had to turn from its set task to engage the Legion.

The Israelis misunderstood Glubb's intentions. They assumed he was preparing to attack Alon's main force and relieve Lydda which was now being threatened by the Yiftah Brigade. In fact Glubb was mainly concerned to protect his Latrun front from a flanking movement in its rear—also he wanted to make a demonstration on the Lydda front for the sake of Arab prestige. But Alon did not know this and the 82nd Battalion became fully engaged in forcing back the Legion, when it might have sufficed to leave a covering screen to prevent the Legion armour from advancing any further.

Meanwhile however the rest of the attack had proceeded according to plan. The Yiftah Brigade was entering Lydda, though its supporting armour had not arrived. The commander was in some difficulty and called urgently to the 82nd Battalion for help. But the 82nd was having its own troubles at Beit Nabala and did not even get the message. Instead the message was received by Moshe Dayan commanding the 89th Jeep Commando force at Ben Shemen. Without explaining that he was not the 82nd Armoured Dayan replied that he was coming immediately. He drove at full speed into Lydda, shooting up the town and creating confusion and a degree of terror among the population and the defenders. But he took the wrong road in the centre of Lydda and was almost in Ramle before he realised his mistake. But his sudden appearance in Lydda had created the desired effect. It had been touch and go until then. But now Lydda fell on July 11th

and its Arab population of 30,000 either fled or were herded
on to the road to Ramallah. The next day Ramle also surrendered and its Arab population suffered the same fate. Both
towns were sacked by the victorious Israelis.

But this was only one part—the most striking—of Operation Danny. Alon's plan unfolded in every direction; south
of Latrun, west of Latrun, east of Latrun, he expanded the
narrow corridor that led to Jerusalem. A second road was
opened, and there remained now only the major objective
itself: Latrun and the open road to Ramallah.

It was only now that the alarmist reports from New York
indicated that there would be no time for the elaborately
planned follow-up. The pressure in the Security Council for
an immediate cease-fire had increased; if there was to be
exploitation of the Lydda-Ramle success it had to come
quickly. The four precious days which had been lost at the
beginning of the second period of the war could not be
recouped. Alon made a determined effort to cut the road from
Latrun to Ramallah. A force from the Harel Brigade had
reached positions overlooking the road when the whistle went
for the second truce. The Legion had been prepared to withdraw but the Harel force was not strong enough to cut the
road without inviting forceful retaliation by the Legion. It
needed more than a forward unit with light equipment to prise
the Legion out of Latrun.

Once again the defence there had stood its ground. The
Israelis had made considerable gains because of this defence
of Latrun at all costs. In Ramallah, Arab Legion soldiers were
stoned and spat upon amidst cries of "traitors " because of
their abandonment of the Arabs of Lydda and Ramle. But
Abdullah still hoped that Jerusalem was to be his and therefore the Latrun blockade had to be maintained even at the
expense of Lydda and Ramle and 60,000 refugees. It was not
so much the strategic and tactical calculations that made
Abdullah abandon the two towns as his determination to hold
on to Jerusalem. More and more the Holy City became the
strategic siren which beckoned both Abdullah and Ben-Gurion.
With the passing of time, Ben-Gurion's generals understood
his insistence and endeavoured to meet it without sacrificing
their broader concepts of strategy. But not Glubb.

Glubb now accepted the purely defensive role of the Legion:

to hold what it already held and to risk neither its men nor its positions. Thus, despite Ben-Gurion's great respect for it, the Legion ceased to be an active factor in the Palestine War after the fall of Lydda and Ramle. Alon had not succeeded in destroying the Legion as he had intended but almost unwittingly he had succeeded (with the help of Glubb's defensive policy) in virtually neutralising it. It was an event that was to have a decisive effect on the battles in the Negev later that year.

In Jerusalem the commander of the Israeli force in the city, Colonel David Shaltiel, was confident. Just before the fighting was resumed, he claimed that he needed no more than four days to take the entire Old City. He had in fact nine days before the second truce was imposed, and he did not begin on his task until the last twenty-four hours of his allotted span. Apparently he too underrated the speed with which Sir Alexander Cadogan could operate at Lake Success—when he so desired. The ambitious paper plan which he had outlined came to nought. The attack was delayed far too long and, when it did come, showed neither finesse nor detailed planning.

At the same time, also rather late in the day, the southern army cleared some villages around Negba in the south, and so widened the corridor to the Negev (which was, however, still blocked by the Egyptians at Huleqiat). The position of Negba, a collective settlement guarding the southern gateway into the complex of Jewish towns and villages South of Tel-Aviv, had been of great importance. It had been under heavy attack from the Egyptians, it had been partly destroyed, and once the Egyptians had broken through the inner defences; but every time the settlers had fought back. And so long as Negba stood, the Egyptians could not risk advancing further with the menace of Negba in their rear. And Negba stood its ground.

Meanwhile, however, the United Nations discussions had become an integral part of the war in Palestine. Each army had its champions, and frequently the moves made at Lake Success had a more profound bearing on the situation than the military moves in Palestine.

The Anglo-American agreement on joint policy in Palestine had not yet reached the Security Council. The Council met on July 8th, to receive a telegram, couched in obscure and evasive language, from the Mediator, Count Bernadotte, announcing the resumption of hostilities. The United States delegate, commenting on this message, said that "had the Mediator's telegram contained a complete text or a flat rejection of the truce appeal by the Arab states, the Security Council would have no other choice than to find that there was a threat to the peace under Article 39." The Syrian delegate disputed the need for such hasty or drastic action. Sir Alexander seemed to share this view. He said nothing. The Council then adjourned for five days, after addressing more lame cables to Israel and the Arabs, calling for a ten-days' truce as from July 10th. Israel replied, accepting the appeal. But the Arabs did not reply. They thought they were still doing well. During the opening days of the fighting there was no evidence of the fate that was to overtake their cause. The attack on the Syrian bridgehead had gone badly; Jewish casualties had been heavy. The Israeli attack in the north seemed to have spent itself in the vain endeavour.

At Lake Success, Sir Alexander Cadogan sat tight and waited; there was no need for haste. It rather looked as if the Jews were now getting their share of the bloody nose. No one on the Council seemed to care. The fatal 13th had not yet dawned.

But at the 334th meeting of the Security Council on the evening of that day, news had come of the turn of the tide in Palestine. Alon had uncovered his cards. His armoured column had captured Lydda airport on July 12th; the key point of Beit Nabala was taken the following day.

The time for letting events take their course had passed. Cadogan went into action, perhaps a little crudely for so polished a diplomat. He complained later, privately, of his unfortunate position of having to dance to the Foreign Office tune. But he danced well.

He informed the Council that in the British view "recent developments" had made it necessary to proceed with haste, to *order* the parties to desist from any further military action, and to consider sanctions against any party not acting in accord with the Security Council's order. But the Council was now in less of a hurry than Sir Alexander. It was not until two days later, on July 15th, that the resolution was voted and agreed upon. The truce was to come into force on July 18th.

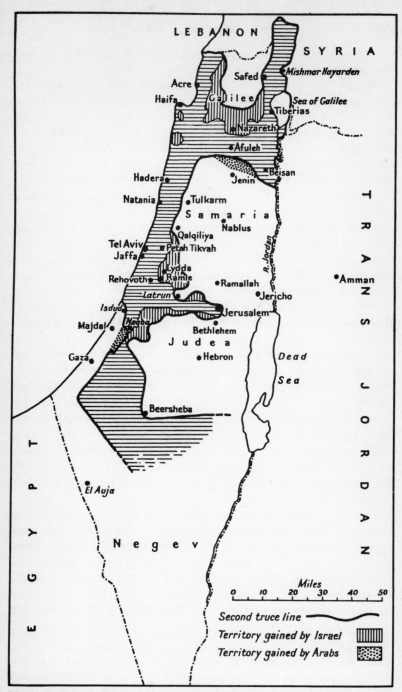

LEBANON

SYRIA

Acre

Safed • Mishmar Hayarden

Haifa

Galilee

Sea of Galilee

Tiberias

Nazareth

Afuleh

Beisan

Hadera • Jenin

Natania • Tulkarm

S a m a r i a

Qalqiliya • Nablus

Tel Aviv • Petah Tikvah

Jaffa

Lydda

Rehovoth • Ramle

Ramallah

Latrun

Jericho

Isdud

Negba

Jerusalem

Majdal

Bethlehem

Gaza

J u d e a

Dead

• Hebron

Sea

Beersheba

T
R
A
N
S

J
O
R
D
A
N

• Amman

E
G
Y
P
T

• El Auja

N e g e v

Miles

0   10   20   30   40   50

Second truce line

Territory gained by Israel

Territory gained by Arabs

Map 13. The position after the second truce on July 18th, 1948, showing territory which had changed hands during the ten days of fighting.

Sir Alexander's rescue operation had come too late; it was only partly successful.

The overall picture showed a considerable Arab reverse. The Israeli army had occupied during these nine days 1,000 square kilometres of Arab-held territory which left Israel in occupation of 1,300 square kilometres of territory allotted to the Arabs in the partition plan. It left the Arabs with 330 square kilometres of territory allotted to the Jews, not including the Negev, which, though effectively cut off by the Egyptians from the rest of Israel, was nevertheless not fully occupied by the Egyptian army.

Altogether, in the thirty-eight days of fighting, Israel had occupied fourteen Arab towns and 201 out of the 219 Arab villages within the Jewish State area. In addition, 112 villages on Arab territory had been captured. The Arabs had captured fourteen Jewish places, including the Jewish Quarter of the Old City of Jerusalem. Only one settlement, Mishmar Hayarden, was within the area of the Jewish State.

The official war in Palestine had come to an end. But the second "cease-fire" in Palestine brought no peace in the land. Neither side thought that this was the end. Both wanted another round. The Jews were determined to "tidy up the loose ends"—such as the Arab road-blocks on the main roads from Tel Aviv to Jerusalem and from Tel Aviv to the Negev settlements—and to make certain other frontier "adjustments." On the Arab side there was also a strong belief that the tide of war would turn again if they were given another chance.

The truce was noteworthy for its incidents and provocations. Firing in Jerusalem, occasional shelling, raids, murders and stealthy encroachments on the other side's territory, were routine features of the uneasy peace in which no one believed.

By the end of August the tension was markedly increasing. On the last day of the month, Jamal Husseini, cousin of the ex-Mufti, chairman of the Arab Higher Committee[1] and for

---

[1] Arab politics in Palestine were dominated by the Arab Higher Committee, which was created in 1936 with the amalgamation of five political parties. The Committee was, from the outset, dominated by the ex-Mufti, Haj Amin el-Husseini, who was elected its chairman. Other leading members were Jamal Husseini, who led the Palestine Arab

many years the leading representative of the Palestinian Arabs, sat down in his exile in Cairo to write a report to his old friend, Faris el Khouri, who was Syria's representative on the Security Council and the foremost Arab delegate at the United Nations.

The following, translated from the Arabic, was Jamal Husseini's description of the Palestine situation on August 31st, 1948:

I have now ascertained from military observers in Damascus, Beirut and here that half of the (Arab) strength now concentrated in Palestine is capable of occupying the entire country within two weeks, provided that the politicians do not interfere in the military operations.

Our manpower in Palestine has attained far larger strength than at any time before.

1. Iraq has now 20,000 men.

2. Syria and the Lebanon, 10,000.

3. The Palestinian irregulars number 10,000.

4. But Transjordan has only 4,000 men.

5. The Liberation Army has 3,000. It was 6,000 strong, under el Kaukji. Now el Kaukji is on long furlough; the army was handed over to Aref Bey Shukeiri, the Lebanese.

Regarding our withdrawals in Palestine. It appears that only one person was killed during the withdrawals, which took place when the situation was still satisfactory. The withdrawals were carried out pursuant to an order emanating from Amman. The withdrawal from Nazareth was ordered by Amman; the withdrawal from Safed was ordered by Amman; the withdrawal orders from Lydda and Ramle are well known to you. During none of these withdrawals did fighting take place. The regular armies did not enable the inhabitants of the country to defend themselves, but merely facilitated their escape from Palestine.

All the orders emanated from one place. The Iraqian people were furious and sent a parliamentary delegation to study the situation in Palestine. Upon their return, the delegation declared that Palestine could be occupied by the Iraqian army in

---

Party, Dr. Khalidi, the head of the Reform Party, and Abd el-Latif Bey Saleh, of the National Bloc. The main opposition to the Husseinis was provided by Raghib Bey Nashashibi, who had founded the National Defence Party. The bitter feud between the Husseini and the Nashashibi families provided one of the main causes of the lack of unity among the Palestinian Arabs during the first months of hostilities.

conjunction with the army of another Arab state. Consequently the feeling in the army reached a high tension. The
Regent, Abdul-Illah, notified his uncle (King Abdullah) of the
gloomy situation and that he (the Regent) contemplates a
decisive deed, and emphasized the necessity of his uncle's taking
part in the operation. Thereupon Abdullah consented to the
unification of both armies under the command of Iraq.
Fortunately el Pachachi happens to be Prime Minister. He is
straightforward and good-hearted. He is now in the Lebanon
and Syria to bring about the unification of their two armies.

Now everyone is convinced that the opportunity is ripe for
the carrying out of large-scale operations in Palestine which, if
launched last March, would have nullified Zionism; Zionism
would now be defunct and an issue of the past. Anyhow, the
illusion of the Jewish power no longer exists. Only the lack of
arms in the hands of the Palestinians and the concentrations
made by the Jews made us appear to be weak; this is a heart-
rendering state of affairs, especially when one bears in mind the
misery which has befallen our people in Palestine.

The Arab League and its secretary (may he be cursed) have
fettered the hands of those who are inactive, and have done
much harm to Palestine. Hence the position of the Secretary-
General is now critical; the Jewish morale is extremely bad,
whereas our morale is strong, and everyone wishes to fight to
the death rather than live in the present conditions.

Confidently believing in this imaginary picture of their
strength and Jewish weakness, the Arab leaders prepared and
looked forward to the next round—the two weeks that would
"liquidate Zionism." Jamal Husseini significantly omitted the
Egyptians from his calculations. He believed that the third
round would be dominated by the Iraqis rather than the
Egyptians. His judgment was sound. The Egyptians were not
anxious for more fighting. They had had all they wanted.
They, and not the Jews or Abdullah, dominated the whole of
southern Palestine, the greater part of it admittedly desert,
but still amounting to two-thirds of the area claimed by the
Jews as theirs. They were content. But they were also foolishly
obstinate and tough with the Jews over the details of their
occupation. It was to cost them dear.

Thus, the Arabs were preparing, and so was Israel. More
arms, guns and planes were arriving. The Israeli Army
Command was impatient to play its successful hand once

more. Foreign Minister, Moshé Sharett, and several members
of the Government were against any resumption of hostilities,
but preparations continued. Ben-Gurion was wavering, but
he was inclined to side with the army. His mind was made
up for him when, on August 12th, a detachment of the Arab
Legion blew up the water pumping station near Latrun.
This was, in his opinion, a clear violation of the truce. The
Legion's Intelligence did not know that shortly before this
action the Israelis had succeeded in laying an alternative
pipe-line parallel to the "Burma Road." Had it not been for
this line, the Jordanian act would have meant that Jerusalem
would be cut off from all water supplies. Ben-Gurion decided
that the Jordanian act provided sufficient cause to renew
hostilities. Plans were prepared for a general offensive against
the Jordanian front in the Judean and Hebron Hills. The
army was alerted; everything was made ready. But final
confirmation of the plans was not forthcoming. A majority
of the Government—including Ben-Gurion's Party—still
opposed the renewal of hostilities, despite the Latrun water-
pump incident. But although the planned offensive was
dropped, or postponed, the tension remained. The army command hoped that the Jordanians might further violate the
truce, and that in this manner the Government might be convinced to give the army a free hand. They began to feed the
foreign press with reports that the Arabs were ready to launch
an assault on Jerusalem on the night of September 15th. On
the morning of the 15th it was "leaked" that the Arabs had
postponed their attack to September 21st. Evidently sensing
or knowing something of the tension in Jerusalem, the Mediator, Count Bernadotte, decided to visit the city himself on Friday, September 17th. While crossing into the Jewish City, he
was assassinated by members of the Stern Gang. The murder
shocked the Israeli Government and a section of public
opinion. But there was no nation-wide outcry or determination
to catch the perpetrators. The attitude of the majority was
that another enemy of the Jews had fallen by the wayside.
Few genuine tears were shed. There was not much normal
indignation. The public was not interested in the hunt for the
assassins.

This mood was further strengthened when, shortly after his
assassination, the contents of Count Bernadotte's last report

to the United Nations were published. The so-called
Bernadotte Report had been completed by him on the island
of Rhodes before leaving on his last, fatal journey. It proposed
that the Palestine Partition Plan of the United Nations
should be altered to take into account the existing military
frontiers: the Jews should retain all Galilee, but give up the
entire south (the Negev) to the Arabs. Furthermore, it proposed that the Arab refugees should be permitted to return
forthwith to the homes in Israel which they had left or from
which they had been driven.

The Report convinced the Israeli Government and army
that a most determined effort would still be made by the
Arabs and the British to wrest the Negev from the Jewish
state. It also convinced them that the only argument that
would count against the last word and testament of the
murdered Mediator was possession and a *fait accompli*. The
Israeli army now prepared with meticulous care to bring this
about, while the unsuspecting Egyptians continued to play
with fire and finally provoked the incident which was to lead
to their virtual expulsion from Palestine.

Watching sadly from his palace in Amman, King Abdullah
sat down on September 30th to write a letter to his friend,
Riadh es Solh, the Prime Minister of the Lebanon. Riadh es
Solh was attending the United Nations General Assembly in
Paris, which was about to debate the Bernadotte Report.
Abdullah wrote:

> The report of Count Bernadotte was never submitted to me
> for examination, but you know that Jordan, in agreement with
> the states of the League, has plunged into the turmoil of the
> Zionist strife in order to crush the power of the Zionists, and
> strives to emerge from the affair with as few losses as possible;
> you will remember that I told you this at lunch during your
> first visit to me.
>
> But while we in Transjordan have been carrying on our
> military campaign and bearing the heaviest of military burdens
> alone, the League decides to set up in Gaza a feeble state for all
> Palestine in order, so to speak, to get rid of its responsibilities.
> This action means the acceptance and execution of partition.
> For my part, I shall not cease to rely on God in carrying out my
> duty. When I saw the Arab armies in Egypt to the west and in
> Syria and Lebanon to the north preparing and proceeding to

carry out this plan, and then failing to send in even a brigade, showing neither sympathy nor regard for the uprooted people of Palestine, but continuing their useless incitement of them and expecting one state to carry out the conquest of Palestine, I kept my place in the vanguard, as I had always determine to do.

Winter is approaching, and the refugees are without shelter. The responsibility for them and for failing to settle the affair rests on those Arab states which, instead of putting forth a military effort, looked idly on. The deeds and steadfastness of my army are sufficient to disprove the slanders that have been fabricated against it.

My greetings to you and to all your brethren.

(signed) Abdullah ibn al-Husayn[1]

Amman, September 30th, 1948.

---

[1] Abdullah, *al Takmilah*, ("*My memoirs completed*") pp. 12–13.

12

THE WAR AGAINST EGYPT

THE offensive against the Jordanians and Kankji had been postponed. The central front was quiet; the stalemate was complete. But not so in the south. The Israelis were beginning to realise that they could no longer consider the southern front to be of secondary importance in relation to the centre. For every day of inactivity further strengthened the Egyptians' position. The Negev settlements were blockaded. Their stocks of food and ammunition were dwindling. And all the while, the Egyptians were consolidating their line of defensive positions, which stretched from the Mediterranean at Isdud to the Hebron Hills in the east. The isolation of the Negev was complete. Unless the Israelis acted quickly the Negev settlements would be starved into surrender or evacuation. Moreover, it seemed increasingly certain that a political settlement would be based on the principle of "what you have you hold." If that was the case the Egyptians might lay claim to the entire Negev.

In its terms for the second truce, the United Nations had provided (on the recommendation of the Mediator) for the supply of food to the isolated Negev settlements. But these arrangements had proved unworkable. They had assumed that both the Israelis and the Egyptians had need of the cross-roads to the west of Faluja: the Egyptians to supply their forces in the Beit Jibrin—Bethlehem area, and the Israelis to send convoys southwards to their settlements. These cross-roads were within range of both Israeli and Egyptian guns The United Nations Mediator had prescribed that the cross-roads were to be used in six-hour shifts: the Egyptians were to be allowed to send convoys eastwards for six hours, and then the Israelis were to send supplies southwards for six hours, and so on. This arrangement, however, failed to work. The

Egyptians refused to allow the Israeli convoys through their territory to the south of the Faluja crossroads, which was in their hands. Repeated protests by Dr. Bunche, the recently appointed Acting Mediator, had no effect. The Israeli convoys were not allowed past the crossroads.

The situation in the Negev settlements steadily deteriorated. This was brought home to the new commander of the southern front, Yigal Alon, when he made a flying tour of the isolated settlements. He returned to Tel Aviv convinced that the whole Negev would be lost unless quick action were taken. As things stood, there was a strong possibility that the "Bernadotte Line" (which gave the Negev south of a line from Majdal to Falujah to the Arabs) would be imposed by the United Nations. Therefore, the *status quo* had to be changed. Next, the Egyptians constituted the largest and most menacing threat to Israeli territory. It had to be removed.

Alon's appreciation was largely shared by the Chief of Staff Yigal Yadin. Together, they set about to persuade Ben-Gurion to agree to the launching of a full-scale offensive in the south. Ben-Gurion, at this time, was still taken up with the idea of offensive action in the Judean Hills. He believed that the decisive front was in the centre and that the crucial battle would have to be fought against the Legion, and not against the Egyptians.

However, Ben-Gurion was quick to see possible implications of the deadlock at the Faluja crossroads. The Egyptians were clearly violating the truce and ignoring the repeated requests of the U.N. to act in accordance with the arrangements made by Dr. Bunche, the Acting Mediator. Ben-Gurion felt that with suitable preliminary preparing of the ground, he could convince the other members of the Government that Israel would be justified in using force to push a convoy through to the besieged settlements of the Negev if the Egyptians persisted in their hostile actions. And once such a breakthrough was forced, and the fighting became general, he could yet carry out his intention of capturing the hills surrounding Jerusalem.

Yigal Alon had been thinking along the same lines. He put to Ben-Gurion a general plan consisting of two phases: the first was to force a way through the Egyptian lines to the besieged settlements in the Negev, to be followed by a wide sweep to the north-east, with the object of reaching Jerusalem from the south, taking Hebron and Bethlehem on the way.

Alon's view regarding the urgency of the situation in the Negev coincided with Yigal Yadin's own opinions. Yadin had for long considered the Egyptians to be the most dangerous enemy. But Yadin opposed Alon's plan of combining a Jerusalem offensive with an attack in the south. In Yadin's view such a combination was impractible and might prevent a complete victory over the Egyptians. At the back of Yadin's mind was the fear that Ben-Gurion, whose preoccupation over Jerusalem was well known to Yadin, would order the switch-back from the southern to the Jerusalem front before the issue with the Egyptians was finally decided. Yadin, therefore, set to work to prepare the draft plan of a purely Negev offensive. He called his plan "Operation Ten Plagues."[1]

It was an ambitious plan. Ben-Gurion was interested. And, in the meantime, the Egyptians themselves took a hand in persuading the more hesitant members of the Israeli Government of the need for action in the south. As the weeks passed the Egyptians were becoming increasingly restless. The number of "incidents" increased. Egyptian reserves were being concentrated, and they showed signs of preparing for an offensive action. The cease-fire on the southern front was now largely a polite fiction. Thus, on October 5th, Egyptian planes bombed most of the Negev settlements, while heavy guns opened up with artillery barrages on several Israeli-held hilltops. The settlement of Ruhama, where there was one of the major air-strips used by the Israelis to keep up connection with the isolated settlements, came under particularly gruelling fire throughout that day.

The following day, the High Command met in Tel Aviv. Ben-Gurion had studied Yadin's and Alon's proposed "Operation Ten Plagues." He now gave it his wholehearted approval. He opened the meeting and concisely stated the case under discussion: "It has become vitally important to send a convoy to the Negev. The Egyptians will interfere. There will therefore be a fight. We have to decide what are the forces we have to concentrate in order to ensure success in as short a time as

[1] The name became so popular that it became a security risk. Too many people "in the know" were talking about it, so the name of the operation was changed to the more modest "Yoav."

possible." "Operation Ten Plagues"—Alon's plan as worked out by Yadin—was confirmed.

But there was still opposition to switching offensive action to the south. "It is possible to attack at only one place at one time. The triangle is more important than the Negev. There still exists a great danger to the Tel Aviv-Haifa road. We could capture a great part of the triangle," declared the opponents of the proposed Negev offensive. Brigadier Carmel supported them, adding: "If we break the strength of the Iraqis then we solve the most serious military problem facing us. Together with the Eighth Brigade as reserve, we can capture the whole triangle." However, strong opposition to the extension of Alon's plan to Jerusalem came from Yigal Yadin. Jerusalem had never yet been captured from the south, he declared. The only danger to the city lay in the north. The entire strength of the Legion was concentrated in the north; they could attack the Tel Aviv-Jerusalem road within an hour. Therefore, in order to capture Jerusalem, the attack must come from the north, not the south.[1]

Despite these history-weighted arguments, it was generally agreed that a convoy had to be sent to the Negev, and that this would mean war. Yadin's plan was therefore approved. But Alon was not given all the troops he wanted. For the great uncertainty for the Israelis, as they made their plans, was what the other Arab armies would do. Would they come to the aid of the Egyptians? Because of this uncertainty, the Israelis could not think in terms of one strategic focal point. They had to consider the possibility of a general Arab counter-offensive on all fronts; therefore Yadin would not denude the other fronts to let Alon have the additional forces which Alon (and Ben-Gurion) wanted for the Negev offensive.

When Alon came to the Army Command to plead for at

[1] These quotations were taken from the verbatim protocol of the G.H.Q. meeting which was shown to the authors by the Historical Section of the Israeli Army. In a subsequent interview with the Israeli Prime Minister, Mr. Ben-Gurion stated that this description of the G.H.Q. discussion was somewhat distorted. General Yadin could also not remember hearing some of these opinions expressed. This is not surprising. All through August and September Yadin had asked his front commanders for plans in case the war was resumed. Understandably, each Commander sought priority for his front and this discussion was in a sense the finale of a debate extending over many weeks.

least part of the 8th Brigade which was being kept in general reserve in case of attacks on other fronts, Yadin told him: "You can have it only over my dead body." Yadin insisted that Alon had sufficient troops for the operation, a fact which, in Yadin's subsequent opinion, was later amply borne out by the events.

This question of the reserve brigade came near to causing another major clash between Ben-Gurion and Yadin. Ben-Gurion was of the opinion that Alon should have the extra brigade, for he was convinced that the other Arab armies would not interfere, but Yadin would not hear of leaving the country without a central reserve force. Yadin felt so strongly on this subject that he was prepared to resign rather than give way. Ben-Gurion realised this and was not prepared to lose Yadin, whom he felt could not be replaced. So Yadin had his way.[1]

Nevertheless, the plans for "Operation Ten Plagues" were pushed forward. In these, Alon exploited to the full the peculiar deployment of the Egyptians. For their front line stretched in a wide arc from Rafah in the south to Bethlehem in the centre. And, although it was well fortified, it had no depth in defence. Moreover, the Israelis had troops both behind and in front of the Egyptian line. In the open space of the Negev, an entire Palmach brigade[2] was operating behind the Egyptian line, keeping contact with the settlements, helping in their defence and raiding Egyptian positions. The Egyptian defensive line from Rafah to Isdud, which protected the coastal road and railway, could be cut by the Negev forces. The line running across country from the Mediterranean to the Hebron Hills in the east could be threatened from both north and south.

Play on two alternatives thus formed the motif of Yadin's plan. He wanted not only to restore communications with the

[1] Later, Ben-Gurion felt that had the extra brigade been sent south the added impetus it would have given to the offensive would probably have enabled Alon to take the entire Gaza Strip in addition to his other conquests. Yadin, however, still insists that he was correct in his assessment of the situation, and that, although it was easy to be wise after the event, there was at the time no way of being completely certain that the central and northern fronts would remain quiet at the time of the Negev attack.

[2] The "Hanegev" (Palmach) Brigade, which had been operating in this area since the beginning of the hostilities, had in the meantime been relieved by the Yiftah (Palmach) Brigade. These troops were infiltrated through the lines of the Egyptians to get to their Negev posts.

settlements, but also to destroy as much of the Egyptian army as possible, and so remove the threat from the south.

For this purpose Alon had a sizeable force under his command: the Givati Brigade, holding the cross-country line facing the Egyptians; the Yiftah Brigade, operating in the Negev itself; two battalions of the Hanegev Brigade, which were returned to the south for the campaign; and an armoured battalion of Yitzhak Sadeh's armoured brigade. Later, during the actual fighting, further reinforcements of the newly-formed Oded Brigade were despatched south. He also had an air squadron carrying supplies to the Negev settlements and an outstanding intelligence organisation under Zerubavel Arbel.

The following figures will give some idea of the changes which had taken place in the armament of the Israeli army since May 15th:

	May 15th, 1948	October 12th, 1948
Men	35,000	80,000
Guns	4	250
120-mm. mortars	none	12
6-inch mortars	none	33
3-inch mortars	105	389
2-inch mortars	682	618
Davidka mortars	16	22
PIATS and anti-tank rifles	75	675
Machine-guns	1,550	7,550
Rifles	22,000	60,000
Sub-machine-guns	11,000	21,300

Facing Alon was a slightly larger force of Egyptians. They were strongly entrenched and had a marked superiority in armour and artillery. The Egyptian force was made up of two brigades of infantry along the Rafah-Isdud axis (one in reserve, based on Gaza, and the second holding the line between Majdal and Isdud); a reinforced brigade, holding the line eastwards from Majdal to Beit Jibrin; and nine so-called battalions of volunteers,[1] holding the Auja-Beersheba-Hebron-Bethlehem axis. In addition, they had two regiments of artillery and an armoured battalion. Altogether about 15,000 troops.

On the morning of October 15th, the Israeli liason officer

[1] Commanded by Brigadier Abd el-Aziz. Most of these troops were members of the Moslem Brotherhood, who had fought in Palestine before the official invasion began on May 15th.

informed the United Nations Observer headquarters that, in accordance with the United Nations arrangements concerning the use of the Faluja crossroads, a convoy would be sent to the Negev that afternoon. Its despatch was confirmed by the United Nations, and shortly afterwards the convoy left its base. This was to be the test. An attack on the convoy was to be the signal for Alon's operation to begin.

The convoy reached the Karatiya crossroads on time and passed the crossing without mishap. As the convoy reached the first houses of the village, strong fire was directed on it from both sides of the road. The first vehicle was set on fire; the rest turned round with some difficulty and retired. It was what the Israelis had expected—and hoped for. The Egyptians had broken the truce by not allowing the convoy (authorised by the United Nations) to go through. Operation Ten Plagues could now proceed.

On that same day, with a speed which took the Egyptians completely by surprise, the Israelis forces went into action. At six o'clock that evening, shortly after the convoy was attacked, the Israeli air force attacked the main Egyptian air base at el-Arish and damaged a number of planes on the ground. At the same time, Gaza, Majdal, Rafah and Beit Hanun were bombed. As night fell, units of the Yiftah Brigade raided the Egyptian communication lines, blowing up the railway line near the Egyptian border, mining the main road between Rafah and Khan Yunis, and generally harassing Egyptian positions in different parts of the Negev. Units of the Givati Brigade attacked Egyptian positions between Faluja and Beit Jibrin. By dawn on October 16th the Yiftah troops had driven a deep wedge to within 600 yards from the main coastal road at Beit Hanun—a threat to all supplies on the western front—while the Givati forces had forced similar wedges into the lateral Faluja-Beit Jibrin road.

But this outbreak of air attacks, raids on Egyptian supply routes and posts, the driving of wedges between Egyptian positions, the direct threat to the coastal road at Beit Hanun, and the general air of menace over the entire Egyptian front on that night of October 15/16th, all had one purpose in Alon's eyes: to confuse the Egyptian commander, to split up his front and thus provide the necessary feint for the main purpose that night. That was the assault on Iraq el Manshiya,

which commanded the possible alternative route to the
Negev settlements. Alon's orders were that Iraq el Manshiya
was to be taken during the night and the capture immediately
exploited by the advance westward to the "Faluja Crossroads".

The first part of the fighting had gone according to plan;
now came the main phase, that of breaking through the
fortified line and joining up with the Negev settlements. Two
roads led into the southern area. One was the main road to
the west of Faluja, through Kaukaba, Huleiqat and Bureir.
The other, a rough track, led from the south of Faluja to

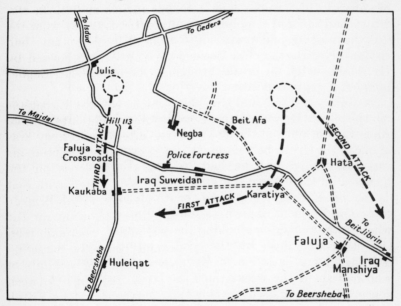

Map 14. The Faluja Crossroads.

Mishmar Hanegev. Alon chose the southern track for his
breakthrough.

At dawn on October 16th a battalion of infantry, supported
by Sadeh's battalion of tanks, attacked Iraq el-Manshiya,
the nodal point of the Egyptian defence on this sector of the
front. This was the first time that the Israelis were attacking
with a force of combined infantry and armour; but they still
lacked experience in co-ordinating the two arms, and they
suffered a major set-back. Two infantry companies advanced
on their objective, but strong Egyptian resistance forced back

one of the companies. As it retreated, it came into the field of
fire of the massed artillery and machine-gun positions at
Iraq el-Manshiya and Faluja. Within a matter of minutes
more than a third of the company had been either killed or
wounded. At the same time Egyptian anti-tank guns scored
direct hits on the attacking armour. Four Hotchkiss tanks
were destroyed, and all the others damaged. By now
the Israelis were in full retreat. The Egyptians had stood
firm.

Alon was now in a difficult position. He had lost the element
of surprise; his armour had been put out of action; his infantry had suffered crippling casualties. The Egyptians would
now be waiting and preparing for his next attack on Iraq
el-Manshiya. He therefore decided on a swift change of plan.
He would switch his break-through to the west. The strongly
fortified Egyptian position covering the "crossroads" would
have to be captured, and the main road to the Negev opened
via this route. By early afternoon, after the dawn catastrophe,
Alon was working out the new plan of attack with commanders
of one of the Givati battalions. It was to begin at sunset. Speed
was everything, and he had to keep Egyptian attention
focussed on the eastern route.

The main "Faluja' crossroads were defended from four hill-
tops; two of them, known as hills 100 and 113, were somewhat to the north, overlooking the settlement of Negba, and
the other two flush by the road crossing. The hills were
defended by a battalion of Egyptians and Saudi Arabians,
who had spent the weeks since the truce was proclaimed in
consolidating and strengthening their positions.

That night began the crescendo of Alon's battle for the
Negev. The second stage of his plan. The overall pattern of
attacks all over the front was resumed, raids were carried out,
and wedges were driven into the Egyptian lines while the Israelis
fought their way onto the hills which covered the crossroads
and held them against repeated Egyptian counter-attacks—
but with heavy casualties—all through that day, October 17th.
But this was only half the operation. Further south, the
Yiftah Brigade was to overrun the Egyptians in the strongly
held village of Huleiqat, taking it from the rear, the south-
west. But it failed to do so.

This left Alon in possession of the crossroads but unable to exploit his gain. For the Egyptians still held a line of strong defence positions, just south and parallel to the main road, stretching from Karatiya to Kaukaba. That night also, the Egyptian commander began to fear that the wedge towards Beit Hanun was the anvil of Alon's operation, and launched a massive artillery barrage against the Israeli positions.

At this point Alon realised that unless he could break through the main Egyptian position at Huleiqat, the whole purpose of the battle for the South would be lost. He had his wedges all over the place, but not a major break-through. Time was short now and Alon concluded that the village would have to be taken by frontal assault. It was no easy decision. Huleiqat with its seven fortified positions was perfectly sited for defence and was known to the Israelis as "the horror of the south".

After much heart-searching Alon persuaded Yadin and his own two principal commanders, Sadeh and Avidan to proceed with the frontal assault on Huleiqat. It was Alon's outstanding military achievement, requiring planning, initiative and guts. After one of the most fearsome encounters of the war, Huleiqat was stormed on the night of October 20th, in a memorable charge by Givati's 52nd battalion commanded by Yaacov Prulov, the same man who was nearly court-martialled for failing to attack at Latrun. Supporting him were the "Shimshon Foxes" commanded by Tchera Tsur. There was no more meaningful message in the records of the Israeli G.H.Q. than Alon's "Huleiqat is ours," which arrived with the early dawn on October 21st.

This proved to be the turning-point. Instead of the Negev settlements being isolated, the Egyptian line was now turned. The troops to the east of the break-through were facing encirclement. The "Faluja pocket" was being formed. And, to the west a second Egyptian brigade was threatened with encirclement by the Yiftah thrust on October 22nd to Bet Hanun and the coastal road. But here the Egyptians countered the threat energetically and successfully. Working against time engineers built a temporary road over the sand-dunes to Gaza and the entire brigade was evacuated before the trap could be closed on them. The towns of Isdud and Majdal fell to the Israelis almost without a battle. The Egyptian "finger " pointing to Tel Aviv had been amputated.

Meanwhile, the Southern Command was almost hourly expecting a new United Nations order to cease fire and halt operations. Speed was now even more essential if the success in opening the road was to be properly exploited. Alon hastily ordered the commander of the Negev Brigade, Nahum Sarig, to plan an attack on Beersheba should time permit. Within 12 hours of the breakthrough at Huleiqat, Alon sent three battalions to Sarig who descended on the surprised Egyptian garrison of Beersheba on the last night before the truce; its commander had not even been aware of the fact that the road to the Negev had been opened by the Israelis. Beersheba fell, and with it any Egyptian hope of maintaining its military hold on the Negev.

While the main battles were being waged in the northern Negev, the Israeli G.H.Q. did not lose sight of the ulterior objective of the offensive—namely, the widening of the southern approaches to Jerusalem. Moreover, the Israelis wished to take the maximum advantage of the brief period of fighting allowed to them before a fresh cease-fire would be imposed by the United Nations. Consequently, even before the outcome of the battle at Huleiqat had been decided, Israeli forces further to the east began an offensive against the Egyptians based in the Judaean and Hebron Hills. While soldiers of the Harel Brigade advanced in a south-easterly direction from Hartuv towards Bethlehem and the Kfar Etzion Group, the Givati Brigade pushed eastwards in the direction of Beit Jibrin and the foothills of Hebron.[1]

It seemed as if the second phase of Yigal Alon's prepared offensive, the advance through Hebron and Bethlehem towards Mount Scopus and Jerusalem, would succeed as fully as the first phase. Resistance was negligible. The Egyptians, after hearing of their defeat further to the west, were retreating everywhere. Their entire defensive position in the Hebron Hills was on the vege of collapse. And, sure portents of what was to come, Arab citizens of Bethlehem and the surrounding villages were already evacuating their homes in their hundreds.

[1] The Egyptian Prime Minister Nokrashy was in Amman to discuss concerted measures to drive the Israelis from the Negev with the other Arab Premiers and rulers. He was outlining his proposals when King Abdullah interrupted him to tell him that Beersheba had fallen to the Israelis. Nokrashy would not believe it. See Abdullah's "*My Memoirs Completed*", p. 26.

But what seemed to be a comparatively simple and straight-forward military campaign for the Israelis was already becoming befogged and confused with political issues. For Abdullah, alarmed at having his entire flank exposed by the possible capture of Hebron and the subsequent threat to Jericho and Jerusalem, hastily sent a force of Legionnaires down to Hebron. Militarily, the force was negligible and could not have affected the outcome of the battle here between the Israelis and the Arabs. But politically, Abdullah's move had the effect of bringing the Hebron area under Transjordan's jurisdiction. Any attack on it would be outside the scope of the Egyptian-Israeli flare-up; it would immediately entail the renewal of hostilities along the entire Transjordanian-Israeli sector, and possibly, if not probably, along the Iraqi and other fronts as well.

Abdullah was aware that the Israelis wished to avoid this at all costs. Moreover, he knew that the Israelis were anxious to commence peace negotiations with at least one Arab state, and thus break the united Arab front against them. He therefore let it be known through unofficial contacts that he might consider entering such negotiations with the Israelis—provided, of course, that they refrained from attacking the Transjordanian sector, including the Hebron Hills.

The Israelis, moving southwards and eastwards towards Bethlehem and Hebron, realised that their advance had become a race against time. They therefore decided to make a supreme effort to attain their objectives before a cease-fire would be forced upon them by the arrival of the Legionnaires. On the night of October 19th, in the midst of the Jewish festival of Tabernacles, a force of three battalions under the command of Brigadier Moshe Dayan began advancing from Jerusalem through the Judaean Hills to the south. Their first objective was the fortified village of el-Wallajah, overlooking the railway to Jerusalem; their second, the village of Beit Jala, the key to Bethlehem and the highest of the imposing range of hills to the south of Jerusalem. But the operation was hastily and badly planned. The zero hour of the attack was postponed three times at the very last moment, and by the time the troops did finally mount their trucks and leave their base in Bakaa and Allenby Barracks, most of Jerusalem knew already that Bethlehem was going to be attacked.

Dayan had been given forty-eight hours to complete the operation, "so as to avoid international complications," but from the very outset the attack became bogged down because of the ineffectiveness of a forward company commander, who failed to deal promptly with the resistance he met. The rest of the night was wasted after the battalion commander on the spot, Lieutenant-Colonel Mart, decided that if he continued the attack that night his forces would be caught in daylight out in the open hills and their retreat would be cut off. Dayan supported this decision, and the front commander, Zvi Ayalon, who thought otherwise, did not press his authority. Thus, by morning, although el-Wallajah and the last remaining stretch of the railway line still held by the Arabs had been captured by the advancing troops, Beit Jala remained in Arab hands.

Throughout that day, October 20th, Beit Jala was shelled in preparation for the assault that was to take place that night. But in the late afternoon an order came through from the headquarters of the Central Front, in the name of General Army Headquarters, to stop all military operations in the area. The Legion had that day taken over from the Egyptians. Abdullah had won the race for the Hebron Hills. Thus, what might have been one of the decisive operations of the war came to an inconclusive end. Had the Israelis pressed home their attack during the first night, or had the cease-fire order come through one day later, the whole ensuing peace negotiations would have taken on a different complexion; Bethlehem and Hebron would have been in Israeli hands and the Hashemite Kingdom of Transjordan in an invidious position. Thus, the procrastination of a serious, rather elderly company commander, in charge of a forward machine-gun unit, who failed to take prompt action when fired on from an Arab position, had unforeseen consequences on the future map of the Middle East.

Twenty-four hours later the cease-fire ordered by the United Nations came into operation over the entire southern front. Bethlehem and the Hebron Hills had been saved from Israeli occupation. The Harel Brigade, which was advancing into the hills from the West, was hardly meeting any resistance and was only a few miles away from the Kfar Etzion Group and Bethlehem. The brigade commander pleaded desperately with the commander of the Central Front to allow him a few more days, but to no avail.

Meanwhile, in Paris, the Israeli delegate at the Security Council fought a covering diplomatic action so as to provide Alon with time to complete his operation. Eban was assisted (or, at least, not obstructed) by the American, Russian and Ukranian delegates, while the Belgian, British, Chinese and Syrian members of the Security Council pressed for speedy intervention. The British were determined. The cease-fire brought Alon to a stand-still on October 22nd, but not British pressure. By November 4th, the British delegation was sure of a majority on the Council to vote for an order to the Israeli troops to withdraw to the original lines which they had occupied on October 14th, before Alon had launched his attack.

At this crucial juncture, Dr. Ralph Bunche, the Acting Mediator, came to the rescue of the Israelis. On November 17th, twenty-four hours before the expiration of the Security Council's time-limit for the Israeli withdrawal, Bunche pro-proposed a new formula to Eban. Israel was to withdraw her mobile forces, but not her garrisons in the Negev, including that in Beersheba. The Israelis accepted the Bunche inter-pretation. Bunche announced that this satisfied the Security Council's terms. The British declared that Bunche had tricked them. They had wanted a demilitarised Negev; now it had been made safe for the Israelis.

Meanwhile, on October 22nd, the United Nations cease-fire had come into operation over the entire front. But Alon's troops on the eastern sector continued their mopping-up operations in the foothills of the Hebron range, where the Egyptians, and not the Transjordanians, were still in com-mand. Beit Jibrin, Ajjur, Dawayima and the entire Lachish area were captured after the truce had come into force. The Egyptians, on their part, successfully made use of the truce by evacuating all their troops and equipment north of Beit Hanun, where they had been threatened with encirclement. In this swift action they showed considerable ingenuity. In the course of this evacuation, for which the Egyptians used naval vessels as well as building a makeshift road over the sand-dunes, a naval engagement took place on the day the cease-fire took effect in which two Egyptian ships were sunk. One of them was the flagship of the Egyptian Navy which had seven hundred troops on board at the time of the engagement. The Egyptians were even less lucky with their 4th Brigade at Faluja, which, when the truce came into effect, found itself completely encircled and cut off from the rest of the Egyptian army.

The Faluja encirclement was a great defeat for the Egyptians: 2,500 men, one of the best brigade groups in the entire army, with all the heavy equipment which normally accompanies a brigade, were trapped, with very little chance of rejoining their army. On the other hand, the "Battle of the Faluja Pocket," as it came to be known, has deservedly been given an honoured place in the annals of Egyptian military history, for the encircled troops, under the command of the Sudanese Brigadier Taha Bey, fought on courageously and determinedly against hopeless odds, refusing even to consider a surrender.

The garrison in the police fortress of Iraq es-Suweidan was a case in point. Six attacks in as many days were mounted by the Israelis against the imposing, fortress-like building which had for months threatened the nearby settlement of Negba. Each time the attackers were repulsed, suffering heavy losses. The Egyptians showed their worth in static defence, at which they excelled throughout the war.

Only in the seventh attack, after the Israelis had laid down an artillery barrage, which was by far the heaviest of the war, did the garrison surrender. But even though it was now deprived of its main prop, the besieged Faluja brigade continued to fight back. Talks were held between Yigal Alon and Taha Bey, during which Taha brought with him some of his staff officers, including Major Gamal Abdel Nasser, but these conversations produced no results. A later attempt at the end of December by the Israelis to storm the eastern sector of the "pocket" and take the village of Iraq el-Manshiya failed after the assaulting Israelis mistook the counter-attacking Egyptian armour for their own. The battalion of the 3rd Israeli Brigade which had mounted the attack had one company wiped out to a man; the other two companies also sustained heavy losses. After this severe setback the Israelis contented themselves with tightening the blockade round the trapped brigade, without attempting any further frontal assaults.

Meanwhile, at the beginning of November, urgent talks were in progress among the Arab Joint General Command in

Amman on how the brigade could best be rescued. Abdullah's description of these meetings in his memoirs illustrates the extent of the distrust and suspicion which had, by then, taken hold of the Arab allies.

. . . the late Prime Minister Nokrashy Pasha (of Egypt), the Syrian Prime Minister Jamil Mardam Bey, and Husni Bey al-Zaim had come to Amman where his Royal Highness the Regent (of Iraq) and the Iraqi Chief of Staff General Salih Saib Pasha were already present. On the night we all met in council over five minutes passed before anyone spoke a word. The Regent motioned to me to begin the conversation, but it was difficult for me to say anything in view of what had happened to the Egyptian army.

Therefore, directing my words to Nokrashy Pasha, I said, "Let us hear what His Excellency has to say."

His reply, word for word, was, "God, I have come to listen, not to talk."

I answered, "I think that your Excellency should do the talking under the present circumstances, in view of the fact that Beersheba has been lost and al-Faluja is besieged."

"Who says so?" he queried. "The Egyptian forces are still holding their positions."

"Perhaps," I countered, "the news has not yet reached the ears of your Excellency. I had thought that you would point out the necessity for military help, as desired by the Egyptian Command, in order to save the situation."

"No," he said, "the Egyptian Government has no need of anyone's assistance. But where are the royal Jordanian and Iraqi forces? And we all know that the Syrian forces are useless." This was said in the presence of Jamil Mardam Bey, who was listening.

"I take it then," I replied, "that your Excellency has come here to accuse us. You have just said that the Egyptian Government needs help from no one, but Azzam Pasha is broadcasting cries for help. Are you heaping scorn on the Arabs in their own house—the house in which Jordan, Iraq, Syria and Lebanon are gathered?"

"I seek forgiveness of God," he said, "I have not come to accuse anyone."[1]

The talks had failed, but efforts to find some means of saving the situation on the southern front continued, for

[1] Abdullah, *al Takmilah* ("*My memoirs Completed*"), p. 26.

Abdullah was quick to see the advantages he might gain from the plight of the Egyptians. His first preoccupation was to strengthen his own precarious position in the Hebron Hills. He therefore asked the Iraqis to take over the Latrun front, so that he could send the Legion to Hebron in force, "in order to bring help to the trapped Egyptians." The Iraqis, however, had their own worries: the most they could do was to send a battalion to Latrun. But the Legion was still determined to play an active part in the Faluja drama. Accordingly, the Egyptian military representative at Amman, Armoured Corps Commander Zabur Bar, was informed of the following proposal made by Glubb Pasha:

1. An attack would be opened by the Iraqi and Trans-jordanian battalions in the direction of Beit Jibrin.
2. While the Israeli forces would be engaged in countering this attack, Taha Bey would destroy all his defence posts, his artillery vehicles and other heavy equipment. After that he would infiltrate his troops on foot, by a secret way known to one of the Legion's officers, through the Jewish lines to the Arab positions in the hills ten miles away.
3. This plan would have to be implemented quickly, as the Iraqis did not want to prolong their stay in the Beit Jibrin sector; they were needed further north.
4. This was to be known as "Operation Damascus."

Shortly after passing on the proposal to Cairo, Glubb sent the Legion officer who was to act as a guide, a British major named Lockett, accompanied by a British sergeant, to Faluja to discuss the details with Taha Bey. But Taha doubted the feasibility of the plan and decided to cable to the newly-appointed Commander-in-Chief at Gaza, General Fuad Sadeq, to ask for instructions. The reply he received was terse and to the point:

It is impossible to rely on a plan whose initiator is Glubb Pasha, and it is impossible to keep the details of the plan from the Jews if it originated in Amman. The evacuation of the troops by foot through areas held by Jews means a massacre for these troops. Reject the plan and drive out the mercenary

Lockett. Defend your posts to the last bullet and to the last soldier as befitting of Egyptian soldiers.

"Operation Damascus" was not shelved there and then, for the discussion continued in Faluja, in Gaza and in Cairo. Should they take the risk and follow Lockett or not? But in the end nothing came of it. This incident, perhaps more than any other, worsened relations between the Egyptians and the Transjordanians. The Egyptians were convinced that the Legion was prepared to lead them into a trap; on the other hand, these suspicions rankled deeply among the Transjordanians. On one point, the Egyptian fears were justified: the Israelis knew all about "Operation Damascus," and, had it taken place, they would have been waiting for the escaping troops. This knowledge, however, did not emanate from Transjordanian treachery; it was gleaned simply by listening in to the radio arguments on the subject. Much later (at the Rhodes armistice talks), Brigadier Yadin once "innocently" referred to "Operation Damascus," thus confirming Egyptian suspicions that the Transjordanians were out to betray them.

Thus, devoid of all hope of help from the other Arab armies, the Faluja brigade grimly fulfilled their general's injunction to fight to the last soldier and the last bullet. The brigade was later evacuated within the framework of the Rhodes armistice talks and given a deserved hero's welcome in Cairo.

Apart from the "Faluja pocket," fighting had died down with the reimposition of a full truce on October 22nd. But hardly had the south quietened down when trouble flared up again in the north. Kaukji's Liberation Army, now reorganised and re-equipped by the Lebanese army, was once more becoming restless. His troops were making an increasing number of forays against the Jewish settlements in Upper and Western Galilee; these came to a climax towards the end of October, when the Liberation Army made a determined assault on kibbutz Menara and the heights surrounding it. These attacks succeeded in isolating the settlement from the rest of Jewish Galilee; they also gave the Israeli Army Command the excuse for which they had been waiting to break the truce in the north and mount an offensive against Kaukji's troops in Central Galilee.

The subsequent offensive, known as "Operation Hiram" and

led by Brigadier Moshe Carmel, proved to be one of the best planned and speediest operations of the war. It began on the night of October 28th, and lasted exactly sixty hours. During that period the 7th Brigade, in conjunction with two other brigades, captured the whole of Upper Galilee and swept into the Lebanon, capturing a number of villages there and reaching the banks of the river Litani. Kaukji's army simply melted away. In this swift campaign the Arabs suffered 400 fatal casualties, of which 200 came from a Syrian battalion ambushed at Jish, to the west of Sassa. Some 500 Arab soldiers were taken prisoner during the campaign.

Operation Hiram ended on October 31st. Here, as in the Negev, the Israeli conquest was safeguarded by the compromise brought about at the United Nations by Dr. Bunche.[1] The matter was to be settled at the proposed Armistice negotiations which the Bunche resolution had proposed in addition to the military compromise in the Negev.

So once more there was a truce in Palestine. But it was artificial, imposed from outside, and could not last. In itself it was no solution, and no move was made to bring about a settlement. It was clear that the truce could not last, so long as there was no alternative to bring the war to an end. Force became inevitable when the Egyptian Government made known that they would not enter into talks with Israel with a view to replacing the truce by a more permanent armistice, as had been requested by the Security Council in a resolution passed on November 11th.

The Israelis duly reacted to this announcement. If this was Egypt's stand, then Israel would reserve freedom of action. For the Israelis were now convinced that they could not rely any more on outside solutions. Their aim was to bring the Arab states to the conference table, and Egypt's latest declaration convinced them that this could only be done after the Arab armies had been decisively defeated, and after they had been expelled from Israeli territory. Consequently, despite the political risks involved in yet another breach of the truce, the Israeli leaders argued that military victory was their only hope, and General Headquarters was authorised to plan a further offensive against the Egyptian army.

[1] See p. 251 above.

On December 23rd "Operation Horev," the largest and most important campaign of the war, was launched. "Horev" proved to be the climacteric; it not only gave the Israelis complete military victory, but it also very nearly brought Great Britain into a war with Israel before it ended with the fulfilment of the Israeli objective: armistice talks between Egypt and Israel.

Once more the execution of the campaign was in the hands of Brigadier Alon. The task given him was the total expulsion of the Egyptian army from Israeli soil, together with as complete a destruction of that army as possible.

The Egyptians were deployed slightly to the north of the international frontier between Israel and Egypt, with two prongs pointing northwards: the western one through Rafah and Gaza, where their headquarters were situated, and the eastern one through Auja-el-Hafir and Bir Asluj, in the direction of Beersheba. In the first of these prongs, two Egyptian brigades were holding the front line; in the eastern prong, two additional brigades held a chain of fortified hills from Auja to Bir Asluj. In addition to these forces, the Egyptian army in the Negev included their 4th Brigade, which was encircled in the "Faluja pocket," and about two battalions of Moslem Brotherhood volunteers in the Hebron Hills—all that was left of the Egyptian forces there. Their western and eastern prongs were joined by a road from Auja to Rafah, through Egyptian territory, along which the Egyptians had their main strategic reserve. It was not very large. They also had a reserve force at their main Sinai base of el-Arish.

Against this force of five and a half brigades, the Israelis had mounted a total of five brigades, of which one was tied down in containing the "Faluja pocket."

Thus, the forces engaged were approximately equal in size. The Egyptians had the advantage of defending well-fortified and well-dug-in positions; the Israelis the advantage of surprise and of choosing the terrain which was best suited for the attack. These advantages were exploited to the full by Alon and by the Director of Operations at G.H.Q., Brigadier Yigal Yadin. They realised that a frontal assault on the Gaza Strip would lead to heavy casualties, require much time, and leave the final outcome uncertain. For the Egyptians had

I

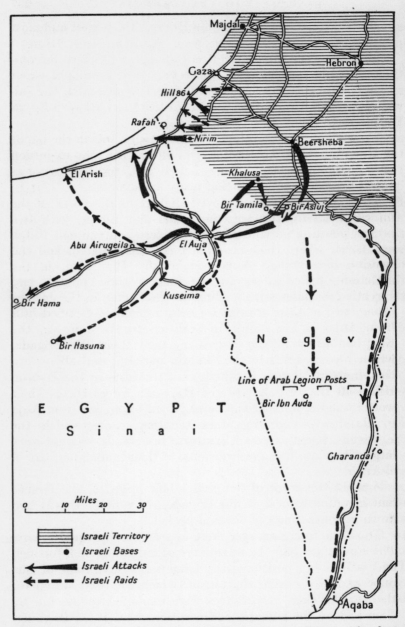

Map 15. Israel completes the conquest of the Negev; the last
battle against the Egyptians and the occupation of the Israeli
shore of the Gulf of Aquaba.

already proved their worth in the static defence of fortified positions.

The plan which they produced was designed to overcome these obstacles and to make the best use of the element of surprise. The Israeli Army Command therefore planned that while the main attack would be on the eastern prong of the Egyptian line—from Auja to Bir Asluj—a strong diversionary attack would first be made on the Gaza Strip. This would make the Egyptians believe that this was the main offensive. The real military objective for the first phase of the attack would be the important road junction of Auja el-Hafir, on the Egyptian-Israeli frontier. Capture of this point would enable Alon's troops to swing in a wide flanking movement through the Sinai desert to the sea and thus threaten the rear of virtually the entire Egyptian army. In this way, the second objective, namely the expulsion of the Egyptian army from the Gaza Strip, and its destruction, would be achieved without the costly frontal assault.

This was the plan. Yadin said of it afterwards: "Strategy decided the issue even before the battle began."

But its implementation raised many problems for Yigal Alon and his staff. The Bir Asluj-Auja heights were situated in barren desert. Advance along the only road from Beersheba southwards to Bir Asluj would preclude any possibility of surprise and would entail attacking the positions where the Egyptians were expecting the attack. On the other hand, the rough desert terrain prevented the use of armoured vehicles, and an attack without the support of armour and artillery would be almost certainly doomed to failure. It was while G.H.Q. was debating this predicament that the scouts of the Hanegev Brigade found the road which Yadin identified as a Roman road from Halutza and Ruheiba straight through to Auja. The road had long been covered by shifting sands, but he believed that it could be prepared to take vehicles. The road was reconnoitered and handed over to the army engineers. They pronounced that it would be touch-and-go, but that with luck the vehicles and armour would get through.

This altered the whole situation. It enabled the Israelis to mount an attack on Auja at the same time as attacks were launched on the fortified hill positions along the Auja-Bir Asluj line. The surprise was complete, for the Egyptian garrison at Auja was convinced that the only direction from which an armoured attack could come was from the north— along the main road, which was heavily defended. When the attack opened with the sudden appearance of Israeli tanks from the seemingly impassable desert the Egyptian defenders were taken by astonished surprise. Even so, the battle for Auja lasted more than twenty-four hours.

Preceding this attack on Auja, Alon had made an impressive diversionary attack on the Gaza Strip. A battalion of Israelis succeeded in cutting the main road linking Gaza with Rafah by taking a vital hill-top, but in one of the sharpest en-counters of the war the Egyptians succeeded in dislodging the Israelis and inflicted heavy losses on them. The attack once more demonstrated the Egyptians' ability to defend their positions.

The fall of Auja on December 27th put the Egyptian army in an impossible position. Its eastern axis had disintegrated; its soldiers surrendered in their hundreds and with all their equipment. Even more serious for them, the road into Sinai lay open before the victorious Israelis, who hastened to exploit this opportunity. Alon had already decided that if political circumstances were favourable he would continue the advance and capture the entire Sinai peninsula; if not, he would return, not to Beersheba, but to Gaza. He realised that there was virtually no organised Egyptian army left to the west of el-Arish, and that if he could take this Egyptian base virtually the entire Egyptian army would be trapped. He acted quickly, for once more the time factor was going to decisive.

Without giving their troops a chance to rest, the Israeli commanders pushed their columns forward, and on December 28th the first Israeli troops crossed the international frontier into Egypt. The same evening the forward troops reached the important desert oasis and crossroads of Abu Aweigeila and, with hardly a pause to reorganise, attacked the surprised Egyptians, taking a large number of prisoners including a camp for Egyptian political prisoners situated nearby.

The next day the column advanced northwards to el-Arish, the main Egyptian base in the Sinai desert. At the same time a secondary force pushed deep into the desert to raid the air-fields at el Hama and Bir Hasana, where, for many centuries, weary travellers crossing the Sinai desert had stopped at the Khan situated there.

By this time, the Egyptians were surrendering on all sides. Complete demoralisation reigned among them. Alon's troops reached the southern airfield at el-Arish on December 30th and captured it. At dawn the following morning his armour and infantry were to capture the town. The greatest victory of the war was now in Alon's grasp as he stood on the sand-dunes some three miles south of el-Arish together with his Chief of Operations, Yitzhak Rabin, and discussed the details of the attack. The Egyptian army's base could be in his hands; the entire army could be trapped. Just then a runner reached the two commanders with a coded message from G.H.Q.: they were to evacuate the entire Sinai desert within a day.

The pill was too bitter to swallow. Telling Rabin to hold everything, Alon boarded a plane and flew to Tel Aviv to plead with Ben-Gurion. First he saw Yadin, who told him: "You needn't try to persuade me; I agree with you already. Try and persuade B.G." Yadin informed the Southern Front commander of the political excitement since he had crossed into Egypt. The Egyptians had appealed to their Arab allies for help, but had met with no response, except for verbal encouragement. Transjordan had not even bothered to reply. Instead, help came from a different quarter. Great Britain saw in this threat to Egypt an opportunity to invoke the long-disputed Anglo-Egyptian Treaty of Friendship of 1936. Such an act, the British Government thought, might induce the Egyptians to cease their attacks on the Treaty. So, shortly after Alon's forces crossed the frontier at Auja, the British sent an ultimatum to Israel calling for her immediate withdrawal from Egyptian territory.

The note, which was sent through Washington, was accompanied by a similar demand from the American State Department. The pressure was on, and the British meant business. It was this ultimatum which had induced Ben-Gurion and Sharett to send Alon the order of withdrawal. Alon pleaded with Sharett at his home in Tel Binyamin (Ben-Gurion was at Tiberias at the time) to allow him to take el-Arish, destroy the base, and then evacuate immediately. But Sharett was convinced that the capture of the town would immediately bring the British into the war, and he would hear none of it.

Alon then asked for four days in the desert in which he would make preparations as if he was going to attack el-Arish; the Egyptians would bring troops from the Gaza Strip, and then he would attack opposite Gaza and Rafah, well within Israeli territory. For Alon felt that the Americans would accept the Israeli explanation that he needed four days to withdraw his forces.

This plan seemed more feasible to Sharett, but when they telephoned Ben-Gurion, he turned it down with a heavy heart. By way of a compromise, Ben-Gurion allowed Alon to use the Auja-Rafah road (which is mainly inside Egyptian territory) in order to mount an attack on Rafah. Its capture would be much more difficult than that of el-Arish, but would have the same effect of bottling up the Egyptian army in the Gaza Strip, without incurring the threat of a war with Great Britain, for Rafah was not in Egyptian territory.

The attack on el-Arish was therefore called off. The troops— who had been incessantly on the move and who had had hardly any sleep since the operation began nearly ten days earlier— were moved against Rafah. On January 3rd the attack began. At first it did not succeed; the Egyptians, realising their danger, fought tenaciously, and the new commander in the Gaza Strip, General Fuad Sadek, personally led the counter-attacks.

But while the Egyptians successfully defended Rafah itself, the Israelis captured the heights of the south of the town which overlooked the road and the railway line to the south. Thus, in effect, they had cut off the Gaza army from the rest of Egypt. Now fully understanding their position, the Egyptian Government, on January 6th, announced its willingness to enter armistice negotiations at the headquarters of the United Nations Acting Mediator at Rhodes. On January 7th all firing ceased on the southern front. The war between Israel and Egypt had come to an end.

The Israelis had good cause to be jubilant. The largest and most powerful of their enemies was suing for peace. Moreover, the capture of the Rafah heights made it virtually certain that the Israelis would obtain a complete evacuation of the Gaza Strip as part of the armistice terms, for the Egyptian position there was now untenable.

The jubilation was premature. To the Egyptian acquiescence was almost immediately added a qualifying rider. Egypt would be willing to discuss an armistice only if Israel withdrew its positions south of Rafah. In Israel, it was commonly believed that Britain was behind this change of front. For almost at the same time as the first Egyptian declaration had been made, five British planes on a reconaissance flight over the front line were shot down in an encounter with the Israeli Air Force. The British reacted violently. They sent additional reinforcements to Aqaba, and then demanded the complete withdrawal of all Israeli troops from Egyptian territory—and this included the Rafah heights.

This was perhaps the most difficult decision of the entire war for Ben-Gurion to take. The order to withdraw meant depriving Israel of its strongest argument in the peace talks. On the other hand, refusal to do so entailed a continuation of the war and a strong risk of direct British intervention. And Ben-Gurion, perhaps alone of all the Israeli leaders, knew how weak and disorganised the young state still was, and what sanctions would entail. Once more Yigal Alon pleaded with him to withdraw his order. Ben-Gurion answered him: "From a military point of view you are correct; from a political point of view you are wrong. The Egyptians refuse to go to Rhodes unless we withdraw the wedge."

There are those in Israel who consider that this was Ben-Gurion's major mistake during the entire war, for, in their opinion, the Egyptians would have been forced to ask for an armistice if their army had still been cut off from their country. And, had the Egyptians gone to Rhodes with the Israeli wedge still in place, the talks could have led to a proper peace settlement, instead of a mere armistice.

But Ben-Gurion was convinced that too much was at stake to take so great a risk. For if the argument of Alon and his friends turned out to be mistaken they might lose all they had gained. And this risk Ben-Gurion would not take. He was content with the achievement of the campaign. It was important to know when one had to stop. This was one such moment.

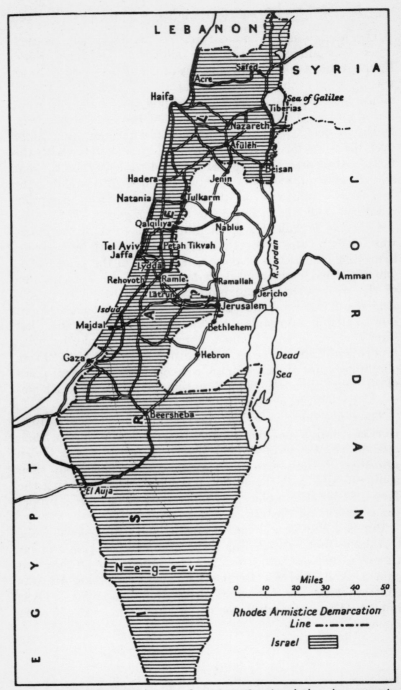

LEBANON

SYRIA

Safed

Acre

Haifa

Sea of Galilee

Tiberias

Nazareth

Afuleh

Beisan

Hadera

Jenin

Natania

Tulkarm

Qalqiliya

Nablus

Tel Aviv

Petah Tikvah

Jaffa

Lydda

Rehovoth

Ramle

Ramallah

Jericho

Amman

Latrun

J O R D A N

Jerusalem

Isdud

Majdal

Bethlehem

Gaza

Hebron

Dead

Sea

R. Jordan

Beersheba

E G Y P T

El Auja

N e g e v

Miles

0   10   20   30   40   50

Rhodes Armistice Demarcation
Line   _._._._._

Israel

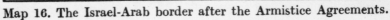

Map 16. The Israel-Arab border after the Armistice Agreements.

13

SHIN-TAV-SHIN: "THE BATTLE THAT REMAINS TO BE FOUGHT"

THE war on the Egyptian front had ended with political intervention by Britain and the United States. But for this, its outcome might have been more decisive and its consequences less troublesome in the future. But even so, it achieved more than a demonstration of the superiority of the now rapidly maturing Israel defence forces. It had established Israel's title to the Negev and, most important of all, it had convinced the Egyptian Government of the urgent need for a *modus vivendi* that would make certain that there would be no further resumption of the war with Egypt as the principal target.

The domestic situation of the Egyptian Government was becoming increasingly difficult. The Prime Minister, Nokrashy Pasha, had been assassinated in the midst of the crisis, and the full weight of the defeat of the Egyptian army had been withheld from the Egyptian public, which was still celebrating the victories in Palestine with special stamp issues and army parades inspected by the King. There seemed, therefore, to be an unbridgeable gap between the Government's fear of an imminent military collapse at the front, and the public joy at the success won in Palestine. And, more than anything, the Government feared lest the real situation should become known to the Cairo "street"—the mob that ruled the rulers. Into this dilemma stepped Dr. Ralph Bunche, the Acting Mediator.

Bunche recalled that the Security Council had passed a resolution—almost eight weeks earlier, on November 11th, 1948—in which it had laid down that "an armistice shall be established in all sectors of Palestine." The Israelis, after their unfinished October campaign, had made no haste to press for the implementation of the resolution. They had other objectives in mind before settling down to an armistice. None of the minor Arab states would make the first move. Abdullah was reasonably content with the existing situation. Neither the Lebanese nor the Syrians would act without the Egyptians. The Iraqis were not directly involved, nor was King ibn Saud. Thus, it was to the Egyptians that Bunche, the Arabs and the Security Council looked for the first indication that they were prepared to consider an armistice. King Farouk and Nokrashy decided to remain firm. There was to be no armistice with Israel.

But now Nokrashy was dead, and Farouk in a state of panic. His personal aircraft was standing by to fly him to the Canal Zone at the first sign of an emergency. The British army was alerted to take over in Cairo and Alexandria in case of serious trouble. This time the Egyptian Government replied with alacrity. The fighting in the Negev and in the Sinai desert had ended on January 7th, 1949. Five days later, on January 12th, a representative Egyptian delegation arrived at Rhodes to begin talks with a view to concluding an armistice with Israel.

Bunche presided and good progress was made after a slow start. The only serious difficulty arose from the fact that the Egyptian public was still in the dark about what had happened. The Egyptian delegation therefore wanted something included in the agreement which would help to foster the pretence that the Egyptians still held the Negev. Their first proposal was that an Egyptian Military Governor of Beersheba should be appointed, though his seat would be in Cairo or Gaza. This was rejected as too absurd. Then the Egyptians wanted a Military Governor for Bir Asluj (a small collection of empty mud-huts on the road from Beersheba to the Egyptian frontier), and lastly for El Auja. They evidently had firm instructions to insist on this appointment. By way of compromise, Bunche proposed a demilitarised zone at El Auja, and agreement was achieved.[1]

For the rest, it gave the Israelis possession of the land they

[1] The full story is told by the principal Israeli delegate, Walter Eytan, in his book *The First Ten Years* (Weidenfeld and Nicolson, 1958), pp. 27–47.

had occupied (with one or two minor exceptions), but it also left some issues too imprecisely formulated and a source of future conflicts. But then the Israeli participants had convinced themselves that this was only a temporary and short-lived arrangement which would soon be replaced by a formal peace settlement.

Once the Egyptians had started, the others were only too anxious to follow. In due course, an armistice was also concluded with the Lebanon (on March 23rd) and with Syria (on July 20th).

But a completely different situation had meanwhile developed in the talks with the Transjordanian delegation. It was of poor personal calibre; it had no authority to act, and it seemed to the Israelis that Abdullah did not want anyone to negotiate for him. At the same time, the Israeli army received intelligence reports that the Iraqi forces were soon to be withdrawn from Palestine and that the Arab Legion would take over from them.

There followed lengthy and detailed discussions in the Israeli General Staff, and with Ben-Gurion. It was decided to use the whole strength of the Israeli army—now well over 100,000 men—in order to occupy the so-called triangle, the whole of central Palestine as far as the Jordan, which was still in Arab hands. The code name given to the operation was "Shin-Tav-Shin." Careful consideration was given to the possible international repercussions, but it was concluded that the over-all gains in the future would far outweigh the temporary difficulties which might have to be encountered at the United Nations and at the hands of the Western Powers. The Russians had shown that anything which the Israelis did to weaken the grip of Western "imperialism" in the Middle East would enjoy their benevolent neutrality, if not their actual (though unpublicised) support.

However, as the preparations for the offensive reached their climax, there were some serious second thoughts among the Israeli political and military leaders: perhaps, it occurred to them, they might be tempting fate once too often. They had been extremely fortunate after the October offensive, and again after the December attack. They had enjoyed both military successes and a favourable world opinion—a novel and refreshing experience for them. Why risk this happy state on the uncertainties of yet another military operation, which would greatly intensify the Arab refugee problem?

It was therefore decided to make the most of the military preparations as a means of exerting diplomatic pressure on Abdullah to settle on frontiers which would be more beneficial to the Israelis. Yadin accordingly arranged that information about the impending attack should reach the Arab Legion command. The information was followed up with an informal communication which was passed to the King through Colonel el-Tel, the Arab Legion's Military Governor in the Arab part of Jerusalem. This said that the Israeli Government considered that it had the same right as the Arab Legion to occupy the area about to be evacuated by the Iraqi troops. This was a narrow but strategically important belt of land from Qalqiliya to Jordan, north of Jenin; for it included most of the important hill-tops along the border.

At first, both Abdullah and the Legion headquarters were inclined to treat this Israeli-inspired information as a diplomatic bluff in order to get better terms at the Rhodes talks. Meanwhile, however, the Israeli High Command had prepared another operation which it wanted to conclude before signing an armistice with Abdullah. The first step in the armistice talks was the signature by both parties of a cease-fire agreement to cover the whole front. But through the opening days of March, the Israelis at Rhodes dallied and delayed. The Transjordanians also seemed in no hurry. Then suddenly, towards the end of the first week of March, the Arab Legion command received reports of two Israeli columns moving southwards in the general direction of Aqaba. Until then no one had paid much attention to the purely token presence of a very small Arab Legion unit on the Gulf of Aqaba and at the police post of Um Resh Resh. The Transjordanian Government cabled the alarming news to Bunche. At first the Israelis said nothing. They had no information, they told Bunche. But by March 9th the columns were on their way, and on the 10th the Israeli delegation informed Bunche that its Government was about to occupy the territory on the Gulf of Aqaba which had been allotted to Israel by the United Nations partition plan.

Diplomatically it was a complicated situation, for the British Foreign Secretary had told Parliament that the Arab

Legion was in possession of this area, and that it was therefore to be considered as Transjordanian-occupied territory. Yadin, Alon and Dori discussed the problem and decided that they had to get to the Gulf of Aqaba without at any point attacking the Legion. If there was to be any fighting, it was the Legion that had to start it. The brigade commanders of the two Israeli columns, Sarig and Golan, had to give written undertakings that they would not attack any Legion position: Alon's last instruction to them was to "defend yourselves all the way to Elath." On these terms, the Israeli Government gave its approval to this delicate operation. Only a small force of Legionnaires barred the road, but, in view of the limitations on the attackers, it was sufficient to require considerable ingenuity on the part of the Israelis to get them to withdraw without engaging them in battle. Once again the scouts of the Hanegev Brigade found a route and an air strip which enabled the Brigade to be airlifted to Ras el Nagib and thus leapfrog Glubb's prepared defences. However, the situation was resolved when Glubb ordered the Legion posts to withdraw into Transjordan. On March 11th the Israeli troops reached the Gulf of Aqaba, and at Rhodes the Israeli delegation signed the cease-fire.

By now, the Israelis had taken up a formal position with regard to the Iraqi withdrawal, which was due to take place on March 13th. Israel's Foreign Minister, Sharett, had informed Bunche that Israel considered herself free to occupy the positions vacated by the Iraqis, and two days later the Israelis informed Bunche that they would consider the taking over of the Iraqi position by the Arab Legion as a breach of the truce. Meanwhile, preparations for "Shin-Tav-Shin" continued with an almost demonstrative lack of secrecy. To stave off what seemed like imminent disaster, Abdullah appealed to the Iraqi Government to delay the withdrawal of their troops. They agreed. But they told Abdullah that it could be for only a few days. For the Iraqi soldiers were on the point of mutiny. They had not received any pay for weeks. They had been on short rations, and they had not enjoyed the rigours of a Palestine winter without the clothing or amenities to help them through it.

Abdullah therefore decided to act, without Glubb. He made direct contact with the Israelis through the Military Governors in the two parts of Jerusalem. The Arab, Colonel el-Tel, contacted the Jew, Lt.-Colonel Dayan. It was not difficult, for they had been in touch for some time; without either Glubb's knowledge or authority el-Tel had a direct telephone connecting him with Dayan's headquarters. It was arranged that a representative Israeli delegation should meet the King at his winter palace at Shune, near the Dead Sea.

El-Tel arranged the crossing of the line at night and the transport to Shune. At the Legion check-posts on the road he identified the visitors as United Nations observers. The Israelis wore civilian clothes, and the only disguise necessary was for Dayan to hide the black patch over his left eye. The first meeting was formal. Abdullah had all his Ministers assembled to greet the Israelis. They stood to the King's right, while the Israelis were grouped on his left. Abdullah then addressed them. Speaking for some twenty minutes, he reviewed the events that had brought them together at this strange meeting.

As the King spoke it became increasingly clear to the Israeli delegation that Abdullah was addressing not them but his own Ministers, and that he wanted the Israelis to hear what he had to say to them. After the first formal polite phrases, Abdullah spoke with extraordinary frankness, so much so as to make Yadin feel embarrassed at the discomfiture of the Transjordanian Ministers. Abdullah said to them that they must now recognise that it was they, together with the Egyptians, who had forced him into a war which he did not want. And he went on in this strain—accusing them, blaming them, condemning them—for the best part of twenty minutes.

When he had finished he asked the Israelis and his Ministers to join him for dinner. The Prime Minister, Abul Huda, asked to be excused as he had a stomach ailment. The King turned to him and with a rude colloquial phrase told him to go. At dinner, Abdullah appeared to be relaxed and enjoying himself and discussed Islamic poetry with Yadin who sat on his left. When they had finished eating Abdullah withdrew, and the Israeli delegation settled down to the serious business of their visit.

Fawzi el Mulki took over as leader of the Transjordanian delegation, but the most active of the Transjordanians was el-Tel himself. Glubb was represented by Brigadier Coaker, his Director of Operations. On the Israeli side, Yadin was accompanied by Eytan, Dayan, Shiloah and Harkabi. After sitting through the night they left in el-Tel's car, so as to reach Jerusalem before daylight.

The nightly journey and the talks continued for about a week before agreement was reached. All the time the Israelis continued their preparations for "Shin-Tav-Shin," and let Abdullah know it. The price for calling it off was that Abdullah should agree to a revision of the border in the area held by the Iraqis. After a great deal of debate, el-Tel drew a line on the back of a cigarette-box which would have given the Israelis the villages as well as the hills which they wanted for security reasons. But Fawzi el Mulki, who had been away, objected. He insisted that at least the villages should remain in Trans-jordan; better to have villages without land, than neither villages nor land. He feared an outcry if el-Tel's frontiers were accepted.

In the end, a map was drawn up by Brigadier Coaker, with Yadin and Harkabi. The agreement was approved by Abdullah and initialled at three in the morning. Dayan and Jundi, the respective delegates, took it and flew to Rhodes. There it was presented in the morning as if it had been negotiated on the spot. On April 3rd it was formally signed in the presence of Dr. Bunche. The Iraqis withdrew, and the Israelis moved forward to occupy the strategic hills which were to give them additional protection on an impossible frontier—a frontier which was to burden them with political problems for the next decade because of the division of the villages from their land.

But such a result was envisaged neither by the Israelis nor by Dr. Bunche. They were convinced that the armistice was but a temporary instrument pending a proper settlement. They assumed that it might last for weeks; they ridiculed the suggestion that it might have to remain in existence for some months, and possibly for half a year. None of the participants at Rhodes or at Shune imagined that this was to be the final settlement that was to last for ten years and more. They would have protested at the impossibility of such a development. But it was not ridiculous nor impossible. The temporary arrangements have become permanent fixtures—and problems.

Thus the Palestine War came to an end with an impossible armistice. "Shin-Tav-Shin" was cancelled. The Arab triangle remained intact in the heart of Israel, and Israel remained intact in the heart of the Arab world. Glubb criticised Abdullah for making this deal with the Israelis. Alon and others criticised Ben-Gurion for abandoning the operation against the triangle in return for so incomplete a settlement.

The claim of Alon and his friends that Ben-Gurion and Yadin were manoeuvred by Abdullah into calling off the operation is no more borne out by the facts of the situation than Glubb's complaint that Abdullah need not have negotiated with the Israelis. There were compelling circumstances on both sides that prevented the battle for the triangle from being decided in the spring of 1949.

But this unfinished battle has haunted the Palestine situation ever since. It has returned to the international scene time and again, but it has never been decided. "Shin-Tav-Shin" was the last element in the first round; it remained the unsolved element of the second round. It had not been removed by Israel's Sinai operation.

EPILOGUE

Israel and the Arab Revolution

THERE was more to it than merely the undecided ending of a local conflict. In another, and far more extensive, sense the Palestine War had ended in a shattering decision, though it was not immediately recognised as such. For just as it had begun—not as an Israel-Arab conflict, but as a rebellion of the Jews against the impositions of the British Mandatory rule in Palestine[1]—so the outcome of war in Palestine was in effect more of a defeat of imperial Britain than of the Arab countries. The Arabs suffered some loss in terms of broad history (however severe the loss may have been to those Palestinians immediately affected by it); but it was imperial Britain which suffered most: within a decade it had lost all its positions of direct control in the Middle East and was on the brink of losing also its direct hold over the rich oil resources of the region.

It was precisely this aspect of the Palestine conflict which Mr. Attlee's administration failed to understand. It assumed that an empire could abdicate at will, and start or stop the process as you start and stop a bus. But in fact, as we have shown, there was not even a conscious policy of abdication to guide the Government of the day. It was mainly a conscious and deliberate policy of drift which was the basis of Mr. Attlee's action on the Palestine question, a mixture of delaying decisions and improvising something when delay was no longer possible.[2] But Attlee was not the only one. The United Nations, both as a secretariat and as an international organisation, also hedged for as long as hedging was practicable. President Truman himself more often avoided decisions than took them. The Egyptian leaders were no less anxious to

[1] Almost exclusively against the restrictions on immigration and less so against the ban on Jewish land purchase in certain parts of Palestine.
[2] Mr. Truman has given a vivid picture of this Attlee technique in the second volume of his *Memoirs*.

273

avoid a situation where they had publicly to take up a position, and the same was true of the Arab League secretariat under Azzam Pasha, who understood the situation better than most and feared the consequences to the League if it were called to take joint action. All these—Attlee, Trygve Lie, Truman, Nokrashy and Azzam—drifted from one position to the next until they had drifted into war and British abdication from Palestine.

They did this because they had all failed to diagnose the main issue which was involved in Palestine: it was not the clash of Jew and Arab, but the inability of Mr. Attlee's Government to maintain the Pax Brittanica on which the Middle East order had been built. They failed to appreciate that what they considered to be a local Palestinian crisis was really the symptom of a much larger imperial crisis. Palestine was not, as they were inclined to treat it, an irritating side-show; it was the first link in the chain of British imperial decline. Whether it held or whether it broke might well be decisive. But the question was never put in this way at the Cabinet discussions in London. It was rated more as a bargaining dispute between Jews and Arabs which called for Ernest Bevin's expertise as a trade union negotiator. This was probably the most significant miscalculation of the Attlee administration.

For in so far as imperial interests had to be retained in the Middle East, these were considered safe in the hands of the Arab allies of the British: Farouk in Egypt, Abdullah in Transjordan Nuri in Iraq—backed by the British positions in the Sudan, on the Suez Canal, in Libya, in Transjordan, in Iraq and on the Persian Gulf. The British attitude during the Palestine conflict had been designed to avoid jeopardising this relationship with the Arab world, even at the cost of annoying the Americans and outraging the Jews. Thus British policy drifted into the Palestine War and drifted on afterwards to the other landmarks of the British decline in the Middle East.

For set against the British position were three men who had strictly limited objectives in the Middle East but who knew what they wanted and were determined to get it. The three were Stalin, Ben-Gurion and King Abdullah.

Stalin had explained his position to Ernest Bevin at an

informal private talk at the end of the Foreign Ministers'
conference in Moscow in March 1947. Stalin wanted to talk
about the Middle East. He was prepared to accept Britain's
legitimate position there. The Russians would make no
difficulties for the British nor aid those who sought to do so.
They would maintain a policy of strict neutrality in the
conflict between Britain and Egypt (which was about to come
before the Security Council), and also in Palestine. Stalin
made only one condition: the British must themselves accept
responsibility for the Middle East; they must not invite the
Americans to share it in any way whatsoever. That was
Stalin's objective. He wanted to keep the Americans out of
the Middle East; and if the British were determined to get
them in, then he would make difficulties for both.

As we know, one of Mr. Attlee's rare decisions on the Middle
East was taken about six months before Stalin's overture to
Bevin. He had then decided that the Americans had to be
compelled, if they could not be persuaded, to share British
responsibility for the Middle East. It was probably this
decision of Attlee's, more than any other, that persuaded
Stalin into the surprise decision to support the establishment
of a Jewish State in Palestine. But simultaneously, Stalin also
attacked the Arab leaders for diverting Arab attention to
Palestine when they ought to concentrate it on the activities
of the "Anglo-American imperialists." One thing was clear,
Stalin's influence was in the scale against the "drifters."

In a class by himself was David Ben-Gurion. His role in the
Palestine War is probably still inadequately appreciated. For
in this conflict, he was possibly the man whose ideas crystal-
lised more quickly and more sharply than those of anyone
else. Once he had become convinced, in the late autumn of
1945, that there was no chance of an agreed settlement with
the British, his mind began to push ahead, way ahead of his
colleagues and of his opponents. For the extraordinary
feature of the establishment of Israel was the suddenness with
which the full measure of the step came to most people who
were involved in it. Only a very few had anticipated it, and
none more so than Ben-Gurion. Had he not done so, the
Palestinian Jews would have been politically and practically,
let alone militarily, unprepared to meet the challenge when it
came.

There had been individuals, groups and parties who had spoken far more about a Jewish State and the need to fight for it; but they had never approached the full measure and size of the effort that would be required. That was as true of the Revisionists as it was of Beigin and the Irgun Zvai Leumi. They thought in terms of commando forces and raids; only Ben-Gurion's imagination visualised a national army and a full-scale war. But his thought also went beyond the military. He provided the ideology, the firmness, the apparently irresponsible demands that were soldered on to his concept of the future. He knew what he wanted. He was not prepared to compromise his fundamentals because at the root his objective was quite different from that of anyone else in this Palestine turmoil. He needed not only victory; he needed not only an army. It was the battle and the army that was to be the foundation of the new Israel. It was in the clash of this life-and-death struggle that he reduced the confusion and contradictions of the Zionist Movement and of Zionist ideologies (often long outdated by events) into the new Israel. It was inevitable that in the process a good deal of the intellectual luggage and tradition of world Jewry should be lost and changed, for the urgencies of the hour left little room for them.

It was an odd fact that living through these historic days in the history of a people, only a small minority were conscious of the occasion, and even fewer appreciated how near Israel had come to the brink of disaster in the process of creation. That the disaster was averted was due almost entirely to the foresight, imagination and determination of Ben-Gurion, and no less to the fact that all Israel accepted him as leader in its hour of crisis. He made mistakes—big ones, as is the wont of great men. He was short-sighted on the Arab question. He was impatient of fools and intolerant of opponents. But his faults were those of a great man—he could afford them. It was unfortunate for the Arabs—and for the British—that they had to meet a man of this calibre. But it was the salvation of Israel.

The third member of the trio, King Abdullah, has generally been regarded as a mere tool of British policy, manipulated by Glubb. This view is quite wrong, as we have shown. Unlike the other Arab leaders (and unlike the British), he knew his own mind. He wanted Jerusalem and he wanted to keep the other Arab states out of Palestine. If anything, he imposed his will on Bevin and Glubb, rather than the other way round. Abdullah achieved his limited objectives. So did Ben-Gurion; so did Stalin—or, at least, his successors.

But not the British. It was they—in terms of history—who were the defeated in Palestine. For the Palestine War was not, after all, the first round of a long series of Arab-Israeli wars, but rather the beginning of the Middle East revolution against the British overlordship. It was followed in the course of the next decade by the assassination of King Abdullah; the expulsion of the Anglo-Iranian Oil Company from Persia; the British withdrawal from Egypt and the Sudan; the overthrow of Farouk; the expulsion of Sir John Glubb from Transjordan, to be followed by the ending of the British alliance; the British Suez fiasco, and then the revolution in Iraq. And in its wake came the rising Soviet star; a new outside influence long held at bay, was staking its claim.

Palestine thus was the watershed for British imperialism— the old and the new; it marked the end of the old order in the Middle East. The Palestine War not only sealed the establishment of Israel, it also signalled the beginning of the real Arab awakening, the Middle East revolution that was to come. But what were the ultimate objectives of this Arab regeneration to be? Was it the destruction of Israel as was claimed at the outset by Zurayk and Musa Alami? It was the question which a new generation—and perhaps a wiser and more understanding generation—of Arab leaders will one day have to answer. On it will depend the fate of the Arab revolution and of the peace in the Middle East.

APPENDIX

(See pages 208-9)

According to Israel Galili, Ben-Gurion reacted to Yadin's and Galili's letters of resignation with a report to the Government in which he hinted, without saying so directly, that a political revolt had broken out in the army. As a result, the Government set up the ministerial committee to consider the causes of the crisis. In fact, Galili maintains that the whole conduct of the war was closely scrutinised by the committee and some of the sessions were highly charged and dramatic. Yadin was particularly outspoken and complained of persistent intervention by Ben-Gurion on the tactical level. But it was the policy for Jerusalem that was the main point of difference between Yadin and Ben-Gurion. Yadin told the committee of his endeavours to delay the attack at Latrun by even a few days. This in his opinion would have made all the difference between victory and set-back.

On the subject of new appointments, Yadin said that Ben-Gurion had ignored the General Staff's proposals and had favoured ex-regular army officers in place of Haganah veterans. Galili and Zvi Ayalon supported Yadin and described Ben-Gurion's directive, that all promotions above the rank of lieutenant must be first cleared with him, as unrealistic over-centralisation. Ayalon expressed himself strongly about Ben-Gurion's lack of trust in the Haganah veterans and he asked for a clearly defined division of authority between Ben-Gurion and Galili, with Galili retaining his function as *de facto* acting chief-of-staff.

Ben-Gurion remained quite unmoved during the proceedings. He answered Yadin briefly and firmly. In his opinion, the battles at Latrun had not resulted in a set-back but in an important victory. They had eased the pressure on Jerusalem when its defences were in danger of giving way. He justified his so-called "interference" in operational matters. They had proved themselves as beneficial to the conduct of the war. He had been persuaded only twice to change his mind about his interventions; and he had later regretted that he had not persisted.

INDEX